AMERICAN DRAMA SINCE WORLD WAR II

AMERICAN DRAMA SINCE

WORLD WAR II by GERALD WEALES

HARCOURT, BRACE & WORLD, INC. NEW YORK

For

LOUISE *(who took me to my first play)*

and **DAVID**

1112666

Contents

"O hell! what have we here?"

—PRINCE OF MOROCCO in
The Merchant of Venice

Introduction

Although the title *American Drama Since World War II* seems specific enough, a book bearing that name might be any number of things. This one is a critical description of the American plays that have been produced since 1945. Not all of them, of course, but more of them than any theatergoer in his right mind would want to sit through. I have no fixed rule about what plays should be included, which ones ignored. For the most part, a play's claim for a paragraph or a line is based on one of three things: (1) its intrinsic merit; (2) its having been written by a playwright who—however mediocre a particular play—has done interesting work; (3) the length of its run. As the third category suggests, Broadway (and off-Broadway) plays provide the material for discussion. Whether one likes it or not, Broadway is a fact of American cultural life. There are a few exceptions—plays that are produced in university or regional theaters, plays that are published and not produced at all, special categories such as children's plays and the outdoor dramas of Paul Green and Kermit Hunter —but for all practical purposes American drama is synonymous with New York production. Since my title provides a beginning but no end to my subject, I have had to be arbitrary about terminal dates. I considered each chapter closed as it came off the typewriter; since much of the book was written during the summer of 1961, very few plays are included that were produced later than the previous season. If the most important play of the decade were to be produced next week or next month, it could not be found here; for one thing, we would not really know that it was the most important until 1970 and, for another, such an exclusion would be a comfort to those people who like to point out that a study is not definitive.

A word about what the book is not but might have been. It is not, except by implication, a cultural history. I have not set out to prove, using the plays as evidence, that the years since the war had this or that character. Still, Broadway theater does not exist in a vacuum; it reflects, as much as movies, television, popular fiction, the tastes and prejudices of its time. It is fairly obvious that American drama, particularly in the fifties, has concentrated on the private instead of the public problem, has been psychological rather than social, has been explanatory rather than dramatic. This is not only an aesthetic but a cultural, a social, perhaps even a political fact, and my comments take that into account.

The book is not a description of the American theater of the last fifteen years. It is not, for instance, about technical innovations. It is true that the single set, the careful representation of a room, has given way to the more complicated set that, through the use of stage machinery or the suggestivity of the nonrealistic, allows the playwright to work in a variety of places and times and states of mind. This change finds its way into the discussions, of course, but details of production are seldom used for their own sake (which would be fine in another kind of book) but to illustrate the workings of a particular play.

Nor is the book about acting. It does not, for instance, consider how much bad acting there is on Broadway today, whether it comes from natural lack of talent, or—more likely—from the chaotic system of underrehearsal before a show opens and the inevitable indifference that sets in if there is a long run. I deal only obliquely with the change in acting style—the influence of the Actors Studio—and its effect on playwriting, and I consider an individual performance only when it has dictated the interpretation or the acceptability of a play.

Nor is the book about economics, although the financial structure of the theater probably has as much as anything else to do with the kind of plays that are produced and, therefore, with the kind that are written. In June 1961, the New York *Times* ran a series of articles that diagnosed the economic troubles of Broadway; the impetus was to find a cure. Although saving Broadway might be important to New York and to the *Times,* since the theater in New York feeds so many other businesses, it is doubtful that the quality of American drama will change much even if the producers, the unions, and the theater owners find a way to work congenially for the greater good of the box office. There might be hope if regional professional theaters, such as those in San Francisco, Washington, and Dallas, became so well established that they gave playwrights a chance both to earn a living and to receive the artistic recognition that today still hangs on New York production. I am offering neither a cure for Broadway's ills nor a restructuring of the American theater as a panacea for American drama. Economics inevitably finds its way into what I have written, but it is not the subject under discussion.

Finally, the book is not a plea for any one kind of theater. I am not committed to either the realistic or the nonrealistic theater, to the play of social conscience or the play of private revelation. There is, then, no ideal drama against which all the others are weighed and found wanting. I am pleased by small virtues in any play, and I am annoyed by shoddy workmanship, obvious venality, copy-cat uncreativity, good intentions that come to nothing, theatrical efficiency with no substance.

If the book is an advocate at all, it is a devil's advocate.

Philadelphia
December 3, 1961

ACKNOWLEDGMENTS

The ideas in this book, and a phrase or two, have been worked out in my graduate and undergraduate drama classes at the University of Pennsylvania, and in articles and reviews for the *Reporter, Commonweal, Commentary, Kenyon Review, Hudson Review, Tamarack Review, Drama Survey, South Atlantic Quarterly* and the USIA.

Some of the chapters have appeared in *Drama Survey, Tulane Drama Review,* and *Antioch Review.*

I want to thank both the Special Research Fund of the University of Pennsylvania and the Yaddo Foundation.

AMERICAN DRAMA SINCE WORLD WAR II

1 ARTHUR MILLER: MAN AND HIS IMAGE

*He's got his stance, he's got his pace, he's got his control
down to a pinpoint. He's almost original sometimes. When
it comes to throwin' a ball, he's all there.*

—AUGIE BELFAST in *The Man Who Had All the Luck*

Arthur Miller is one of those playwrights, like Thornton Wilder, whose reputation rests on a handful of plays. The quality of that reputation changes from year to year, from critic to critic, but now, five years after the production of his most recent play (the revision of *A View from the Bridge*), it is generally conceded, even by those who persist in not admiring his work, that Miller is one of the two playwrights of the postwar American theater who deserve any consideration as major dramatists. Tennessee Williams is the other.

There are many ways of approaching Miller's work. In the late forties, after *All My Sons* and *Death of a Salesman,* popular reviewers tended to embrace him enthusiastically, while consciously intellectual critics, displaying the carefulness of their kind, hoped that in explaining him they might explain him away. For a time, his plays were lost in discussions of the author's politics, past and present, or were buried beneath the pointless academic quibble about whether or not they are true tragedies. Miller's own defensiveness on these two points helped feed the controversy. In the last few years, however, with no new Miller play to stir up opinion, his work has begun to be considered outside the immediate context that produced it.

Even so, there is no single handle by which to grasp his works. Because each of his four chief plays is built on a family situation —*Sons* and *Salesman* on the father-son conflict, *The Crucible* and

View on the triangle—the plays can be treated as domestic dramas. Because they obviously criticize or comment upon the structure of society, they may be considered conventional social plays; still, as Eric Bentley has pointed out, noting the chief motivating force in most of the plots, they are as much sexual as social dramas. There are probably enough biographical reflections in the plays to send the psychological critic in search of personal analogies; Maurice Zolotow, for instance, interrupts the psycho-anecdotage of *Marilyn Monroe* long enough to point out that both *Crucible* and *View* deal with marital problems caused by the attraction of an older man to a younger woman and to suggest that they stem from the fact that the author could not get Miss Monroe out of his mind between his first meeting with her in 1950 and his marriage to her in 1956.

Any of these approaches, even Zolotow's, may manage to say something valid about Miller's plays. To me, however, the most profitable way of looking at his work is through his heroes and through the concern of each, however inarticulate, with his identity —his *name,* as both John Proctor and Eddie Carbone call it. Perhaps the simplest way to get at what Miller is doing in these plays is to force a path through the confounding prose of his general comments on contemporary drama and on the kind of play he hopes he has written. Although his opinions on the nature of drama are scattered through interviews, introductions, and occasional articles for the New York *Times,* the bulk of his theoretical writing is contained in four essays: "On Social Plays," printed as an introduction to *A View from the Bridge* (1955); "The Family in Modern Drama," originally a lecture given at Harvard (*Atlantic Monthly,* April 1956); Introduction to the *Collected Plays* (1957); "The Shadows of the Gods" (*Harper's,* August 1958). Although each of these essays has a particular job to do, a recurring idea about the possibilities of modern drama seeps through the ponderousness of all of them, climbs over the barriers of Miller's Germanic fondness for definition and redefinition. For Miller, the serious playwright writes social drama, but that genre, for him, is not simply "an arraignment of society's evils." Just as he refuses to accept the standard definition of the social play, a product of the thirties, so too he rejects the drama which he sees as most representative of contemporary American theater, the play in which the characters retreat into self-preoc-

cupation and give little hint that there is a society outside themselves. The true social drama, the "Whole Drama," as he calls it,
must recognize that man has both a subjective and an objective
existence, that he belongs not only to himself and his family, but to
the world beyond.

Since Miller's plays were written before these essays were, it is
probably safe to assume that the theorizing is *ex post facto* in more
ways than one, and that his general conclusions about the drama
are based, in part, on what he thinks he has done as a playwright;
his ready use of *Salesman* as an example strengthens such an assumption. I have no trouble accepting his belief that the best of
drama has always dealt with man in both a personal and a social
context, but his generalizations are most useful as approaches to
his own work. His plays are family-centered, obviously, because
our drama the last few years has been uncomfortable in any context larger than the family; his heroes, however, are more than
failed husbands and fathers because he has recognized that the
most impressive family plays, from *Oedipus* through *Hamlet* to
Ghosts, have modified the concept of the family and of the individual under the pressure of society.

Each of his heroes is involved, in one way or another, in
a struggle that results from his acceptance or rejection of an image
that is the product of his society's values and prejudices, whether
that society is as small as Eddie Carbone's neighborhood or as wide
as the contemporary America that helped form Willy Loman.
Miller's work has followed such a pattern from the beginning.
Even Ben, the hero of *They Too Arise,* a now happily forgotten
prize winner from the mid-thirties, has to decide whether he is to
be the man that his middle-class, small-businessman father expects or the comrade that his radical brother demands; the play
ends, of course, in leftist affirmation, but the conflict has been in
terms of opposed images, both of which are assumed to have validity for Ben. The hero of *The Man Who Had All the Luck* (1944),
Miller's first produced play, accepts the town's view of him as a
man who has succeeded through luck not ability; he assumes that
all luck must turn and, in his obsession, almost brings disaster on
his head until his wife convinces him that he should reject the
town's rationalizing bromide and accept the principle that man
makes his own luck. In his novel *Focus* (1945), a fantasy-tract,
his anti-Semitic hero finally accepts the label that his neighbors

force on him; he admits that he is a Jew. Most of Miller's short
stories reflect the same kind of preoccupation with the self that
someone else expects the hero to be; in one of his most recent stories, "I Don't Need You Any More" (*Esquire,* December
1959), the five-year-old hero's idea of himself is formed on half-
understood perceptions picked up from his parents and the adult
world they live in, the only society that he recognizes outside himself. The lament and the longing implicit in Martin's thought—"If
only he *looked* like his father and his brother!"—is a small echo
of the bewilderment that haunts all the Miller heroes who do the
right things and come to the wrong ends.

In *All My Sons* (1947), Miller's first successful play, Joe Keller,
who is admittedly a good husband and a good father, fails to be the
good man, the good citizen that his son Chris demands. "I'm his
father and he's my son, and if there's something bigger than that
I'll put a bullet in my head!" Chris makes clear that, for him, there
is something bigger than the family, and Joe commits suicide.
Much more interesting than the unmasking and punishment of
Joe's crime (he shipped out cracked cylinder heads during the war
and let his partner take the blame and go to jail) is Joe as a pecul-
iarly American product. He is a self-made man, a successful
businessman "with the imprint of the machine-shop worker and
boss still upon him." There is nothing ruthless about Joe, no
hint of the robber baron in his make-up; his ambitions are small—
a comfortable home for his family, a successful business to pass on
to his sons—but he is not completely fastidious in achieving his
goals. Not only has he accepted the American myth of the primacy
of the family, his final excuse for all his actions, but he has adopted
as a working instrument the familiar attitude that there is a difference between morality and business ethics. Not that he could ever
phrase it that way. "I'm in business, a man is in business. . . ."
he begins his explanation, his plea for understanding, and moves
on to that dimly lit area where the other man's culpability is his
forgiveness.

When Miller at last moves in on Joe, brings Chris and discovery
to destroy him, there is no longer any possibility of choice. His
fault, according to Miller and Chris, is that he does not recognize
any allegiance to society at large; his world, as he mistakenly says
of that of his dead son Larry, "had a forty-foot front, it ended at
the building line." Joe's shortness of vision, however, is a product

of his society. Even Chris shares his goals: "If I have to grub for money all day long at least at evening I want it beautiful. I want a family, I want some kids, I want to build something I can give myself to." The neighbors, in the figure of Sue, respect Joe's methods: "They give him credit for being smart." At the end of the play, finally confronted with another alternative ("But I think to him they were all my sons"), Joe Keller, in killing himself, destroys the image that he has accepted.

There is a disturbing patness about *All My Sons,* an exemplary working out of the conflict that is as didactic as Chris's more extended speeches. With *Death of a Salesman* (1949), Miller escapes into richness. The ambiguity that occasionally touches the characters in the earlier play, that makes the supposedly admirable idealist son sound at times like a hanging judge, suffuses the playwright's second success, his finest play. It might be possible to reduce the play to some kind of formula, to suggest that Biff's end-of-the-play declaration, "I know who I am, kid," is a positive statement, a finger pointing in some verifiable direction, a refutation of all the beliefs to which Willy clings and for which he dies. Miller suggests, in his Introduction to the *Collected Plays,* that Biff does embody an "opposing system" to the "law of success" which presumably kills Willy, but there are almost as many contradictions in Miller's Introduction as there are in his play. Since the last scene, the Requiem, is full of irony—Charley's romantic eulogy of the Salesman, Linda's failure to understand ("I made the last payment on the house today. . . . We're free and clear"), Happy's determination to follow in his father's failed footsteps—there is no reason to assume that some of the irony does not rub off on Biff. We have been with the lying Lomans so long, have seen them hedge their bets and hide their losses in scene after self-deluding scene, that it is at least forgivable if we respect Willy's integrity as a character (if not as a man) and suspect that Biff is still his son. The play after all, ends with the funeral; there is no sequel.

When we meet Willy Loman, he, like Joe Keller, is past the point of choice, but his play tells us that there are at least three will-of-the-wisp ideals—father figures, all—that Willy might have chosen to follow. The first is his own father, the inventor, the flute maker, the worker-with-his-hands, who walked away one day and left the family to shift for itself. His is the flute melody that opens the play, "small and fine, telling of grass and trees and the horizon." From what we hear of him, he was a man who did not make his fortune because he did not know that a fortune was a thing worth making and, if his desertion of his family means anything, he needed the world's good opinion as little as he needed its idea of conventional success. The chances of Willy's going the way of his father are as dead as the frontier, of course; so when the flute appears in the play it is no more than a suggestion of a very vague might-have-been. Nor is the second possible choice, that embodied in the figure of Ben, a likely one for Willy; it is difficult to imagine him among the business buccaneers. For that reason, perhaps, Miller has chosen to make a comic caricature of Ben: "Why, boys, when I was seventeen I walked into the jungle, and when I was twenty-one I walked out. And by God I was rich." Ben, with his assurance, his ruthlessness ("Never fight fair with a stranger, boy"), his connections in Africa and Alaska, looms a little larger than life in Willy's mind, half cartoon, half romance. There is romance enough—liberally laced with sentiment—in the ideal that Willy does choose, Dave Singleman, the old salesman who, at eighty-four, could, through the strength of his personality, sit in a hotel room and command buyers. Willy admires Singleman for dying "the death of a salesman, in his green velvet slippers in the smoker of the New York, New Haven and Hartford," without ever recognizing that there is more than one way to kill a salesman.

Willy can no more be Dave Singleman than he can be his father or his brother Ben. From the conflicting success images that wander through his troubled brain comes Willy's double ambition—to be rich and to be loved. As he tells Ben, "the wonder of this country [is] that a man can end with diamonds here on the basis of being liked!" From Andrew Carnegie, then, to Dale Carnegie. Willy's faith in the magic of "personal attractiveness" as a way to success carries him beyond cause and effect to necessity; he assumes that success falls inevitably to the man with the right smile, the best line, the most charm, the man who is not only liked, but well liked. He has completely embraced the American myth, born of the advertisers, that promises us love and a fortune as soon as we clear up our pimples, stop underarm perspiration, learn to play the piano; for this reason, the brand names that turn up in Willy's speeches are more than narrow realism. He regularly confuses labels with reality. In his last scene with Biff, Willy cries out, "I am not a dime a dozen! I am Willy Loman, and you are Biff Loman!"

The strength and the pathos of that cry lie in the fact that Willy still thinks that the names should mean something; it is effective within the play because we have heard him imply that a punching bag is good because "It's got Gene Tunney's signature on it," and that a city can be summed up in a slogan—"Big clock city, the famous Waterbury clock."

The distance between the actual Willy and Willy as image is so great when the play opens that he can no longer lie to himself with conviction; what the play gives us is the final disintegration of a man who has never even approached his idea of what by rights he ought to have been. His ideal may have been the old salesman in his green velvet slippers, but his model is that mythic figure, the traveling salesman of the dirty joke. Willy tries to be a kidder, a caution, a laugh-a-minute; he shares his culture's conviction that personality is a matter of mannerism and in the sharing develops a style that is compounded of falseness, the mock assurance of what Happy calls "the old humor, the old confidence." His act, however, is as much for himself as it is for his customers. The play shows quite clearly that from the beginning of his career Willy has lied about the size of his sales, the warmth of his reception, the number of his friends. It is true that he occasionally doubts himself, assumes that he is too noisy and undignified, that he is not handsome enough ("I'm fat. I'm very—foolish to look at"), but usually he rationalizes his failure. His continuing self-delusion and his occasional self-awareness serve the same purpose; they keep him from questioning the assumptions that lie beneath his failure and his pretense of success. By the time we get to him, his struggle to hold onto his dream (if not for himself, then for his sons) has become so intense that all control is gone; past and present are one to him, and so are fact and fiction. A suggestion becomes a project completed; a possibility becomes a dream fulfilled. When Biff tries to give him peace by making him realize, and accept the realization, that he is a failure and a mediocrity and see that it makes no difference, Willy hears only what he wants to hear. He takes Biff's tears not only as an evidence of love, which they are, but as a kind of testimonial, an assurance that Willy's way has been the right one all along. Once again secure in his dream ("that boy is going to be magnificent"), he goes to his suicide's death, convinced that, with the insurance money, Biff will be—to use Willy's favorite nouns —a hero, a prince.

Joe Keller and Willy Loman find ready-made societal images to attach themselves to and both become victims of the attachment. Society is not nearly so passive in Miller's next play, *The Crucible* (1953). Salem tries to force John Proctor to accept a particular image of himself, but he chooses to die. Although there are occasional voices in the earlier plays (the neighbors in *All My Sons,* the bartender in *Death of a Salesman*) who speak for society, Miller operates for the most part on the assumption that his audience knows and shares the ideas that work on the Kellers and the Lomans. He cannot be that certain in *The Crucible.* Whether we are to accept his Salem as historical or as an analogy for the United States in the early fifties, Miller needs to create a mood of mass hysteria in which guilt and confession become public virtues. For this reason, Proctor is not so intensively on stage as the protagonists of the earlier plays are; the playwright has to work up a setting for him, has to give his attention to the accusers, the court, the town.

Now that Joe McCarthy is dead and Roy Cohn is running Lionel trains, it has become customary to consider *The Crucible* outside the context in which it was written. Since the play is not simply a tract, there is good sense in that attitude; whatever value the play comes to have will be intrinsic. Still, there is something to be learned about John Proctor from Arthur Miller's opinions at the time the play was written. About six months after the play was produced, the *Nation* (July 3, 1954) published Miller's "A Modest Proposal for Pacification of the Public Temper," a not very successful attempt at Swiftian satire. What the piece does do is make quite clear that Miller believed that the America of that moment, like the Salem of his play, was going in for a kind of group therapy that demanded each man's *mea culpa.* It would be simple enough to dissect Miller's use of Salem and to show, as so many critics have, that the Massachusetts witch hunts are not analogous to the postwar Communist hunts, but such an exercise is finally beside the point. The important thing is that Miller found Salem both relevant and dramatically useful. A resurrection of the political situation at this time is valuable only because it is quite obvious that Miller's involvement with that situation dictated his treatment of the material. I am not thinking of the villainous Danforth, the ambitious Parris, the greedy Putnam, the envious Abigail, each of whom uses the cryings-out to his own advantage, although Miller was plainly intent on questioning the sincerity of accusers and investigators in general. It is John Proctor who shows most clearly Miller's attitude. His hero might have been another Willy Loman, another Joe Keller, an accepter not a defier of society, and his play would have had just as much—perhaps more—propaganda value. There is such a character in the play—the Reverend John Hale, the witch expert, who breaks under the strain of the trials—and one can make a good case for Hale as the protagonist of *The Crucible*. Although Hale is a much more interesting character than Proctor, it is Proctor's play and here Miller has produced, as he has not in his earlier plays, a romantic hero. It seems likely that Miller's opposition to the investigations and particularly to the form they took, the ritual naming of names, made him want a conventional hero, not, as usual, a victim-hero. When he appeared before the House Committee on Un-American Activities in June 1956, there was dignity in his refusal to give names, in his willingness to describe his past without apologizing for it, in his simple, "I accept my life." Ironically, not even Elizabeth's "He have his goodness now" can make Proctor's dignity convincing. The simplicity of the real situation is impossible on stage. Miller's need to push Proctor to his heroic end causes him to bring to *The Crucible* too many of the trappings of the standard romantic play; the plot turns on that moment in court when Elizabeth, who has never lied before, lies out of love of her husband and condemns him by that act. This is a sentimental mechanism almost as outrageous as the hidden-letter trick in the last act of *All My Sons*. There is excitement enough in the scene to hold an audience, but the attention that such a device demands is quite different from that required by John Proctor's struggle of conscience.

Although Proctor is never completely successful as a character, Miller makes a real effort to convince us that he is more than the blunt, not so bright good man he appears to be; and once again Miller works in terms of societal concepts. The Proctor who appears in the novelistic notes that Miller has sprinkled through the text of the published play is not quite the Proctor of the play itself; but there are similarities. We are to assume that Proctor is a solid man, but an independent one, not a man to fit lightly into anyone else's mold. When we meet him, however, he is suffering under a burden of guilt—intensified by his belief that Elizabeth is continually judging him. Miller makes it clear that in sleeping with Abigail Williams, Proctor has become "a sinner not only against the moral fashion of the time, but against his own vision of decent conduct." In Act III, when he admits in open court that he is a lecher, he says, "A man will not cast away his good name." When he is finally faced with the choice of death or confession (that he consorted with the devil), his guilt as an adulterer becomes confused with his innocence as a witch; one sin against society comes to look like another, or so he rationalizes. In the last act, however, Elizabeth in effect absolves him of the sin of adultery, gives him back the name he lost in court, and clears the way for him to reject the false confession and to give his life: "How may I live without my name?"

Eddie Carbone in *A View from the Bridge* (1955; revised, 1956) also dies crying out for his name, but when he asks Marco to "gimme my name" he is asking for a lie that will let him live and, failing that, for death. Eddie is unusual among the Miller heroes in that he accepts the rules and prejudices of his society, an Italian neighborhood in Brooklyn, and dies because he violates them. Early in the play, Eddie warns Catherine to be closemouthed about the illegal immigrants (the "submarines") who are coming to live with them; he tells her with approbation about the brutal punishment meted out to an informer. By the end of the play, the "passion that had moved into his body, like a stranger," as Alfieri calls it, so possesses Eddie that to rid himself of the presence of Rodolpho he is willing to commit an act that he abhors as much as his society does. Miller's own comments on the play and the lines that he gives to Alfieri, a cross between the Greek chorus and Mary Worth, indicate that he sees Eddie in the grip of a force that is almost impersonal in its inevitability, its terribleness, "the awesomeness of a passion which . . . despite even its destruction of the moral beliefs of the individual, proceeds to magnify its power over him until it destroys him." The action in *View* seems to me somewhat more complicated than the clean line Miller suggests; its hero is more than a leaf blown along on winds out of ancient Calabria. Eddie chooses to become an informer; his choice is so hedged with rationalization—his convincing himself that Rodolpho is homosexual, that he is marrying Catherine for citizenship papers—that he is never conscious of his motivation. He comes closer and closer to putting a label on his incestuous love for Catherine (although technically she is his niece, functionally she is his daughter) and his homosexual attraction to Rodolpho (how

pathetically he goes round and round to keep from saying *queer*).
By comparison, informing is a simpler breach of code, one that has
justification in the world outside the neighborhood. It is almost as
though he takes on the name *informer* to keep from wearing some
name that is still more terrible to him, only to discover that he
cannot live under the lesser label either.

"It is not enough any more to know that one is at the mercy of
social pressures," Miller writes in "On Social Plays"; "it is necessary to understand that such a sealed fate cannot be accepted."
Each of his four heroes is caught in a trap compounded of social
and psychological forces and each one is destroyed. Miller is concerned that their deaths not be dismissed as insignificant, the crush-
ing of little men by big forces. His description of Eddie Carbone
expresses his opinion of all his heroes: "he possesses or exemplifies
the wondrous and humane fact that he too can be driven to what
in the last analysis is a sacrifice of himself for his conception, however misguided, of right, dignity, and justice."

Playwrights, however, have always been better at telling men
how to die than how to live. A dramatist in opposition is always
more comfortable than one in affirmation. When Miller chooses
to be a social critic, in the old-fashioned sense, it is apparent what
he is against. Although he disavows any blanket attack on capital-
ism, both *Salesman* and *Sons* contain explicit criticism of a business-
oriented society in which corruption, selfishness, indifference, are
the norms. The political and governmental targets are obvious
enough in *The Crucible*; in *View* there is an implicit condemnation of a social system that turns men into submarines. Back in the
childhood of his career as a playwright, the days of *They Too
Arise,* Miller might have been able to conceive of some kind of
political action as a cure for such societal wrongs, but it has become increasingly clear that his concern is with personal morality,
the individual's relation to a society in which the virtuous goals
(Joe Keller's sense of family, Willy Loman's idea of success) are
almost as suspect as the vicious methods. When there is a concrete
situation, a problem like that of Joe Keller's cylinder heads, Miller has no difficulty; who in the audience is going to suggest that
Keller was right in sending them out? It is with those other alter-
natives—the ones embedded in generalizations—that the trouble
arises.

Biff can say, at the end of *Death of a Salesman,* "He had the wrong dreams," but we have seen enough of Willy to know that for this man there is probably no right dream. Still, Biff suggests that there is: "there's more of him in that front stoop than in all the sales he ever made." And Charley seems to agree: "He was a happy man with a batch of cement." The play is filled with references to Willy's pride in working with his hands, his desire for a garden. This theme that so pervades *Salesman* is hit glancingly in some of the other plays, in John Proctor's obvious love for his farm and in Eddie Carbone's pleasure in working a shipload of coffee. Smell, touch, taste, the physical contact between a man and his work, a man and the thing created—this is at least part of the alternative. It is a sentimental possibility, a compounding of two quasi-literary myths—the thirties' insistence on the dignity of labor coupled with the older back-to-nature idea. Reduced to its simplest, it is the respectable commonplace that a man is happiest doing work that he likes.

The rest of the "right dream" is not so concrete. It has to do with the relation of one man to another (a man to society, Miller might say), but it can only be defined in terms of the great words, the words that we use on state occasions. The fascination of Miller's plays is that he knows so well the way a society edits the meaning of the grand abstractions and forces (or entices) men to embrace them. Implicit in his work, however, is the possibility of a society that might not lead the Willys of this world astray. In *Situation Normal,* a volume of reportage that grew out of his army-camp research for the movie *The Story of G.I. Joe,* Miller insists that the main purpose of the book is to find the Belief (he uses the capital letter) that is sending men into war. When he finds it ("And that Belief says, simply, that we believe all men are equal"), it is traditional and it is honorable, but it is as amorphous as Chris Keller's *brotherhood.* Chris embodies the idea that a good society will follow when men choose not to live only for themselves. Vague as this idea is, it does represent a kind of commitment; Miller's characters, however, can effectively express or represent that commitment only in terms of opposition.

In Miller's most recent work, *The Misfits* (1961), both in the movie and the cinema novel (as his publisher calls it), there has been a change of attitude. It can be seen most clearly in two ideas that have preoccupied Miller the last few years: one is his assumption that in our society the hero is reduced to the misfit; the other is the chief dramatic cliché of the fifties, faith in the curative powers of love. To understand this change clearly, one must go back to *Death of a Salesman,* begin with Biff, who is, after all, the prototype of the Miller misfit. Uncomfortable in Willy's competitive world, Biff goes west, becomes an outdoors bum—like Gay, Guido, and Perce in *The Misfits.* Although *Salesman* is too ambiguous, too good a play to allow Biff to wear a single label, it implies at least that there is something positive in Biff's choice. Certainly, as late as 1955, in the novelistic notes he added to the Bantam edition of the play, Miller was to describe Happy as "less heroically cast" than Biff, a phrase that suggests that Biff is somehow heroic. The same year, however, in "On Social Plays," Miller shook his head sadly over the state of the hero, said that "our common sense reduces him to the size of a complainer, a misfit." *Salesman* suggests reasons for this reduction in size in Biff's case; he is "lost," to use a cliché that Miller shares with Linda Loman, the queen of the bromides, but the implication is that he is incapacitated by his sense of guilt at having rejected his father and his father's dream. Although there are suggestions of psychological dislocation in the story version of "The Misfits" (*Esquire,* October 1957), it is primarily the story of three men who have no place in the world of job, home, and family. "Well, it's better than wages," says Gay of their pathetic roundup of wild horses, and Perce answers, "Hell, yes. Anything's better than wages." Using the roundup as plot, the story insists that, even though the West might once have been big enough for a man or horse to be proud and free, the mustang has become dogfood and the mustanging hero, a dogfood-hunting bum. In this form, "The Misfits" is a kind of twilight of the gods, and it has the dignity and sadness that such a theme demands.

In the later versions, the movie and the novel, the regret turns to therapy. Although Miller has often criticized the sentimentality of contemporary drama, his commitment to the generalized good seems finally to have forced him to embrace the last decade's faith in love as an anodyne. In the Introduction to *Collected Plays,* published the year that "The Misfits" first appeared, Miller says that in *Salesman* he wanted to set up "an opposing system which, so to speak, is in a race for Willy's faith, and it is the system of love which is the opposite of the law of success." There is no such thing in the play. Biff obviously loves Willy as much as he hates him, but this fact hardly constitutes a system; nor is it presented as a

possible opposite to Willy's desire for success. Miller is simply trying to read back into the earlier play a concept of love that comes
too late to save Willy, but just in time to destroy the hero-misfit.
The movie and the novel pick up the psychological hints of the
story, develop them at great length and indicate that these men
are not misfits in the grand tradition of Daniel Boone and Kit Carson; they are would-be conformists looking for a home. At the
end of the movie, Perce is going back to wages, to the mother and
ranch he lost when she remarried after the death of his father.
Guido is still crying out in anger, but there is more frustration than
principle in his cries. It is with Gay that the sentimentality is most
obvious. As he and Roslyn drive off at the end of *The Misfits,* after
he has released the wild horse and with it any claim he has to in-
dependence, she says, "How do you find your way back in
the dark?" He answers, "Just head for that big star straight on. The
highway's under it; take us right home." It has been suggested that
this end is as ironic as the Requiem of *Salesman,* but there is too
much evidence against such an interpretation: Miller's remarks
about love and Biff, the sudsiness that pervades the prose and the
characters in the novel, the clichés (John Huston's as well as Miller's) that fill the movie.

It is too early to tell whether *The Misfits* is an anomaly or an indication, whether—when and if he returns to the theater—Miller
will again concern himself with society and its effects on men or,
like so many of his contemporaries, crawl into the personal solution to public problems. Whatever happens, it is necessary to say
that Miller's early work for the theater has earned him an important place in American drama. The faults of his plays are obvious enough. *All My Sons,* for all its neatness, tends to go to pieces
in the last act when the recognition of Joe's guilt no longer comes
from the interaction of characters, but from the gratuitous introduction of Larry's letter. In *Death of a Salesman,* peripheral characters such as Howard and Bernard are completely unbelievable
and Miller has not saved them, as he has Ben, by turning them into
obvious caricatures. There are distressing structural faults in *The
Crucible,* violations of the realistic surface of the play, such as the
unlikely scene in Act I in which Proctor and Abigail are left alone
in the sick girl's bedroom. Nor was it such a good idea for Miller
to attempt, in that play, to suggest the language of the period; the
lines are as awkward and as stagily false as those in John Drink-

water's *Oliver Cromwell.* The pretentiousness of Alfieri's speeches in *A View from the Bridge,* the conscious attempt to make an analogy between Red Hook and Calabria, reduces the impact of Eddie Carbone's story; any connection between Eddie and the passion-ridden heroes of old should have been made implicitly.

Miller's virtues, however, outweigh these faults. The theme that recurs in all of his plays—the relationship between a man's identity and the image that society demands of him—is a major one; in one way or another it has been the concern of most serious playwrights. A big theme is not enough, of course; Miller has the ability to invest it with emotion. He is sometimes sentimental, sometimes romantic about both his characters and their situations; but sentiment and romance, if they can command an audience without drowning it, are not necessarily vices. Even in *A Memory of Two Mondays,* in which he peoples his stage with stereotypes, he manages, in the end, to make Bert's departure touching. The test of the good commercial playwright is the immediate reaction of an audience; the test of the good playwright is how well his plays hold up under continuing observation. Each time I go back to *All My Sons,* to *The Crucible,* to *A View from the Bridge,* the faults become more ominous, but in each of these plays there are still scenes that work as effectively as they did when I first saw the play. *Death of a Salesman* is something else again. It does not merely hold its own, it grows with each rereading. Those people who go in for good-better-best labels—I am not one of them—would be wise, when they draw up their list of American plays, to put *Death of a Salesman* very near the top.

2 TENNESSEE WILLIAMS' FUGITIVE KIND

We are the gooks and geeks of creation;
Believe-It-or-Not is the name of our star.
Each of us here thinks the other is queer
and no one's mistaken since all of us are!
  —*Carrousel Tune*

"At the age of fourteen," Tennessee Williams wrote in the Foreword to *Sweet Bird of Youth,* "I discovered writing as an escape from a world of reality in which I felt acutely uncomfortable." In the thirty-odd years since that discovery, his has been a busy escape mechanism. He has written a dozen long plays, some twenty short ones, six film scripts (in and out of collaboration), a novel of sorts (*The Roman Spring of Mrs. Stone*), two books of short stories, a volume of poems and a handful of short pieces, half autobiography, half aesthetics, which usually do double duty, as New York *Times* articles heralding the production of his plays and as introductions to the published versions. There is also, presumably, a large body of unpublished work from his embryonic years as a writer—in some of his introductions, notably the one to *Orpheus Descending,* he has described his early plays; but the *juvenilia* need not detain us here. Aside from its therapeutic value to the author, Williams' writing—or the products of it—has, justly or unjustly, given him an international reputation as the leading American playwright since World War II.

Although there have been recognizable shifts in emphasis and in method in Williams' work in the course of his career, it is impractical to treat him chronologically, to use the standard critical approach that stalks a writer from his youthful inadequacies to the flowering of his mature years. For one thing, Williams suffers from a familiar affliction of American playwrights—first-play afflatus.

Although *The Glass Menagerie* was not his first play, it was his Broadway debut and his first success, and it is still his best play. For a second thing, Williams re-uses so much material that the past and the present sometimes lie side by side in a single work, uncomfortable bedfellows. In *Baby Doll,* for instance, which is presumably set in 1955 when it was written, there are lines about the good-neighbor policy and the President's speech that belong to the thirties of the film's short-play source, *27 Wagons Full of Cotton.* That kind of slip is easy enough to catch. It is the private anachronism that causes the trouble; for instance, it is difficult to tell whether the broadly comic depiction of the demented Mrs. Winemiller in *Summer and Smoke* is a hangover in tone from "The Yellow Bird," the short story in which Alma got a first, farcical workout, or whether Williams thinks that his characterization of the mother adds to the portrait of the daughter. So many characters, situations, scenes, lines, in the later plays are carried over from the one-acters, the short stories, the poems, that it is simpler to think of Williams' work as a single unit than to try to break it up into bite-size bits.

Under some circumstances it might be a little unfair to treat twenty years of a man's work as though it were all of a time, all of a piece, but Williams' writing reflects a continual preoccupation with the same themes, the same kinds of characters. The distance from Dorothy Simple in *The Case of the Crushed Petunias* (1941) to Isabel Haverstick in *Period of Adjustment* (1960) may be measured in years and in sophistication of technique, but it cannot be measured in terms of the author's changing view of the world. The boy of fourteen that Williams conjured up in the Foreword to *Sweet Bird* was father to the man in more ways than one; the playwright of fifty is still uncomfortable in the world of reality, providing that that world can be described in Harold Clurman's words about *A Streetcar Named Desire,* as one in which "aspiration, sensitivity, departure from the norm are battered, bruised, and disgraced. . . ."

Clurman has Blanche DuBois in mind, of course, but Blanche is not the first of the Williams victims and certainly not the last. The word *victim* comes easily when one begins to talk about the characters in Williams' plays, for the rape of Blanche and her subsequent insanity hangs like a banner over Williams' work, proclaiming him the spokesman for the defeated, the frustrated, the beaten. It is easy to forget that Hadrian rescues Matilda in *You Touched Me!* (which Williams wrote with Donald Wind-ham); that *The Rose Tattoo* ends triumphantly with Serafina's rejection of death and ashes; that *Camino Real* sends Kilroy, a patsy turned hero, out across the desert with Don Quixote; that *Baby Doll* manages an upbeat ending at the expense of the heroine's characterization; that *Period of Adjustment* puts two couples to bed in an attempt to solve their problems; that even *Cat on a Hot Tin Roof,* providing you accept the Broadway, or Elia Kazan, last act, ends on an ambiguous note of reconciliation. Despite the re-strainedly happy endings, there is enough blackness in even the lightest of these plays—*The Rose Tattoo,* say—to make plain that their action takes place in the world of Tennessee Williams. His characters, then, are related by the nature of their struggle, not by the outcome.

All of Williams' protagonists and many of his subsidiary charac-ters are outsiders, unable or unwilling to conform to the dull or cruel world in which they find themselves. Cora and Billy, the slut and the homosexual who join forces in the short story, "Two on a Party," are militant examples:

> It was a rare sort of moral anarchy, doubtless, that held them to-gether, a really fearful shared hatred of everything that was restrictive and which they felt to be false in the society they lived in and against the grain of which they continually operated. They did not dislike what they called "squares." They loathed and despised them, and for the best of reasons. Their existence was a never-ending contest with the squares of the world, the squares who have such a virulent rage at everything not in their book.

The generic name for these characters in Williams is "the fugitive kind," a phrase that turns up first as the title of his second full-length play, which was never published. The use of the words in the story "One Arm" is specifically homosexual. By the time Carol Cutrere adopts the phrase in *Orpheus Descending,* as she takes Val's snakeskin jacket, a token by which "the fugitive kind can always follow their kind," the label belongs to the outsider who seeks the freedom that Val describes metaphorically when he tells Lady about the legless bird that lives all his life on the wing. The movie version of *Orpheus Descending,* of course, became *The Fugitive Kind.*

To go to the stories for a definition of the Williams outsider is to do his protagonists a disservice; the short fiction is redolent with a kind of lip-smacking perversity, lingers lovingly over the details of the trade, to use a "trade" term. In the plays, the preoccupation is not so narrow. The leading characters are different from (implicitly, superior to) their neighbors, but there is variety in the differences. The one thing that all of them seem to have in common is the combination of sensitivity and imagination with corruption—physical, spiritual, sexual disability. From the beginning, the plays have suggested that the heroes are abnormal and that there is something vaguely damnable about normality.

Tom in *The Glass Menagerie* describes Jim, the gentleman caller, as "an emissary from a world of reality that we were somehow set apart from." Neither Tom, who is in some ways Williams himself, nor his creator, who calls Jim a "nice, ordinary, young man," seems aware that the gentleman caller is a much more important symbol than the pretentious "long delayed but always expected something that we live for." Jim, much more than the romantic Tom, is a condemnation of the world Tom wants to escape from; he is an Arthur Miller character, dead wrong and almost certain, expecting optimistically that he will find success just beyond the next correspondence course. Although Williams has given him space to operate in, lines enough to be damning in their glibness and pathetic in their naïveté, it is apparent here and later that Williams cannot really come to care seriously about the Jims who try to operate in the real world. He is more concerned with those who reject or are rejected by it. The three Wingfields are Williams' kind although only Tom becomes a fugitive. Tom is supposed to be a poet, a spirit too free for the confines of the warehouse that encloses him; before the play is over, no longer able to find escape at the movies, he leaves his family "attempting to find in motion what was lost in space." That is, he joins the merchant marine. His sister Laura is a painfully shy girl with a slight limp, a physical and emotional cripple, who takes refuge in her glass collection and in the old records that belonged to their father, who deserted the family years before the curtain rises. Amanda, the mother, the strongest character in the play, has one foot in reality in her struggle to hold the family together and the other in the illusionary world of her girlhood, the genteel tag end of the aristocratic South. Her past, the play suggests, may be as imaginary as its application to her present, for there is never any evidence that Amanda's memories are real ones. Amanda and Laura are defeated by the world, fade at the end of the play into an amorphous future, all scrim and lighting effects; Tom survives to tell the story, but he is fated to be a stranger in the world. Among them, the three Wingfields manage to display most of the characteristics of the later Williams characters.

Both Laura and Tom have the sensitivity; with Laura it is allied to physical fragility and virginal withdrawal, with Tom it is part of his poetic temperament. Other Lauras turn up in Matilda in *You Touched Me!,* Alma in *Summer and Smoke,* and Isabel in *Period of Adjustment.* Brick in *Cat on a Hot Tin Roof* is also a kind of Laura; Williams even gives him a broken ankle, like Laura's limp, to serve as a visual symbol of his "moral paralysis." Most of the heroines, whether they are Laura's type or not, have their glass menageries, which, like Amanda's Blue Mountain memories, keep them from seeing the ugliness of a frightening world. Blanche has the mythical Shep Huntleigh as a potential gentleman caller and she acquires a Chinese lantern to put over the naked bulb in the Kowalski apartment. Matilda has the silver to polish; Serafina, in *The Rose Tattoo,* her urn of ashes; Lady, in *Orpheus,* the simulation in her confectionery of her dead father's wine garden; Alexandra, in *Sweet Bird,* her hashish and her oxygen.

Tom's poetic temperament turns up again and again in the later plays and, for the most part, it is as ambiguously presented as it is in *The Glass Menagerie.* All that we really know about Tom as an artist is that he jots verses down on the lids of boxes in the warehouse where he works, and that Williams did the same thing when he worked in a warehouse in his youth. It may be that Tom, like the young man in *Long Day's Journey into Night,* has the habit of the poet without the makings. For Williams, that does not seem to matter. Sensitivity is implicit in the character who, like Billy in "Two on a Party," manages to be "a sort of artist *manqué*" and has "a touch of homesickness for what that was." His pseudo-artistic characters aside, Williams seems to have only a flaccid idea of what art is. He describes the interior set of *The Glass Menagerie* as "dim and poetic" and, fifteen years later, suggests that a cyclorama be used in *Sweet Bird* to achieve "a poetic unity of mood"; a good many of his general comments on writing that fall between the two stage directions display the same fondness for the vague. Williams uses the word *poetic* as loosely and as enthusiastically as Blanche might; so it is hardly surprising that his characters need only cultural and artistic pretensions, not achievements, to indicate their differentness from the people around them. Thus, Blanche can display the high-school teacher's namedropping familiarity with literary figures ("Only Poe! Only Mr. Edgar Allan Poe!—could do it justice!") and Alma can take part in the meeting of a literary club, which Williams presents satirically, without either of them losing her standing among the Williams near artists. Both Mrs. Stone, of the spring in Rome, and Alexandra in *Sweet Bird* are ex-actresses, and even though their success depended more on their beauty than their artistry, they belong to Tom Wingfield's fraternity. So, too, does Vee Talbot, the primitive painter of *Orpheus Descending,* even though (or because) her painting is the objectivization of her sexual frustration. The most preposterous of the Williams artists are Sebastian, the poet of *Suddenly Last Summer,* and Val Xavier, the Orpheus who does the descending. The first may well be intended satirically—at least I cannot take seriously the poet who produces one poem a year, each time after a nine-month gestation period —but Val, I am afraid, is serious. In *Battle of Angels,* the embryonic version of *Orpheus,* Val is, incredibly, writing *the book;* in *Orpheus,* Williams wisely takes away his pen and hands him a guitar, which not only better suits his mythic origins, but which can be worked less portentously into the action of the play. Even so, Val insists on calling the instrument his "life's companion," fondles it so lovingly that he ends by suggesting Christopher Fry's charming Chaplain in *The Lady's Not for Burning,* who calls his violin "my better half . . . my mistress . . . my angel." The only dead-certain poet in the body of Williams' plays is Byron, who turns up in *Camino Real,* but it is his manner and not his matter that gets him into that play.

Just as Laura the recluse and Tom the poet turn up in other plays, bearing other names and faces, so too does Amanda the faded aristocrat. The short plays and stories are loaded with serious or comic, New Orleans or deep South, versions of the Amanda character—*The Lady of Larkspur Lotion,* Miss Collins in *Portrait of a Madonna,* Mme. Duvenet in *Auto-Da-Fé,* the two ladies in *Lord Byron's Love Letter,* Cornelia Scott in *Something Unspoken,* Miss Jelkes in "The Night of the Iguana." All of them must be hounded in some way—by poverty, by age, by frustration—and all of them must look back fondly on better days, either real or fictional. Blanche in *Streetcar* is certainly the most famous of the Williams faded ladies. Much of her manner—her pretense at gentility, the affectations of her speech, her verbal withdrawal from Stanley—goes back to an imaginary Belle Reve, one that existed, if it existed at all, in the years before Blanche was around to know it; the Belle Reve she describes, the plantation Stella escaped from, was a place of slow death and decay ("Crumble and fade and—regrets—recriminations"). Blanche, more than she knows, is a product of Belle Reve, true descendant of those "improvident grandfathers and fathers and uncles and brothers" who "exchanged the land for their epic fornications. . . ." When *Streetcar* first appeared in 1947, we were still within shouting distance of those days when critics thought of plays always in social terms; it was not surprising that Blanche became a symbol of the Old South, that romantic invention of Southern ladies and Northern historians, whose cultural and human virtues were doomed to destruction in the face of the vitality and vulgarity of the New South—Stanley. Although Williams' plays have, from the beginning, often contained specific social criticism, his attachment to the Blanches is more than a search for a social symbol. Her corruption is as important to him as her sensitivity; both characteristics make her an uncomfortable visitor in a middle-class world. He consistently uses the shell of the Southern aristocracy for the double value it gives him. This is made quite clear in "The Night of the Iguana" in which he describes Miss Jelkes's "historical Southern family of great but now moribund vitality": "There had been an efflorescence among them of nervous talents and sickness, of drunkards and poets, gifted artists and sexual degenerates, together with fanatically proper and squeamish old ladies of both sexes. . . ." The sentence reads like a cast list for a Williams play. Sandra in *Battle of Angels* makes the same point when she describes herself as rotten and neurotic, but identifies with Val, "You—savage. And me—aristocrat. Both of us things whose license has been revoked in the civilized world. Both of us equally damned and for the same good reason. Because we both want freedom." This kind of leaden explicitness disappears in the rewrite, in *Orpheus Descending,* in which Sandra has become Carol

Cutrere, but Carol's actions and many of her lines still say the same thing.

The once elegant Mrs. Venable in *Suddenly Last Summer* is a variation on the type. Her connections are not with a historical past, but with a personal one. She is one of the ex-beauties, like Mrs. Stone and Alexandra Del Lago and Camille as she appears in *Camino Real,* although—unlike the other ladies—she is not feeding (nor can she) the illusion of youth by buying love. Chance Wayne is a male version of the aging women and so, too, is Brick, although the ex-athlete in him brings him closer to the ex-actress in Alexandra than to the ex-beauty.

Two other important identification marks for the Williams outsiders are their physical and mental sicknesses and their preoccupation with sex. The first of these is apparent in *The Glass Menagerie* in Laura's limp and in the description of Amanda as "not paranoic, but her life is paranoia." Blanche is specifically identified as a "neurasthenic personality." Alma has to have her tablets ("The prescription number is 96814. I think of it as the telephone number of God!"), and Lady, Alexandra, Chance, Sebastian, Isabel Haverstick are all pilleaters, too. Kilroy in *Camino Real* has a weak heart; Brick, a broken ankle; Big Daddy, cancer. Mrs. Venable has had a stroke, but in *Suddenly Last Summer* that is hardly noticeable, for in that play Williams' fondness for medical mumbo jumbo runs rampant; not only is Catharine threatened with a lobotomy, she is given a truth injection on stage and the audience is offered a parody paradigm of the scientific process as solemn as that of the mad scientist in old horror films. It is obvious that the mental and physical diseases, real and imagined, that afflict the characters are partly symbolic; all of them, like Laura, are crippled in the face of a world that is cruel and demanding. Williams is not completely consistent in his use of disease—and I am not suggesting that he should be—for Jabe, who is king of the hell Orpheus descends into, who represents death against the life in Val, is dying of cancer.

The Glass Menagerie is an unusual Williams play in that sex has no part in it; the plays that follow it add up to a kind of sexual *smörgåsbord,* if Sebastian will forgive the phrase. Williams seems to use sex in two different ways. The most characteristic, the one that is most identified with his work, is desperation sex, which gives the plays the lurid ingredients that probably help make them popular—nymphomania, rape, homosexuality, voyeurism, prostitution (male and female, in and out of marriage), and flagellation (in *27 Wagons Full of Cotton*; in *Baby Doll,* Vacarro still carries the riding crop, but he only uses it to tease with). Implicit in his gallery of deviates is Williams' conviction—almost the only subject of his stories and poems—that human beings can make contact with one another only tentatively, momentarily, and that even if the touch be agonizing it is better than no communication at all. Blanche, who tries, through promiscuity, to reach and get forgiveness from her dead homosexual husband, killed she believes by her cruelty, is the most famous of these lost ones; Carol Cutrere is the most articulate. In a scene with Val, she makes clear that sex is physically painful to her, but she hunts it in the "jook" joints along the Mississippi roads because, "What on earth can you do on this earth but catch at whatever comes near you, with both your hands, until your fingers are broken?"

If the broken-fingered ones continue to reach out hungrily, but not with hope, there are also Williams characters for whom sex is consolation and comfort. His most affirmative statement comes at the end of *The Rose Tattoo* when the newly pregnant Serafina, shouting her love, goes off with Alvaro. It is possible that he manages so determined a declaration for love and life here because the characters are Sicilian. Williams has been quoted (New York *Post,* April 24, 1958) as calling himself a Puritan, although a rebellious one, and he does seem to share that Anglo-Saxon myth, probably Puritan in origin, that is so sure that Latin people are richly capable of uncomplicated sex lives. Thus, the end of *Baby Doll* suggests that Vacarro, another Sicilian, may be able to break through the infantile virginity of the heroine. Thus, Myra in *Battle of Angels* becomes Italian in *Orpheus Descending*; the part of Lady was supposedly written for Anna Magnani, which would explain the shift in national origin, but so simple an explanation is somewhat complicated by the fact that the transmutation began earlier with Rosa Gonzales in *Summer and Smoke,* a Mexican halfway house between Myra and Lady. Lady, incidentally, is the only Williams character, other than Serafina, capable of shouting in favor of life, and she, like Serafina, is pregnant when she lifts her voice. In terms of affirmation through sex, the plays are similar, although there is a slight reversal in roles. In *The Rose Tattoo,*

Serafina has put aside sex after the death of her husband and is re-awakened by the need of Alvaro. In *Orpheus,* Val has put aside sex, having never found in physical love the mystery that he is searching for, and is reawakened, or once again made willing, by the need of Lady. The plays have different jobs to do; so the re-birth in Val and Lady proves abortive. The destructive world that appears only on the periphery of *The Rose Tattoo*—the traveling salesman who calls Alvaro *wop* and kicks him in the groin—is triumphant in *Orpheus Descending.*

There is a double use of chastity in Williams, too. It can be a psychological withdrawal, a fear of contact, or it can be a symbolic withdrawal, a refusal to make contact. In the first case, the chaste character must be rescued, as Matilda is in *You Touched Me!* from the "aggressive sterility" of her Aunt Emmie. So, too, Baby Doll will probably finally get out of her crib in time to avoid the fate of Alma in *Summer and Smoke,* who at last gets Dr. John's message about the body, but too late to get Dr. John with the mes-sage; Alma, it appears, is going the way of Blanche, or—re-membering the Alma of "The Yellow Bird"—heading for a crib rather different from Baby Doll's. The therapeutic aura that hangs over all these rescues is made explicit in *Period of Adjustment,* where the virginal newlyweds finally get together on Isabel's words, "The whole world's a big hospital, a big neurological ward and I am a student nurse in it." The chastity on principle is that of Serafina before Alvaro reaches her, that of Val when he has de-cided to put all corruption behind him. It is explicit in Brick's re-fusal to sleep with Maggie in *Cat on a Hot Tin Roof* (the homo-sexuality is only implicit), and it is frankly symbolic in *Camino Real* in which Kilroy's enlarged heart makes sex dangerous for him. All of these withdrawals are expressions, in Brick's words, of disgust with the mendacity of the world. Although chastity can be one of the marks that the fugitive kind bears, just as often Williams uses it, under not so pure a guise as chastity, to represent the fugitive-kind-hunters from Emmie, the genteel symbolic castrater of *You Touched Me!,* to the sex-envy boys in St. Cloud, the real castraters of *Sweet Bird.* But, then, healthy sex has also been on the side of the brutes, to use Blanche's word, for Stanley and Stella must surely be the most sexually compatible couple in all of Williams' work.

In trying to pin down the shifting form of the Williams outsider,

I have inevitably suggested something about the world that has pushed him outside. It shows three faces in the Williams plays: one dull and vulgar, one hypocritically complacent, and one ugly and violent. The first is the ordinary middle-class world in which material success and status are important. This is the world that Jim aspires to in *The Glass Menagerie*; its symbols are the neon-lighted warehouse where Tom worked and the building in which he lives, "one of those vast hive-like conglomerations of cellular living-units that . . . are symptomatic of the impulse of this largest and fundamentally enslaved section of American society to avoid fluidity and differentiation and to exist and function as one interfused mass of automatism." Although Williams is quite specific about what it is from which Tom wants to escape—the horror of routine and the concern with conventional success—the play is set in the Depression years and he cannot here show, as he does in the later plays, the material symbols of getting ahead and the vacuity implicit in them. He makes much in his stage directions in *Cat* of the "*huge* console combination of radio-phonograph (Hi-Fi with three speakers) TV set *and* liquor cabinet . . . a very complete and compact little shrine to virtually all the comforts and illusions behind which we hide. . . ." What Williams has to say directly in *Cat,* Serafina says for him in *The Rose Tattoo* when she describes the ordinary housewives: "Instead of the heart they got the deep-freeze in the house." In *Period of Adjustment,* Ralph Bates has achieved what Jim was working for in *Menagerie,* the complete suburban existence (the subdivision, called High Point, is built over a cavern and is slowly sinking into it), but, like Tom, Ralph wants to escape. Ironically, *Period,* for all its attempts at satire, is Williams' most conformist play, for the attack on suburbia is the chief badge of the Broadway insider today.

For the Williams birds of passage, like Tom, the dullness and grossness of middle-class life may be reason enough to escape; for Williams, particularly in the later plays, the materiality becomes more ominous. In *Cat on a Hot Tin Roof* greed is as much his subject as mendacity. Gooper and Mae, who want so desperately to get their hands on Big Daddy's plantation, are Williams' harshest caricatures of lust for property, at least until Mrs. Holly and her son George turn up in *Suddenly Last Summer,* willing to sacrifice Catharine to Mrs. Venable to protect an inheritance. As though Gooper and Mae and their parody of family affection were not enough, Williams underlines the connection between greed and hypocrisy by introducing into the play the Reverend Tooker, "the living embodiment of the pious, conventional lie," with his continual harping on stained-glass windows and other bequests to the church. He is drawn so broadly that it is impossible to accept him as a character; he is either a thematic variation or comic nonsense, or both. The only property-hungry character in the play who manages to hold the sympathy of the audience is Maggie, who is no longer the emasculating woman that she was in the short story, "Three Players of a Summer Game"; Williams goes to some lengths to provide her with a genteel-poverty background by way of motivation. (I should have said that Maggie is supposed to retain the sympathy of the audience; my own reaction to *Cat* is one of complete boredom, utter indifference to Brick, Maggie, and booming Big Daddy; once Maggie's opening soliloquy is over, nothing in that play touches my sympathy or even my curiosity until Gooper's one honest speech in which he blurts out his desire for money and shows, inadvertently, that he would have liked love.) In *Orpheus Descending,* Williams also emphasizes the connection between cupidity and pretense; Beulah says, ostensibly talking about Lady, perhaps talking about herself, "I've always noticed when couples don't love each other they develop a passion for money." In that play, however, money is more closely connected with the harsher evil of Jabe, who, according to Beulah, bought Lady and "bought her cheap."

The problem of mendacity is a difficult one if one considers Williams' work as a whole. In *Cat* it is presented as a crippling force. Big Daddy finally makes Brick see that he has been lying to himself, that he has deserted Skipper by a refusal even to consider the possibility of homosexuality in himself. The reason, of course, is that society condemns the homosexual and demands that he conform or face rejection. Brick chooses to reject rather than to be rejected, to drink in disgust at society, but he carries with him the pretenses of that society, the need to lie about his sexuality, just as the rest of the characters lie about family, money, position, affection, disease. The suggestion in the play is that there is something to be condemned in a mendaciousness that, looked at another way, is simply the collection of polite lies by which society exists. Those lies become impolite when they become the myths of Sebastian by which Mrs. Venable lives in *Suddenly Last Summer* and when they must be preserved against Catharine's truth at the cost of the girl's sanity. The difficulty is largely one of connotation. The words *mendacity* and *lie* are not so soft, so appealing as the word *illusion*. Amanda and Blanche have been prodigious liars, but the audience has been expected to share in and sympathize with those lies. In the early plays illusion is a defense against an essentially harsh world; in the later plays, it has become mendacity and is one of that world's weapons.

The ugly face that the world turns on the Williams outsiders can best be characterized in Blanche's words "deliberate cruelty," which she insists is "not forgivable." Williams is aware that it is difficult to decide which cruelty is deliberate and which is not. Blanche, for instance, is one of the cruelest characters that Williams has created. She is aware that she has been deliberately cruel to her husband and has caused his death, but, in her way, she has tried to atone for that act; if she is right that such cruelty is "not forgivable" then her end may be as ironic a piece of self-judgment as that of Oedipus. Her treatment of Allan lies in the past, however; the Blanche we meet in the play is supposed to be pitied not blamed. Even so, her involvement in her own sensitivity is so complete that she refuses to recognize that she offends Eunice, who is goodhearted if garrulous; that Stanley may have feelings; that she is destroying the marriage of Stanley and Stella. Williams knows too much about the behavior of men, the self-defensive gesture that becomes attack, to make his division completely black and white. Marguerite in *Camino Real,* distressed at having missed The Fugitivo, the possible escape, warns Casanova, "if you stay with me now, I'll say cruel things, I'll wound your vanity, I'll taunt you. . . ." The strength of the early plays, of *The Glass Menagerie, A Streetcar Named Desire* and even *Summer and Smoke* (although its mechanical division into conflicting drives finally defeats it), is that the forces of cruelty, even Stanley, have not become the brute evil of the later plays.

The later group might be characterized by Baby Doll's words to and about Archie Lee: "Men that blow things up and burn things down because they're too evil and stupid to git along otherwise." Hatred is what drives them. Their chief representatives are Jabe in *Orpheus Descending* (and in *Battle of Angels*: I have placed this group in the late plays but they are amply in evidence in the very early work) and Boss Finley in *Sweet Bird of Youth;*

their instrument is the lynch mob. They are specifically identified with sex envy (*Orpheus, Sweet Bird*) and success envy (*Baby Doll*), with racial bigotry (*Sweet Bird, Orpheus*) and national bigotry (*Baby Doll, Orpheus*). Their only possible action, individually or communally, is violent. Thus, in *Camino Real,* the Survivor is shot when his thirst drives him to the hotel. In *Baby Doll,* Archie Lee burns down the competing cotton gin and contemplates organizing a lynching. In *Orpheus,* the Mystic Crew (in *Battle* the references are specifically to the Klan) burns Lady's father and his wine garden, Jabe shoots Lady, the mob uses a blowtorch on Val. In *Sweet Bird,* Boss Finley's thugs (respectable townsmen all) beat the heckler and presumably, after the curtain, castrate Chance.

The violent death of Sebastian in *Suddenly Last Summer* stands a little apart from these other evidences of violence. His destruction at the hands of the children in Cabeza de Lobo is part of the Williams metaphysic; their devouring of the poet's body is a symbol of a cannibalism that Sebastian also represents (there is something inevitably ludicrous in the symbol, however, since Sebastian's sexual taste conjures up a visual image of the sense in which he was an eater). The blackness that hovers over all the Williams plays suggests that the author may share with Sebastian the vision of the universe implicit in the sight he witnessed in the Encantadas, the "flesh-eating birds" destroying the baby turtles as they made their "desperate flight to the sea." Mrs. Venable explains that at that moment Sebastian was certain that he had seen God: "He meant that God shows a savage face to people and shouts some fierce things at them, it's all we see or hear of Him." Catharine, in her description of Sebastian's death, identifies the children with the birds of the Encantadas; they are "black plucked little birds" and apparently no more guilty than the real birds: "*He!—accepted!—all!*—as—how!—things!—are!" Williams has always been attracted to predator images, particularly birds, and he has often used them ambiguously. Camille and Casanova are "captive hawks" in *Camino Real;* when we see them, they are more preyed on than preying. In *The Roman Spring of Mrs. Stone* the heroine is frequently described as a predatory bird although she is as much a victim as she is a victimizer. This confusion makes it possible for Williams to move beyond the Jabes and the Boss Finleys and to find the universe the real destroyer, to discover that the fact of existence is inevitably opposed to the possibility of existence. For this reason, his work has always introduced an unbeatable opponent, Time; his victims, from Blanche to Chance Wayne, have struggled not only against the Stanleys and the Boss Finleys, but against inevitable aging. Almost twenty years ago he warned, "That time is short and it doesn't return again. It is slipping away while I write this and while you read it, and the monosyllable of the clock is Loss, loss, loss, unless you devote your heart to its opposition."

Catharine reports that Sebastian saw himself as "a sort of!— *image!* . . . *sacrifice* to a!—*terrible* sort of a—" When Dr. Cukrowicz prompts, "God?," Catharine finishes her sentence: "Yes, a—*cruel* one, Doctor!" If Sebastian's universe seems to him to demand a pagan sacrifice, perhaps of propitiation, Williams' seems to be willing, eager, to accept a vaguely Christian sacrifice, one of atonement. The early plays are sprinkled with references to purification by sacrificial death—in the pseudo-Lorca *The Purification,* for instance, and in the accidentally funny *Auto-Da-Fé.* In the story "Desire and the Black Masseur" the Christian analogy is much more specific; not only is Anthony Burns killed by the masseur, after a week of passion "toward the end of the Lenten season," but the death occurs while the congregation in a church across the street celebrates the Passion: "All of them are involved in a massive atonement." Finally, the Negro eats Anthony's body, a macabre parody of communion. The Christ figures that turn up in the plays are not much more attractive than Anthony Burns—but their sacrificial deaths (or mutilations) are more clearly acts of atonement (if accidental ones) that bring salvation of sorts (a temporary reinvigoration of freedom) to the fugitive kind. The most obvious of Williams' Christ figures is Val Xavier (read Savior) in *Orpheus Descending.* His identification with Christ is much more specific in *Battle of Angels,* where much is made of his name, whether or not it is spelled with an "s"; where Vee paints him as Christ; where, twice, moved to inarticularity by a kindness of Myra's, he stutters, "God, I—! Lady, you—!"; where the lynching takes place on Good Friday. The analogy is clear enough in *Orpheus,* although the crucifixion has been moved to Saturday; here Vee sees him in a vision as "JESUS CHRIST RISEN! . . . I mean Crucified and *then* RISEN!" and the exclamation "Christ" turns up more than once in the off-stage voices of the lynchers. Here, too, Val's snakeskin jacket, a relic,

passes on to Carol, one of the surviving faithful. Chance Wayne in
Sweet Bird is also a Christ apparently, since his castration takes
place at Easter; castration is as good as crucifixion for a Williams
Christ because the confusion of religious and sexual passion, so
important in "Desire and the Black Masseur," runs through all his
work. For instance, when Vee has her vision of Val as Jesus, she
cries out, momentarily blinded, "Light, oh, light! I never have
seen such brilliance! It PRICKED my eyeballs. . . ." If we are to
take the crucifixion analogy as anything other than a playing about
with religious sexuality, an echo of Oscar Wilde and the French
decadents, then it is necessary to emphasize that resurrection (despite Vee's vision) has little to do with these crucifixions. The one
character in any of the plays who makes something of the holy-day
analogy is Boss Finley in *Sweet Bird,* who points out that he was
burned in effigy on Good Friday and "Today is Easter Sunday and
I am in St. Cloud." In the Williams theology only evil is resur-
rected; Orpheus is always in descent. Perhaps there is tempering
of the death without resurrection in *Period of Adjustment,* which
takes place at Christmas with the Infant of Prague (there is a
statue in the Bates bedroom) presiding over the joining of the two
couples.

In good part, the form of Williams' plays grows out of his commitment to their matter. He has, from the beginning, insisted on
nonrealistic staging, but his refusal to work in the realistic tradition
extends to his development of character and plot. The characterization, with a few exceptions, borders on caricature, comic or horrifying; and incident, after *The Glass Menagerie,* becomes grandiloquent, operatic. In an Afterword to *Camino Real,* in what is apparently a crack at Eric Bentley, Williams points out that he is not
a "thinking playwright," that he is "permitted only to feel." This
is true, of course. In the pages above, I have tried to put the matter
of the Williams plays in a form that is useful for purposes of discussion, but any coherence that the ideas have has been forced on
them. Williams is not intellectual certainly; he is visceral. The
irony is that he is also didactic. Any playwright, I suppose, is
eager to communicate his vision of the world to an audience, but
Williams operates with some of the insistence of a "message" playwright. Since his universe is largely intuitive, his sense of horror
interior, he cannot expect to communicate to an audience in realistic terms. The real, the identifiable horrors do not interest him as

much as symbolic ones, cannibal feasts in Cabeza de Lobo or
Christ lynchings in the Delta country. He is less interested in the
event than in what it represents; for this reason, he filters it through
a macabre imagination. "My cornpone melodrama is all my own,"
he told Arthur Gelb in an interview (New York *Times,* May 1,
1960) in which he insisted "that I want to reach a mass audience.
I feel it can dig what I have to say, perhaps better than a lot of intellectuals can." The laughter—not nervous, but honest, amused
laughter—that filled the theater in which I saw the movie version
of *Suddenly Last Summer* may cast some doubt on Williams' conviction that he is getting through to a wide audience.

It was the pedagogic side of Williams apparently that devised
the elaborate mechanical framework, legends, and pictures to be
flashed on a screen, which he suggested should be used in the production of *The Glass Menagerie.* These devices were not to be
used for the fun of them, like the lantern slides that Thornton
Wilder introduces into *The Skin of Our Teeth,* or to enrich the
thematic intention of the play; they were to be as baldly explanatory as the same devices are in the teaching plays of Bertolt Brecht,
to make clear to a presumably unintelligent audience what is going
on in the scenes it is witnessing. Eddie Dowling wisely dumped the
gadgetry in the initial production of the play and so too have most
professional and amateur productions of *Menagerie* since then.
Although Williams never returned to so obvious a device as visual
aides to prop up his characters, the plays that follow *Menagerie* all
show evidence of an internal conflict between the characters and
action and an explanation of them.

His use of significant names, which began simply enough with
Blanche DuBois ("It means woods and Blanche means white. so
the two together mean white woods. Like an orchard in spring!")
and Alma ("Spanish for soul!"), is an attempt to define the characters directly or ironically. Occasionally, when the names are as
stridently obvious as Chance Wayne and Heavenly, he lets them
do their work alone, but ordinarily, as the parenthetic quotes above
indicate, he steps in with his pointer and explains; not that it is
inappropriate for Blanche or Alma to so identify themselves, but
the need that they do seems more the playwright's than the character's. Williams displays the same relentless explicitness in his use
ing in the growing, and then enrich the characters and the actions.
of symbols; they do not grow out of dramatic situations, gain mean-

Compared to Mrs. St. Maugham's chalk garden or Madame Ra-
nevsky's cherry orchard, Sebastian's jungle garden hangs on the
play like a decoration; nor is the comparison an unfair one, for
Williams, for all his allegiance to nonrealistic forms, does not (except in *Camino Real*) completely divorce himself from naturalistic
plot and characterization.

His most famous symbol, of course, is Laura's glass menagerie.
In one scene, Jim and Laura dance into the collection and break the
horn off the unicorn; the point is obvious, and is made even more
so by Laura's speeches, but the scene is touching and at least, for
this once, the symbol is used dramatically. In the first speech in the
play, Tom says, "I have a poet's weakness for symbols"; he might
have added that, in so far as he is Williams, he has a teacher's
weakness for explaining them. Thus, after we learn in the first
scene of the play that Blanche has ridden a streetcar named Desire on her way to Stella's, the two characters pick up the reference
and use it once again, more explicitly, in Scene Four. His other
symbols—the fox in *You Touched Me!*, the medical chart and the
angel in *Summer and Smoke,* the endless profusion of roses in *The
Rose Tattoo,* the bed in *Cat on a Hot Tin Roof,* the knocking on
the ceiling and Val's guitar in *Orpheus Descending,* the shaking
of the house in *Period of Adjustment*—are introduced, repeated,
explained, until they die of overexposure; besides, most of them
never had the poetic health to flourish in the rocky soil of an imagination that, for all the attraction to the exotic and the romantic, is essentially literal. *Camino Real,* Williams' one attempt at un-
fettered expressionism, is a case in point. In his Foreword to the
play, Williams insists that the philosophy is not the important thing
in it, but the sense of freedom and wildness that the form gives
him. The play cries out for surprise and suggestion, but all it gets
is the patient repetition of its not very abstruse idea. "He is analyz-
ing his play at the same time he is writing it," Walter Kerr said in
How Not to Write a Play; "or, rather, he is giving us the analysis
without ever having written the play."

When Williams' work first began to appear, it was the poet in
him, the player with symbols and language, who was often singled
out for praise—incredibly, when we look closely at the symbols,
listen carefully to the lines ("The cities swept about me like dead
leaves. . . ."). The real appeal of the early plays, however, lay
in the characters—particularly in Amanda and Blanche. In these

two, the playwright created a type that is almost a Williams trade-
mark: the Southern woman, with a pretense to gentility and culture, caught in a context in which the pretense is meaningless and
so is forced to use her mannerisms of vivacity and charm as a defense. Isabel Haverstick's first entrance in *Period of Adjustment,*
the nervous bubbling with the hysteria peeping through, indicates
that Williams can still write the character although he no longer
has any special use for her. The strength of Amanda and
Blanche is that we get to see them fully, their crudity and cruelty
as well as their gentleness, their foolishness as well as their pathos.
The reason that this is true is that Williams, in the early plays, has
not yet completely succumbed to demonstration as a dramatic
method, he still creates fine scenes—the fights between Tom and
Amanda, and the dinner with the gentleman caller in *Menagerie*;
the ghastly birthday party in *Streetcar,* in which revelation comes
through the clash of personalities.

The kind of sympathy, even empathy, that an audience feels
for Amanda and Blanche (even while feeling it for Tom and Stanley) disappears in the later plays. Alma, who is after all one of the
Southern ladies, can still command the audience through much of
her play, but Williams finally forces her into the reversal that the
play's pattern demands, the ironic peroration to the lecture on
the duality of body and soul, and she slips sadly into abstraction.
After *Summer and Smoke,* as the plays become more nonrealistic,
the characters tend to become exhibits; Williams, who still wants
audience identification, begins to try to get it from the outside, to
insist on it, say, in stage directions. Even in *Cat,* the most realistic
of his post-*Streetcar* plays, he has to assure us that Brick has "the
additional charm of that cool air of detachment that people have
who have given up the struggle"; Maggie, too, insists that he has
"the charm of the defeated." Unfortunately, the Brick of the play
has no charm at all, is simply a petulant, pouting, thirty-year-old
boy, and all Williams' insistence that he is lovable cannot make him
so. What Williams tries to do for Brick in the stage directions to
Cat, Chance Wayne tries to do for himself in *Sweet Bird*; apparently aware that the character is unrealized, Williams sends
Chance forward at the end of the play and gives him the curtain
speech: "I don't ask for your pity, but just for your understanding
—not even that—no. Just for your recognition of me in you, and
the enemy, time, in us all." But a character cannot be recognized,

as a convention delegate can, by the label he wears. The compassion in Williams' early work has given way to stage gestures that represent pity; the understanding has been replaced by lurid effects and rhetoric cum philosophy. I do not find in Chance Wayne the shock of recognition but only the recognition of Williams' shock, and that sense of horror ceased to move or even to interest me several plays ago.

Although Chance Wayne is one of the dullest of the Williams clichés, the priapic young man, all muscle and no matter, his play provides, in Alexandra Del Lago, the Princess Kosmonopolis, one of the two best characters to come out of Williams' work since the *Streetcar* quit running. The other is Archie Lee in *Baby Doll*. These two are obviously not characters like Blanche and Amanda, capable of commanding our sympathy; they are grand grotesques, monumental comic figures, often as horrifying as they are funny. A reading of *Sweet Bird* indicates that Williams may not have intended that Alexandra be quite so broad as Geraldine Page played her, wheezing, snuffling, gesturing all over the stage, but the actress was probably more right than the author. Williams says in *Baby Doll* that Archie Lee's violence "should give him almost a Dostoevskian stature"; what it does give him, as Karl Malden played him, is the bitter force of a Ben Jonson character. In the Foreword to *Sweet Bird,* Williams misuses Aristotle, talks about the purgation of violence through its "poetic representation" on stage, opts for "the tragic intention." He seems not quite ready to admit that what he has been doing the last few years, sometimes accidentally, is communicating the violence and horror that he finds in the world not by its poetic representation, but by its comic transmutation into grotesquerie. Now that he seems to have passed beyond the pathos of the early plays, his best vein other than the comic, he has depended more and more on melodramatic climax and decadent *frisson* for his effects. It is here that the unconscious comedy begins to take over. The line between the farcical and the melodramatic, between the parodic and the decadent, is so thin that only the most delicate performer can walk it, and a romanticist like Williams is too fond of grand gestures to retain his balance. For this reason, *Sweet Bird,* much of *Orpheus,* practically all of *Suddenly Last Summer,* are more ludicrous than horrifying. Even the rape scene in *Streetcar,* effective as it was at the time, grows preposterous in retrospect, mainly because of Stanley's line,

"We've had this date with each other from the beginning!" In the face of what is happening to his serious effects, and what is likely to happen to them in the near future, Williams would better serve himself and his audience by following the lead of Archie Lee and Alexandra; the kind of frightening comedy that they represent is not only a valid reaction to the world as he sees it, but a more viable dramatic presentation of that reaction.

Although I have suggested that some of Williams' most recent plays are accidentally laughable, he has used comedy consciously from the beginning. Amanda, for instance, is often as funny—consider the telephone scenes in which she tries to sell magazine subscriptions—as she is pathetic; Williams is even willing to kid her a little from the outside, as he does in his suggestion that "Ave Maria" be used under the breakfast scene in which she and Tom finally settle their quarrel. Blanche is occasionally and Stanley often intentionally funny; although the second scene builds to Blanche's outburst about Belle Reve and her dead husband, a good part of it, all Stanley's talk about the Napoleonic code and his expert friends, is gauged for laughter. Most of the other plays have scenes or characters that are supposed to be funny: the literary party in *Summer and Smoke,* much of *The Rose Tattoo,* Kilroy's scene with the Gypsy and the parody love scene with Esmeralda in *Camino Real,* much of the incidental horseplay of *Cat,* the Temple sisters in *Orpheus.* Not all of Williams' attempts at comedy succeed. He is not a successful bawdy writer as Big Daddy's tiresome robustness indicates, and the kind of bittersweet, dully witty comedy that *Period of Adjustment* is might have been written by any of a dozen Broadway regulars. Nor is he a conventional satirist. Alma's literary friends in *Summer and Smoke* and Reverend Tooker in *Cat* are examples of the kind of satiric overstatement that is finally self-defeating. What the comedy demands is a context in which it can operate. Alexandra is possible in *Sweet Bird,* even though the play is tragic in intent and chaotic in fact, because the whole conception is bizarre. It is *Baby Doll,* however, that most effectively displays Williams' comic talent. Despite the sentimentality of Baby Doll's sudden and unlikely emergence as a mature young lady, the film is conceived and played as grotesque comedy. Baby Doll's crib, Archie Lee's peephole, Aunt Rose's hospital visits and her fantastic supper, the sex play between Archie Lee and Baby Doll, and between Vacarro and Baby

Doll, the hide-and-seek chase through the house, all of these provide a comic continuity so broad and so tough that the hysterical end, Archie Lee's drunken scene with the shotgun, is a true culmination of the action and the mood. He is terrifying, but he is still a comic character; he is the Pantaloon run mad; he is the comic cuckold in a farce that is more frightening than most of Williams' serious attempts to conjure up the terror of human existence.

The Williams of *The Glass Menagerie* and *A Streetcar Named Desire*, the playwright who could so effectively present the pain and the sad comedy of the fragile trapped in an insensitive world, has long since given way to the strident exotic of *Suddenly Last Summer* and *Orpheus Descending*. Williams appears to be dedicated to offering us pictures of hell. How rewarding it would be if he came to recognize that the comic camera of *Baby Doll* presents a tougher, cleaner, clearer picture than the Aubrey Beardsley brush with which he painted Sebastian's garden.

3 THE NEW PINEROS

In his review of *The Notorious Mrs. Ebbsmith* (*The Saturday Review,* March 16, 1895), Bernard Shaw characterized Arthur Wing Pinero's work as "an attempt to reproduce that peculiar stage effect of intellectual drama, of social problem, of subtle psychological study of character, in short, of a great play. . . ." He went on to define the nature of Pinero's success: "In this way he conquered the public by the exquisite flattery of giving them plays that they really liked, whilst persuading them that such appreciation was only possible from persons of great culture and intellectual acuteness."

Shaw's words have a perennial applicability. Every period produces playwrights whose ability to judge public taste is so fine they seem always a step or two ahead of the audience they are actually following. Such men are not simple hacks, turning out standard products because they assume that particular kinds of plays will go that year. They are men so involved in the prejudices and the preoccupations of their society that their work reflects the values of its audience. Inevitably, in their attempts to be serious, they get sidetracked into sentiment, romance, theatrical and ideational cliché, but, for a time at least, their new dressing of old bromides wins them commercial and critical success. Under ordinary circumstances their vogue is short-lived, for changing fashions in ideas render them obsolete; genuinely serious playwrights break through and bury them in the rubble, as Shaw did Pinero. Still,

there are always new Pineros in the wings, ready to step forward
and receive the applause of audiences who want to be in the know
without being uncomfortable, who want advice not truth, stage
effect not art.

Although Robert Anderson and Arthur Laurents are among the
leading new Pineros, the success of William Inge and his attitude
toward his work demand for him first consideration. Until the
appearance of *A Loss of Roses* (1959), Inge had a reputation as
a playwright whose work did not fail. Following the modest success of *Come Back, Little Sheba* (1950), Inge's next three plays,
Picnic (1953), *Bus Stop* (1955), and *The Dark at the Top of
the Stairs* (1957), established him as one of Broadway's most successful playwrights; because of our strange belief in the corollary
relationship between income and reputation, Inge also came to be
accepted as one of America's leading dramatists. His own ambiguous sense of his position is made clear in the Foreword to *4 Plays*
in which he dwells on his longing for both big success ("but none
of them has brought me the kind of joy, the hilarity, I had craved
as a boy") and artistic success, a feeling of having contributed
something to the theater.

If the self-image that Inge projects in that Foreword—the playwright who went into analysis after the first hint of success with
Sheba—tags him as a representative American (intellectual, artistic
variation) of the fifties, it is not surprising that his plays should
embody the theatrical commonplaces of the decade. *The Dark at
the Top of the Stairs* is almost a casebook of clichés for our time.
It has, in Reenie, a sensitive adolescent girl who takes refuge in
her music ("All you do is *pity* yourself at the piano") or in books,
a kind of Laura Wingfield without a limp; in the early version of
the play, *Farther Off from Heaven,* which was produced at Margo
Jones's theater in Dallas in 1947, Reenie has, at least, a broken
front tooth. Another Inge adolescent, Millie in *Picnic,* sits around
reading Carson McCullers, so she is more Frankie Addams than
Laura, but funnily sad or shiveringly sad the lonely adolescents,
male and female, have been as busy on the stage in the past fifteen
years as they have been in novels. The basic pattern in these plays
is to confront the child with a situation that must push him or her
toward maturity (see Moss Hart's *The Climate of Eden,* Julian
Funt's *The Magic and the Loss,* Robert Anderson's *All Summer
Long,* above all McCullers' *The Member of the Wedding*). In

Dark, Reenie has to discover, through the off-stage suicide of Sammy, that her fear is a kind of selfishness. Her little brother has his lesson to learn, too. A ten-year-old with a passion for collecting photographs of movie stars, Sonny does a relentlessly specific Oedipal double with his mother ("For a moment, mother and son lie together in each other's arms") until, at the beginning of Act III, she takes him aside and explains that he is too big to share her bed any longer. *Dear Dr. Franzblau: My son is ten years old and all he does is lie around looking at movie star pictures and the other boys tease him and . . .*

Act II, the therapy and diagnosis act, is particularly rich in bromide. In the first half, Sammy arrives to escort Reenie to a party. Presumably because he is a Jew and the neglected son of a much-married movie bit player, he is able to understand Reenie, with whom he is politely shy, and Sonny, whom he stops in mid-tantrum. The off-stage anti-Semitism responsible for Sammy's death and the on-stage anti-Catholicism of Lottie are atypical of the fifties, an echo of the immediate postwar period, the years of Laurents' *Home of the Brave* and N. Richard Nash's *The Young and Fair,* when playwrights mistook a healthy social conscience for healthy theater.* Although there is something a little old-fashioned in Sammy's presence on the stage in 1957, he is contemporary enough to be more a tortured adolescent than a victim of bigotry.

Once the children are sent off to their party, the stage is cleared for the long confessional scene in which Cora, the play's heroine, listens to her bawdy-talking sister Lottie explain the failure of her marriage, her own frigidity ("I never did enjoy it the way some women . . . say they do") and the accompanying emasculation, spiritual and sexual, of her husband. The old problem of character development has been solved here and in much of the theatrical writing of the last decade by allowing characters to indulge in the favorite contemporary sport of analysis, self and other. The articulate self-awareness that Inge and most of his contemporaries give to their characters disposes of the virtue of revelation through

---

* The social effectiveness of such direct propagandizing is as doubtful as its dramatic validity. I still remember the woman who sat behind me at *Lost in the Stars,* crying copiously as the stiff-necked South African white man walked across the stage to shake hands with the Negro preacher after both men had lost their sons; in her unmistakably Southern voice, choked with tears, she told her neighbor: "Of course, I'd never shake his hand."

dramatic action, through the conflict of personality, through the interaction of one man's life on another. Walter Kerr likes to blame the leadenness of so much of the talk that goes on in contemporary drama on the ghosts of Ibsen and Chekhov, but the audience at an Ibsen or Chekhov play has to be alert to keep from being taken in by any one person's speeches because the characters in their plays, like most of us, have a way of lying to themselves and to others. Speeches, such as those of Lottie's, are hardly Chekhovian revelation; they are much more like the show-and-tell period at the neighborhood kindergarten. Behind Lottie's self-definition and those of Sammy in *Dark,* Hal and Rosemary in *Picnic,* Dr. Lyman in *Bus Stop,* and Doc and Lola in *Sheba* (these last two are not always as conscious of what they are saying as their brother confessors are) lies the remnants of a first-year course in psychology or an incompletely digested analysis. At least, Inge, in his psychologizing, avoids the kind of jargon that some of his fellow playwrights use. The line that most incredibly typifies this tendency in contemporary plays is that of the young girl in Paddy Chayefsky's *The Tenth Man*: "I'm a little paranoid and hallucinate a great deal and have very little sense of reality, except for brief interludes like this, and I might slip off any minute in the middle of a sentence into some incoherency." She does not quite follow this with "Now tell me about yourself," but she does not have to because the author and the audience know that nothing could keep the young man from offering a reciprocal self-diagnosis.

Although Inge's characters spend a good part of their time explaining their motivations (in *Picnic,* for instance, although one good scene between the two sisters would make everything clear, Millie must indicate frequently that she resents Madge's beauty and Madge must have a speech in which she complains that beauty is not enough), they still have to go through the regular expositional hoops to give the audience the past out of which the dramatic present has grown. Some of the less conservative playwrights have tried to find technical ways to escape the awkwardness of such exposition. Arthur Miller has made the past and present contemporaneous in Willy's brain in *Death of a Salesman* and Arthur Laurents has used the expressionism of *A Clearing in the Woods* to let his heroine exist simultaneously at four different ages; Tennessee Williams, in *Sweet Bird of Youth,* has simply dropped any pretense at realism and lets his characters speak directly to the audience. Inge, who is far too wedded to naturalism to try anything unusual, falls back on a trick of characterization by making Lottie in *Dark* and Lola in *Sheba* uncontrollably garrulous women. "Did I ever tell you about the first time she met Rubin?" Lottie asks her husband; although he answers, "Yes, honey," she plows on into a long narrative, prefaced by "I did not!" Although the postman and the milkman in *Sheba* give every indication that they have heard the story before, Lola reminds them and tells us about Doc's alcoholism. The clumsiest exposition in the early Inge plays comes in *Bus Stop* in which Elma Duckworth, another of the adolescent yearners, wanders from character to character, gathering information as though she were a researcher for *Current Biography*. The logical end product of Inge's tendency toward explanation is *A Loss of Roses,* in which practically nothing happens except in the narrated past.

One of the recurring criticisms of American drama in the last fifteen years is that in it action has given way to talk. There is a kind of validity in that position, but since good talk in the theater is often a kind of action, the difficulty lies not in the fact of but the quality of the talk. The naturalistic tradition seems to have spawned a host of dull people who are bromidic and repetitive, inarticulate except at those moments of high whine when they grind out their tales of woe; Inge's plays have their quota of such characters. My generalized carping about the people who walk our stage today does not mask an implicit longing for the tragic tradition that supposedly demands that heroes be kings; I would as happily spend the afternoon with Prince Hal hanging around a tavern in Eastcheap as eavesdrop on King Henry's guilty musings. It is not status I yearn for, it is interest. I could throw a handful of paper clips out of the window of the third-floor walk-up in which I am now writing and hit a half-dozen ordinary people who have more life, more vitality, more originality, and more serious problems than the lonely, longing people who infest the Inge plays. My disapproval is too blanket, of course. There are characters in the early Inge plays, particularly Lola in *Sheba,* who are strong enough, in their pathos or comedy, to insist that their ties to life are stronger than their ties to soap opera. Inge, who has an ear for Midwestern speech, apparently built Lola consciously out of the clichés of common usage, but they are only the vehicle of her expression; she

transcends them—and not simply in Shirley Booth's performance
of the role—because Inge can allow himself a certain comic indulgence that would be impossible with Doc, whose pretensions
really demand a satirist. The result is that Lola is more endearing
and more unpleasant than Doc; she is, in short, a realized character in a way that Doc never is. Rosemary, in *Picnic,* has some of
Lola's virtues as a character; although she is solidly based on the
stereotype of the old-maid schoolteacher, Inge's conception of her
as comic allows him more easily to bring the submerged pathos
into the open, makes her more touching than the romanticized Hal
and Madge. There is a kind of tough funniness about Cherie and
a certain charm about the bumptiousness of Bo in *Bus Stop* that
makes that out-and-out comic couple more theatrically palatable
than many of Inge's other characters.

By *The Dark at the Top of the Stairs,* in which everyone is
something and no one is, the casebook had triumphed over characterization. This is nowhere more evident than in *A Loss of Roses,*
in which Lila turns up with the remnants of the dramatic company
with which she has been touring. What the play needs at this point,
having just passed through the dinner scene between Helen and
Kenny, one of the dullest passages in the Inge canon, is some big,
boozy theatrical caricatures that might wake up the play. What
we get are thin suggestions of the *grande dame* manager, the aging
homosexual juvenile, the company cocksman. I have used Pinero
as the type of the unserious serious playwright, but there are two
sides to Pinero's talent. Inge equals him as a purveyor of popular
ideas; it is too bad that he could not catch up with him in theatrical
flamboyance, could not make his wandering actors at least half as
much fun as the company that Pinero provided in *Trelawney of
the "Wells."* Inge, who after all once traveled with a Toby company himself, should have provided Lila with associates as interesting as Cherie, but *Loss,* like *Dark,* talks itself to death, not to
life.

Of all the clichés that keep *Dark* afloat, the most blatant is the
ending, when, having got the children off to the movies, Cora
mounts the stairs to join Rubin who stands (we just see his feet)
where the dark once lurked, waiting to take her to bed. In one
sense, this is the ending to all of the plays except *A Loss of Roses*
and, even in that play, Lila goes off with Ricky to keep from being
completely alone. In *Sheba,* Doc and Lola agree on their mutual

need; in *Picnic*, Madge follows Hal and Rosemary traps Howard; in *Bus Stop*, Cherie goes off with Bo, and Grace settles for the momentary comfort of Carl. Inge's recurrent theme, as Robert Brustein has pointed out (*Harper's*, November 1958), is that man finds his "salvation from fear, need, and insecurity only through fulfillment of domestic love." He qualifies this theme as surface and finds "a psychological sub-statement to the effect that marriage demands, in return for its spiritual consolations, a sacrifice of the hero's image (which is the American folk image) of maleness." Brustein points out that each of the plays has a scene in which the hero pleads his weakness to win the heroine's love, although that scene in *A Loss of Roses*, which came after his analysis of Inge, is simply a technique of seduction. Although Brustein's description of Inge's work is a convincing one, I am less interested in and less annoyed by the substructure—after all, serious drama, unless it ends catastrophically, is almost always about what a man must give up of himself for the consolations of home, state, church— than the surface solution. Broadway's prevailing belief that love conquers all, which as the earlier chapters indicate has spread to Arthur Miller and Tennessee Williams, is as fatuous a solution to dramatic problems as an age is likely to come up with. *Bus Stop* is after all a romantic comedy, so it is proper that Cherie and Bo exit together for a Montana ranch where, according to the conventions of the theater, they will live happily ever after. Unhappily, Inge, like so many of his fellow playwrights, has transferred the roman- tic-comedy ending to all of his plays. He has done so diffidently, as though he were unsure that the evidence at the box office really proved the validity of the sentimental fade-out. In the original ver- sion of *Picnic*, Madge did not follow Hal, and in *Sheba*, still his best play, the joining of Doc and Lola at the end is more of a truce than an embrace. Even so, the prevailing message of the plays is that love is a solution to all social, economic, and psychological problems.

The final scene of *Dark* is not only an example of the love- panacea ending, it is representative of a popular variation within the general type—the sex-as-salvation conclusion. The dramatic purpose of Lottie's detailed analysis of her marriage, in so far as it has any, is that it convinces Cora that she is happy with Rubin. Although Inge takes the trouble to indicate that the couple have radically different ideas about social and personal goals, although the father and his children have lost any ability to communicate with one another, and although the family is faced with a genuine economic crisis, the suggestion is that sexual compatibility will carry the day. This kind of phallic romanticism is also evident in *Picnic* in which Hal, who has been a kind of "Male at Stud," to use Val's phrase from *Orpheus Descending,* suggests that his future is likely to be rosier than his past after one night of love with Madge: "Not like last night, baby. Last night was . . . (*Gropes for the word*) *inspired.*" Tennessee Williams and *A Streetcar Named Desire* are almost certainly responsible for the currency of this dramatic myth. Stanley and Stella overcome all differences of taste, erase all evidences of personal history, when they get "them colored lights going!" Stella's words to Blanche are almost a slogan for the new movement: "But there are things that happen between a man and a woman in the dark—that sort of make everything else seem—unimportant." It was Speed Lamkin who finally carried the whole idea of sexual sufficiency to its ridiculous end. In *Comes a Day* (1958), a play ostensibly about whether or not a young girl should marry for love or money, he not only made the poor boy sexually capable, he made the rich one a psychopathic sadist; you see what happens, the play seems to say, if you are not good in bed, as likely as not you will break down, foaming at the mouth, and chew up an expensive set. Inge is not so silly about the whole thing as Lamkin is; even so, the *Dark* is gross enough, particularly if it is played smirkingly as it was in the Elia Kazan production on Broadway. All joy to Cora and Rubin, but, when the curtain comes down, the harness business is still on the rocks.

There is, also, still dark at the top of the stairs. Inge's titular metaphor for every man's fear of the uncertain future is indicative of an intrusive symbolism that he had not used since *Sheba*. In that play, the missing dog, so insistently equated with Lola's lost youth, stands out incongruously in a simple naturalistic play that has no need of it. There is the same kind of obviousness in the symbolic use of Turk's javelin and the excessive explicitness of Lola's dreams. It may well have been *The Glass Menagerie,* which, as Inge has admitted, brought him to the writing of plays, that caused him to sprinkle *Sheba* with symbols that do not grow out of the drama, but are grafted onto it. In any case, such devices are not evident in *Picnic* and *Bus Stop*.* With *Dark,* Inge reverted to his earlier practice. Too much is made in terms of set, lighting, and action of the area at the head of the stairs. If we must have an Inge symbol, I prefer Sammy's sword in Act II, which is introduced, does its work, and then is forgotten. Sammy, who is in the uniform of the military school he attends, answers Sonny's question: "I wear a sword to protect myself! . . . To kill off all the villains in the world!" Sonny then borrows the sword and does a mock-suicide. Both gestures of childish reaction to the real or imagined oppressions of the world, they tell us all we need really know about Sammy and Sonny and render a good part of Sammy's exposition unnecessary.

By trying to reach Inge's work through *The Dark at the Top of the Stairs,* which for me is one of his least attractive plays, I have perhaps been unfair to the playwright. He has (or had in the early plays) a genuine talent for small, touching effects; this is a real theatrical virtue. Still, *Dark* is a play that received both critical and popular approbation, and it is certainly typical of his work. One of the difficulties with Inge and with other playwrights who ponder heavily over the same concerns is that Paul Osborn's *Morning's at Seven* makes it almost impossible to take them seriously. This play, which was first presented unsuccessfully in 1939, jumbles together enough clichés of situation and language to provide Inge with material for four or five plays; Osborn, however, although he occasionally reaches for a pathetic moment, presents the whole thing as wry comedy, almost a parody of the idea of lonely lostness in the Midwestern backyard. It is a kind of judgment on Inge that Eileen Heckart, who was Rosemary in *Picnic* and Lottie in *Dark,* could play Myrtle Brown in the Play of the Week production of *Morning's at Seven* with very little broadening of the mannerisms she used in the two Inge plays. In his Foreword to *4 Plays,* Inge wrote: "I deal with surfaces in my plays, and let whatever depths

---

* *Bus Stop* is loaded with significant names, a kind of symbolism. The drunken professor is Dr. Lyman; the forceful sheriff, Will Masters; the cowboy who sends Bo and Cherie off with his love, Virgil Blessing; even Cherie, as the lines indicate, is a comic play on *cherry.* It was a student in one of my classes who first pointed out Inge's use of significant names in this play; he was intent on proving that Elma was a satirical figure because her last name is Duckworth. That way lies exegesis.

there are in my material emerge unexpectedly so that they bring something of the suddenness and shock which accompany the discovery of truths in actuality." He might well have stopped at the end of the first clause.

For a new voice in the American theater, to borrow a phrase from the title of Brooks Atkinson's Modern Library anthology, Robert Anderson has had remarkably little to say. He made his reputation on the long run of *Tea and Sympathy* (1953), which Louis Kronenberger, in his seasonal summary in *The Best Plays of 1953–1954,* correctly characterized when he asked, "Can this resemble what William Archer had in mind in contending that the same piece of writing can be bad literature but a good play?" *Tea and Sympathy* is a good play in the sense that it is a workable theater piece; it makes use of almost as many clichés as *The Dark at the Top of the Stairs* does, but it handles them with such skill that, when I saw it, it was not until I got out on the street that I realized just how empty the play is. Its success stems from two quite different theatrical sure-things: the fashionable sex-as-therapy ending and the old-fashioned cowboy-movie division of the world into the good guys and the bad guys. Set in a boy's school, where false accusation of theft would once have initiated the action, Anderson's play is up-to-date enough to suspect its hero of homosexuality. After Tom Lee, certainly the most naïve young man to hit the stage in years, goes swimming with a homosexual instructor, his schoolmates remember that he sings French folk songs and refuses to take part in sports, and, by their logic, any man who is not a mixer is no man at all. He fails in an attempt to sleep with the campus doxy, by which he hopes to prove himself, and is apparently wrecked for life until Laura Reynolds, his housemaster's wife, who is supposed to give the boys no more than tea and sympathy, offers her body as a platform on which he can assure his manhood. After what he has just been through, the sudden appearance on the edge of his bed of Laura, unbuttoning her blouse, might well shock him into a trauma; but Tom and Laura live in the world of sentimental melodrama, not in the real world, and on Broadway all fairy stories have happy endings. Her last line, "Years from now . . . when you talk about this . . . and you will . . . be kind," is Laura's version of "It is a far, far better

thing that I do, than I have ever done." The unbuttoned blouse
and the unblushing schmaltz of that last line allow the audience to
mix titillation with a joyful tear.

While the effeminate boy is being revealed as a real man, the
mountain-climbing, handball-playing master, all muscle and moral
rectitude, is discovered to be the real homosexual. If this eventual-
ity is familiar it is because so many Westerns have let the stranger
ride in from the range, suspect, and become the savior of the
ranch, the town, the girl, after the banker or the sheriff has been
unmasked as the mysterious villain. In quoting Thoreau's familiar
remark about the man who follows a different drummer, Anderson
has suggested (*Theatre Arts,* September 1954) that his play is
about the nonconformist in a demanding society. A case can certainly be made for that subject in *Tea and Sympathy,* but the conventional black and white of Anderson's characters makes impossible any serious consideration of moral problems.

Anderson has had only two other Broadway productions—*All
Summer Long* (1954) and *Silent Night, Lonely Night* (1959). The
first of these, an adaptation of Donald Wetzel's novel *A Wreath
and a Curse,* was acted at the Arena Theatre in Washington,
D.C., in 1953 and may well have antedated *Tea and Sympathy.*
The play, like the novel, is the story of a boy who spends a summer building a retaining wall that fails to save his home from a
flooding river; the point, in both cases, is that a child is forced to
do a job that the adults, self-preoccupied, fail to do. Wetzel kills
the boy off in the novel, but Anderson saves him and assures him,
through the crippled older brother, that the wall has been as educational as Tom Lee's afternoon with Laura Reynolds: "it was the
most important thing you ever did in your life." There are a few
effective scenes, taken over almost directly from the novel, such
as the one where the confused and irascible father decides not to
bury himself in a newspaper, to give his children a chance to talk
to him. For the most part, the play is as diffuse as it is sentimental,
not nearly so efficient as its more successful predecessor.

After five years of film scripts, Anderson returned to Broadway
with *Silent Night, Lonely Night,* a relentlessly dull play that could
not be saved even by its author's trickery. Katherine Johnson, who
does not believe in adultery, and John Sparrow, who has not slept
with a woman he could care for in five years, meet—lonely, lonely
—in a Colonial Inn in a New England town on Christmas Eve and

finally get to bed together after a fakery feint in which Anderson
suggests that they will not make it. The audience expects the couple to get together at the end of Act I, but Anderson, working for
a touching analogy with the story that John tells of a wartime encounter that ended this side of copulation, keeps them apart until
the end of the first scene of Act II where they and he finally suc-
cumb to the various needs of their psyches and his box office.
Their love-making, in good *Tea and Sympathy* tradition, is therapeutic; it saves Katherine's marriage and makes John more content
with his misery, his guilt about his wife's insanity. The incredible
thing about the play is that it has no dramatic material in it at all;
it is simply a long double narrative in which each of the leads takes
a turn at telling his lugubrious story. It makes *A Loss of Roses*
seem like a hotbed of action.

Until Arthur Laurents emerged as a book writer for musical comedy with *West Side Story* (1957), he had never achieved the kind
of commercial success that came early to both Inge and Anderson.
Of the four plays—*Home of the Brave* (1945), *The Bird Cage*
(1950), *The Time of the Cuckoo* (1952), and *A Clearing in the
Woods* (1957)—that preceded *West Side Story* only *Cuckoo* was
a success in Broadway terms. Still, since the appearance of *Home of
the Brave,* Laurents has been considered as one of the serious playwrights trying to operate on Broadway. His dramatic limitations
are as obvious as those of Inge and Anderson, yet, to me at least,
he is a more interesting playwright, perhaps because, for all his
psychological orientation, he seems aware that his characters operate in a world that is peopled with more than mirror images of
their own suffering hearts. All of his plays—including the two musicals (the second is *Gypsy,* 1960)—are given a social context.

Home of the Brave is concerned with anti-Semitism, in and out
of the army. *The Bird Cage,* the story of a petty tyrant who runs
a night club as though it were a satrapy, is given specific allegorical
significance through Wally's words about the place: "Well, to me,
it's a—city, Ferdy. A country, a big, beautiful whole damn world!
. . . here *I'm* God!" The end of the play is properly heroic,
when a chorus girl with a conscience leads a supposedly cynical
war veteran and the tyrant's own son in a defiant march-out, but
much of the play is about the ways that ordinary, likable people,
caught in their own pattern of fear and failure, feed dictatorial

power. *The Time of the Cuckoo* is another treatment of the perennial American theme of innocence abroad; although the choice of
the spinster schoolteacher in search of romance traps the playwright into a deal of sentimentality, he does manage to give some
force and some flesh to his twin targets: the Puritan confusion of
guilt and sex, and the destructiveness of American idealism. Despite the borrowings from *Romeo and Juliet* and sometimes, as in
the fire-escape balcony scene, they edge on the ludicrous, *West
Side Story* is about juvenile delinquency and race hatred on the
streets of New York; *Gypsy,* for all the fun it has with vaudeville
parody, is the story of a driving show-business mother, a particularly flamboyant variation on the common American phenomenon,
the destructive parent who, as the song says, "had a dream, / A
dream about you, Baby!" *A Clearing in the Woods,* particularly in
the relationships between Virginia and Andy, and Ginna and Pete,
touches on the American wife as upholder of status, as pusher of the
success ethic. Laurents' recent comedy, *Invitation to a March*
(1960), through which a little boy wanders beating a toy drum,
is a fantasy-satire that suggests, without invoking, Thoreau's other
drum. The division, as Camilla makes clear in one of her speeches,
is not Thoreau's between one drum and another, but between
marching and dancing; in either case the choice is between doing
what others want you to do and doing what you want. Although its
use of the Sleeping Beauty story—the heroine falls asleep at every
suggestion of the conventional future that she is to share with her
respectable fiancé—is a fine comic invention, Laurents' play is remarkably flat; all his work, including the musicals, indicates that
he is romantic, sentimental, even evangelistic, but not often funny.

If my insistence on Laurents' use of social themes seems to separate him somehow from Inge and Anderson, his primary concern, the one that runs through all the plays, puts him comfortably back in their camp. In a Preface to *A Clearing in the Woods,*
he wrote:

The loneliness afoot in this country must be staggering—unless only
writers and their lovers are lonely—but I do not believe it a natural or
inevitable state of man. I think the man who is lonely is the man who
is lonely with himself because he has not accepted himself for the imperfect human being he is. Until he makes that difficult acceptance
(and so many of us are startlingly unaware that we have not), he

cannot feel very much, he cannot give very much, he cannot have very much.

This is Virginia's problem in *Clearing*; in each of the guises in which we see her—as a little girl, as an adolescent, as a young bride, as a frightened woman edging into middle age—we get an example of her own enlarged self-image and the demands that that image makes on others to live up to it. Similarly, Coney in *Home of the Brave* is physically paralyzed when he lets his sense of Jewishness, his suspicion of bigotry, keep him from accepting and giving friendship. Leona in *Cuckoo* rejects love that does not come with the trappings of romance. Wally is revealed at the end of *The Bird Cage* as the tyrant *manqué*, burning his world because he discovers, having rejected all human contact, that he is not strong enough to go on alone. The much-married Rose of *Gypsy* can be neither wife nor mother because those roles may throw shadows over the bright lights. Even the boys in *West Side Story* form a gang, an artificially conceived communal image that is larger than life size ("And when your gang is the best, when you're a Jet, buddy boy, you're out in the sun and home free home!") because they are unable individually to admit, as Tony and Maria do by falling in love, that they are "imperfect human."

Read one way, the Laurents quotation above could be just another indication of the familiar contemporary psychological and social advice to face facts, be practical, get small. Dramatically, it could result in a series of couples, like those in Inge, Anderson, and Chayefsky, huddling together for warmth. Laurents does not intend that it should. Whether his plays end in conventional affirmation (*Home of the Brave*) or bittersweet pathos (*The Time of the Cuckoo*), all of them embody the suggestion that the acceptance of human limitations is not the choice between being an ant or being a giant, but the recognition of being a man and the possibility of a new beginning. This is made quite specific— perhaps too specific—at the end of *A Clearing in the Woods,* when Virginia insists, "But I don't want to be a groundling! I want to rise in the air just a little, to climb, to reach a branch, even the lowest— Can't I try for that?" and Ginna comforts her, "Why not? An end to dreams isn't an end to hope." As though he suspects the littleness of his whole concept, he puts it into the mouths of the lost ladies, Lily and Deedee, in *Invitation to a March* and sends his lovers dancing off at the end, the dream finish that his plays have been cautioning against for fifteen years. The best dramatic statement of his strange ambiguity, the acceptance that still contains protest, comes in *Gypsy,* in Rose—an intensification of the character as she appears in Gypsy Rose Lee's biography—whose wonderful vitality makes her admirable without making her likable or nice, without saddling her with any of the current namby-pamby virtues. Rose's vitality, however, is not simply a product of Laurents' book; Jule Styne's music, Stephen Sondheim's lyrics, and, most of all, Ethel Merman's performance make the woman the attractive monster she is.

As a playwright, Laurents shares a number of the virtues and a number of the faults of his contemporaries. He is capable of writing an extremely effective scene, such as the start of Leona's cocktail party in the second scene of Act II of *Cuckoo,* in which the expectation of disaster bubbles through the beginning of drunkenness of all the characters, but the explosion when it comes —the business of the counterfeit money and the unpaid-for necklace—is less exciting than the build to it. He can let himself slip into the corniest melodrama—Wally's smashing Vic's hands at the piano in *The Bird Cage*—and he can dip into the most blatant kind of theatrical hokum. At the end of *Home of the Brave,* Coney goes off with the crippled Mingo to open the bar that he once had planned with the dead Finch, and the curtain comes down on a Coney-Mingo variation on the Coney-Finch word game involving *charming* and *delightful;* at the end of *Cuckoo,* the tearful Leona, still toughly smiling, goes out with Mauro, who is in the play only for the cute-little-boy scenes that he plays with the heroine, after he has given her the fountain pen that he has been trying to sell her all play long. Both are tear-jerking fade-outs and both effective of their kind. Laurents' most egregious fault as a playwright, one that he shares with his contemporaries from Arthur Miller down, is a suspicion that he has not done his job dramatically and a concomitant insertion of explanatory speeches. Thus Coney is given a long, unnecessary speech about anti-Semitism. Leona, who is a perfectly obvious character, is explained at length by both her Italian lover and her Italian landlady. Even in *A Clearing in the Woods,* where the timeless form gives him the opportunity to do everything directly, he succumbs to diagnostic speeches which he places in the mouths of Virginia's father and her one-time fiancé.

One of the main difficulties with *Invitation to a March* is that the chief device in the play, the direct address to the audience, which might give another playwright a chance to be funny, becomes, in Laurents' hands, a kind of message service. In many ways, Laurents' two musical books are his most effective dramas, largely because the music and the lyrics often do, without strain, the work that in his own plays falls to the long, intrusive speeches; it took much exposition in *A Clearing in the Woods* to make evident about Virginia what is clear about Rose after her first song, "Some People."

Williams aside, Laurents is the contemporary dramatist most willing to break the realistic form that still attracts the near seriousness of the new Pineros. *The Time of the Cuckoo* is the only one of his plays that is completely conventional. He is not experimental; he uses devices that have been used often enough before. Still, he borrows with an eye to fitting form to content. Thus, he uses flashbacks in *Home of the Brave*. In *The Bird Cage,* he suggests a nonrealistic set, a cage of sorts, that will put his melodrama in a symbolic setting. *A Clearing in the Woods,* which looks like expressionism to the unwary eye, is, he insists, a fantasy in which the action happens as we see it, not in a dream or an hallucination, or in Virginia's memory or her mind: "To seek some such explanation is to seek a realistic approach, to cling to naturalism because it is familiar and, thus, safe." *Invitation to a March* serves up a fairy story in a structure that is one part *Strange Interlude,* two parts the lecture-platform method of Elmer Rice's *Not for Children.* There is no evidence in Laurents' work that he is breaking any new ground, pointing a direction that younger playwrights may want to follow, but the variety that seems to attract him, to save him from burial in the familiar living-room or apartment setting, may explain why he could fit himself so comfortably into the demands of musical comedy.

Louis Kronenberger once wrote of Laurents (*Partisan Review,* Fall 1959): "Amid the honest intentions of an Arthur Laurents's *A Clearing in the Woods,* which is most depressing?—his attempting a kind of crude stream-of-consciousness so late in the day; or in so wrong and resistant a medium; or with such uneven and limited gifts." The most depressing thing about *Clearing,* even accepting that all of Kronenberger's strictures are true, is that it should have died so quickly in uncongenial Broadway air where slicker, sweeter love potions, like *The Dark at the Top of the Stairs* and *Tea and Sympathy,* ran for months. For all that his talent is uneven and limited, Laurents is finally more attractive than some of his even and limited contemporaries.

No other playwright has either the reputation for seriousness or a body of work large enough to demand consideration with Inge, Anderson, and Laurents. A few individual plays, because of their success or because of an incidental virtue, should perhaps be mentioned with the new Pineros. Joseph Kramm's *The Shrike* (1952) is a good example of an empty melodrama dressed in the popular trappings of medical reporting—a kind of *Angel Street,* plus hospital procedure. Much about Julian Funt's *The Magic and the Loss* (1954) is trite, but the central character is a reasonably forceful portrait of a career woman on the edge of hysteria, and the play has the incidental virtue of using an advertising agency as something more than a comic butt. Michael V. Gazzo's *A Hatful of Rain* (1955), which has at least one effective scene between the addict and his father, is, as Arthur Miller has said (*International Theatre Annual,* No. 1), "so full of illogical behaviour, so evasive in its confrontation with its theme, so unevenly finished in almost every department." The last word on *Rain* comes from another play, Jack Gelber's *The Connection,* in which Jim, the producer, tells the audience: "I can assure you that this play does not have a housewife who will call the police and say, 'Would you please come quickly to the [name of theatre]. My husband is a junkie.'" *Blue Denim* (1958), by James Leo Herlihy and William Noble, makes its adolescents far too articulate about their difficulties and occasionally, particularly with Ernie, the tough guy, dresses them in Andy Hardy cuteness, but at least it does not smother them in sensitivity. The best things in the play are the cross-purpose family scenes, such as the one in which Arthur tries to tell his parents about Janet's being pregnant, and the best character is the father, a happy surprise in these knowing days, who never really understands his failure with his children.

Small virtues should not be ignored in the theater, but after a decade and a half of Pineros, one gets restless. Where in the world is Shaw?

4 THE VIDEO BOYS

ESMERALDA: *Look, Mama! Look, Mama! A tear!*
GYPSY: *You have been watching television too much. . . .*
—*Camino Real*

In 1954, six television playwrights—Paddy Chayefsky, Horton
Foote, Tad Mosel, N. Richard Nash, Robert Alan Aurthur, and
David Shaw—joined Fred Coe, then a television producer, to form
an organization rather like the Playwrights' Company to produce
the plays of the members. The group is much more interesting as
a phenomenon of the mid-fifties than it is for its motivation (to
bring the writers more money than they could get as hirelings) or
its success (nothing much came of it). This gathering of forces and
the publicity that grew out of it is an indication of the respect with
which the television dramatist (not to be confused with the man
who provides jokes for TV comics and scripts for filmed series)
was treated at that time. By then, the contempt for television that
had been a necessary intellectual appendage a few years earlier
had collapsed under the weight of social pressure; even academic
children persuaded sets into their homes and academic parents
began to look over small shoulders at what was going on on the
small screen. A light breeze is a blessing on a heavy hot day, so it
was not surprising that the work of men like Chayefsky and Foote
seemed impressive. It was a simple step to decide that their quality was an absolute, not a matter of context. For a time, there was
a school of thought—more properly, an amorphous feeling—that
saw the artistic future of American drama in television and the
men who wrote for it. This was a point of view that the television
dramatists happily accepted.

Within two years of the formation of the abortive producing group, three of the participating writers published collections of their best plays. There had been a few volumes of assorted television scripts issued earlier, but those, like similar collections of radio plays and film scripts, were designed not to display a particular writer's work, but to show examples of what the medium could produce; some of them were aimed frankly at the aspiring writer, samples to emulate. With the appearance of Paddy Chayefsky's *Television Plays* in 1955, ephemeral video drama achieved the permanence of print; the implication was that a trade had become an art. Horton Foote's *Harrison, Texas* and Tad Mosel's *Other People's Houses* followed in 1956. In the same year, Gore Vidal's *Visit to a Small Planet and Other Television Plays* and Reginald Rose's *Six Television Plays* were published; Rod Serling's *Patterns* came out in 1957. Other television playwrights—William Gibson and James Costigan, for instance—issued their work in less fat volumes, but the six collections I have mentioned best represent what is sometimes called the golden age of television drama. By the time the volumes appeared, the situation that produced them had changed. The number of television programs that accepted original material had dwindled, first in the face of quiz shows and then in competition with the filmed series—Westerns, private-eye melodramas, situation comedies. The few remaining dramatic programs seldom offered anything but adaptations. The dwindling market certainly had something to do with the defection of the men who had written and defended television drama, but they were headed toward Broadway and Hollywood in any case. Foote and Nash had been writing for television and the theater at the same time; by 1957, Chayefsky, Vidal, and Aurthur had moved to Broadway, stretching television scripts to fit the requirements of the stage. Most of them had begun to write movie scripts. Serling was the only one still working regularly for television and he was responsible for *The Twilight Zone,* a fantasy-science-fiction series of so little interest dramatically that, instead of issuing the scripts, he published paperback collections of stories based on the program.

Except for occasional theorists, such as Maxwell Anderson and Arthur Miller, American playwrights have been remarkably reticent about their work. This is not the case with television dramatists. Most of the collections contain prefaces—part autobiography, part aesthetics—and additional comment on the individual plays.

For the most part, the playwrights are quite aware of the defects of individual scripts, although generally—no father has an ugly baby—they assume that their work is both serious and successful. Few are quite as blunt as Rod Serling, who says of *Patterns,* "it was good, perhaps better than good," and who has a habit of using the word *tragedy* when he talks about his scripts, but none of them, except perhaps Gore Vidal, would quite accept what appears true on a rereading of the published plays: that they are reasonably efficient dramatic journeymen working in a medium congenial to the kind of realism that had already become old-hat on stage and in the movies.

The plays share certain characteristics that come obviously from the medium rather than from the personality of the dramatists. Television, Tad Mosel says, is "suited to what I call the 'personal drama'—that is, a play wherein the writer explores one simple happening, a day, or even an hour, and tries to suggest a complete life." Chayefsky says much the same thing when he points out that the medium demands that the playwright focus on one or two people, on a situation in which the events are ordinary. *Intimacy* is the word most often used to describe the effect of television drama, and as Rod Serling points out, it is a strength that results from a weakness, the lack of space in which to spread out. The plays, then, are almost all concerned with the problems of a particular individual, usually in relation to a group no larger than the family; if there is a community around the protagonist, it exists only by implication. "The author must often probe vertically," Serling writes, "because there just aren't enough inches to let him spread out horizontally." The vertical probe, so often invoked by the television-drama enthusiasts, is an ideal rather than a fact. In some cases—Mosel's *Ernie Barger Is Fifty,* for instance, or Chayefsky's *Marty*—playwrights manage effective character portraits, but even these are not complicated personalities. The best of them approach stereotypes that allow the author to indicate who and what they are by means of familiar, even stock, analyses. More often, as Vidal says of the family in *Visit to a Small Planet* and as Reginald Rose admits of the jurors in *Twelve Angry Men,* characterization is sacrificed to some other concern—as often as not, just getting the plot introduced and worked out.

Television puts other restrictions on its playwrights. One is the stringent demands of time. The dramatic situation must be

shaved or, infrequently, padded out to fit the half-hour or hour
(more recently, hour-and-a-half) program—minus advertising
time, of course. Such a restriction would hardly seem crippling to
the Broadway playwright who has to get his curtain down in time
to send the audience to the suburbs and to avoid overtime pay for
the stage crew. It is the organization of the time, rather than its
limitation, that works most unfavorably on the television playwright. In an hour show, for instance, the sponsor has two com-
mercials, besides the opening and closing ones. This means that
there will be two breaks in the play whether or not its structure or
subject has any need of them; in most cases, the playwright tries
for an artificial climax—a good act curtain, to use a stage term. Although Andy Sloane, in *Patterns,* is circumspect about his drinking, Rod Serling brings Act I of that play to a close in a pantomime
scene in which Sloane's secretary discovers an open bottle on his
desk and, sadly, puts it out of sight. The scene is a teaser, not
really necessary to the play, but one that the author hopes will stick
in the viewer's mind until the commercial is over. Rose's *Twelve
Angry Men* is an even better example of a play in which the act
breaks are artificially contrived; the discussion in the jury room,
the slow conversion of the eleven jurors by the holdout, is or
should be a continuous process.

The problem of agency and network censorship is another restricting influence on the television dramatist. Sometimes the nig-
gling worries of the sponsor and the programmer involve no more
than picking at lines; sometimes the whole conception of a play
must be shifted. Most of the dramatists have commented unfavorably on the difficulty of having to please too many people, but
the harshest words on the subject are in Serling's Introduction to
Patterns, in which he describes what happened to his own script,
Noon on Doomsday, and Reginald Rose's *Thunder on Sycamore
Street,* in which the playwrights had to find acceptable minorities
to substitute for the victims in their antibigotry plays: "But in the
meantime, a medium best suited to illumine and dramatize the
issues of the times has its product pressed into a mold, painted lily-
white, and has its dramatic teeth yanked one by one." The problem of tooth-yanking is not simply a television one. Gore Vidal,
in the Preface to the play version of *Visit to a Small Planet,* says
of his role during the pre-Broadway tryout: "I was more dentist
than writer, extracting the sharper (but not always carious)

teeth." The commercial theater certainly has a freer use of vocabulary than television does, and it may have a greater choice of subjects (although it seldom exercises it), but the theatrical producer and director who feed the prejudices and vanities of tryout audiences, coaxing smiles and sniffles, are really doing the same thing that the television executive and the soap salesman do when they worry about insulting a hysterical maiden lady in Dubuque. Both attitudes have a great deal to do with merchandizing and very little to do with healthy drama. Vidal, who takes such a refreshingly venal attitude toward all his dramatic work (he does not talk art and poor mouth at the same time, like Chayefsky), is not particularly upset by what television will not let him say. He compares the television play to the nineteenth-century novel and suggests that both forms force the writer to work by indirection and suggestion: "With a bit of patience and ingenuity there is nothing that the imaginative writer cannot say to the innocent millions." Judging by the television plays that I have seen and read, Vidal's included, not enough patience and ingenuity have yet been exercised. The analogy to the nineteenth-century novel is a sensible one; it would be more convincing if Vidal were Dickens.

Beyond the pressures of the medium that give all television plays a family resemblance, there are similarities that come from particular programs. Despite the surface differences among Chayefsky, Foote, and Mosel, their work is very much alike. Perhaps the plays were chosen for the Philco-Goodyear Television Playhouse, where most of them appeared, because the subjects were congenial to producers Fred Coe and Gordon Duff and to directors Delbert Mann, who did most of the Chayefsky scripts, Vincent Donehue, who did most of Foote's work, and Arthur Penn. Perhaps the staff put its own imprint on the men who wrote for the program. In any case, Horton Foote's description of his work and its common themes, "an acceptance of life or a preparation for death," would serve as well for Chayefsky or Mosel. The standard Foote character, like the standard Chayefsky or Mosel character, is one who is suddenly aware of a situation that has long existed, one in which he or she is uncomfortable and which he or she must come to understand; in terms of the tough but sentimental realism of all these playwrights, the understanding seldom brings the conventional happy ending, although ordinarily the suggestion is that the protagonist is better or stronger for his

new knowledge. Foote's characters, as he points out, are usually
very young or very old; Mosel's are often middle-aged and under
the impression that their life has a meaning that they discover it
does not have; Chayefsky's may be any age, but they are almost
always lonely and openly intent on finding out why.

Not only are these three men operating in an old-fashioned
realistic tradition, their plays reflect a regionalism that—for all of
William Inge's thriving Midwest—suggests an earlier period in
American drama. Stark Young, in a Foreword to Foote's play,
The Traveling Lady, testifies to and praises the accuracy of the
language that Foote uses for his characters, residents of an
imaginary town on the Gulf Coast of Texas. Whether Chayefsky's
characters are Jewish, Italian, or Irish, all of them reflect the playwright's ear for the accuracy of Bronx speech, an ear that seems
to have gone a little deaf in *The Tenth Man.* Mosel's characters
usually inhabit a generalized Midwest. All three men use the
clichés of ordinary speech, risking dullness for the sake of an assumed reality, sacrificing imagination to the small rightness of word
and gesture. Since their kind of play has generally been more effective on television than anything more demonstrative or rhetorical—in fact, a new generation of actors has developed, able to invest the simplest phrase with a pathos not inherent in it, even in
the context of the play—they have perhaps found the correct form
for the new medium. This is rather different from making a permanent contribution to the corpus of American drama.

The work of Vidal, Rose, and Serling, written for other programs, does not have the group feeling that emanates from the
Philco-Goodyear contributors. Vidal has tried a variety of things:
adaptations; "good melodrama without pretensions," to use his
description of *Dark Possession,* which is certainly not pretentious
although it is not much good either; myth-making (*The Death of
Billy the Kid*); fantasy-satire (*Visit to a Small Planet*). All of
Vidal's work for television suggests an imagination unwilling to
follow ideas to completion; even at his best, in *Visit* for instance,
his scripts are amorphous. Rose and Serling are more concerned
with social problems, at least on the surface, than are the rest of
the television playwrights. On close look, however, Rose's *Twelve
Angry Men* turns out to be a rather ordinary detection melodrama in an unusual setting. Its only comment on the jury system,
an implicit one, boils down to an ironic statement that justice is

done only by accident. His juvenile-delinquency play, *Crime in the Streets,* dissolves in sentimentality when the protagonist, who has been carefully drawn as a young man completely without social or family feeling, does not commit his murder because the little boy says, "You're my brother."

Rod Serling backs away from the possible implications of his most famous play when he writes: "*Patterns* is a story of power . . . it is not truly a big-business story . . . there is, in the final analysis, nothing Marxist in the message of this play." Elsewhere in his commentary, he says that "it is simply an indictment of the imposed values of a society that places such stock in success and has so little preoccupation with morality when success has been attained." The contradiction here, the gratuitous mention of Marxism, and the insistence that his depiction of the business world has nothing to do with the business world are evidence of a contemporary reluctance to be caught saying something specific. In the thirties, in *Golden Boy,* Clifford Odets wrote a boxing play that tried to suggest the corruption in a whole culture; in the fifties, Serling examines the destructiveness of executive competition and then disavows his script, insists that it has no more significance than his boxing play, *Requiem for a Heavyweight.* Somehow the end of *The Strike,* a 1954 Studio One script, typifies Serling as a social playwright. Having spent the hour showing us Major Gaylord struggling between his conscience and his responsibility, trying to bring himself to order an air strike that will kill a patrol but will allow what is left of the battalion to escape, Serling closes the play with the order, as he should, but he refuses to leave it there. Although all of Gaylord's lines to the chaplain suggest that he has no faith in God, Serling has him say, "God rest their souls . . . and God forgive me." The chaplain assures him, "He'll do both, Major. I know He'll do both." An interpretative vertical probe might suggest that the final exchange is ironic; actually it is a cheat, a pulling away from the play itself, a chance for the audience to nod comfortably and prepare for the closing commercial.

Now that the practitioners of television drama have passed on to other things, most of them to Broadway, their contribution to American drama, such as it is, extends beyond the small body of their video plays. Their influence is evident in the television plays that have been adapted for Broadway, in certain techniques that have been transferred from television to the stage, and in the Broadway playwrights who made their beginning or their first reputation on television. The list of adaptations from television is a long one, too long for anyone who suspects that adaptation in any form is only vaguely related to the creation of a drama of quality: Robert Alan Aurthur's *A Very Special Baby,* Paddy Chayefsky's *Middle of the Night,* James Costigan's *Little Moon of Alban,* Horton Foote's *The Trip to Bountiful,* William Gibson's *The Miracle Worker,* Ira Levin's *No Time for Sergeants* (an adaptation of an adaptation), N. Richard Nash's *The Rainmaker,* Arnold Schulman's *A Hole in the Head,* Gore Vidal's *Visit to a Small Planet,* Shimon Wincelberg's *Kataki.* This is only a small sample. The reasoning of producers, I suppose, is that material (one tends to talk about American drama in terms of product rather than art) that has been pretested has a good chance for commercial success. The number of theatrical failures in my brief list should, but will not, shake that conviction. Success or failure, the plays adapted for Broadway are seldom very different from their original (only in the sense of not being adaptations) neighbors.

There are incidental virtues in even the worst of the plays listed above, and I am willing to admit a fondness for *The Rainmaker* as a romantic comedy and *Visit to a Small Planet* as a satirical farce. The only one of the group that is particularly unusual, however, is *Kataki,* which not only failed on Broadway, but again in an off-Broadway revival. Wincelberg's adaptation of his script *The Sea is Boiling Hot* places an American soldier who has jumped from a burning plane on an island with a Japanese survivor of a torpedoed ship. All that the play does is show the mutual suspicion and growing friendliness of the two men, neither of whom speaks the other's language. In one sense, *Kataki* is a kind of gimmick play, a long monologue punctuated by lines in Japanese and decorated with pantomime, but the gimmick—unlike that nonsense of two people and two telephones that made William Gibson's *Two for the Seesaw* endearing to everyone but me—makes sense within the situation. The real strength of Wincelberg's play is its young American; since he cannot keep from talking, he reveals himself as a particular kind of late adolescent, very Midwestern to my Midwestern ears, compounded of arrogance and inferiority, self-pity and swagger, stupidity and knowingness—likable and hateful at once. Perhaps the play failed to attract audiences because the portrait is too good, because Wincelberg's Alvin is a distant relative to the stereotype of the American boy as we know him in cartoons and light comedies, and the playwright insists on making him distasteful instead of cute and lovable.

One of the pet tricks of the theater reviewers, faced with an adaptation from television, is to blame any weaknesses of the play on its origin in another medium or on padding that presumably was necessary to make it the right length for Broadway. The assumptions, unless the reviewer has seen and remembered the television version clearly, are likely to be wrong. In *The Trip to Bountiful,* for instance, it would be sensible to assume that a good part of the scene on the bus, the discussion between Mrs. Watts and Thelma, had been added for the sake of length, since much of what is said is clear in the situation itself; actually, their conversation is almost word for word from the television script. If that scene is a weakness in the play, and I think it is, the fault has nothing to do with adaptation but with Foote's original conception of what was necessary to his depiction of Mrs. Watts. On the other hand, as William Gibson points out in the prefatory note to *Two Plays,* many reviewers blamed television for the clumsy device of aural flashback in *The Miracle Worker,* voices in Annie Sullivan's mind that are audible in the theater, although the whole unnecessary business was added in the stage version. In a few cases—*The Trip to Bountiful, Visit to a Small Planet,* and *The Miracle Worker*—both the theater and the television versions of a play have been published, and it is possible to see what changes were made. Even here, the alterations cannot be traced exactly because the published script is not a working one, the printed version not the same as the acted one; Gibson says specifically in a note to the television *The Miracle Worker* that the reading version contains things that had to be dropped or changed in production. These variations are probably no greater than those that separate any play in print from its other self on stage; certainly they are not great enough to keep the reader from reaching certain generalizations about the transfer from television to the stage.

The most obvious thing about the three plays is that they are essentially the same in both versions. If there is a vast difference in acceptability of subject matter and treatment between stage and television, these plays give no evidence of it. The greatest change in plot is in *Visit to a Small Planet,* but the play is still doing what the television script did—using Kreton, a visitor from another planet, to make Vidal's point about the meaninglessness, the childishness even, that lies beneath the horror of war. On stage, Vidal uses Ellen instead of accident to prevent the war, letting mankind save the world. The most important differences between the two versions of *Visit* lie in the details. The minor figures, only vague sketches on television, have become vivid farce figures— particularly the General, a standard military bumbler, lifted above his fellow officers in *No Time for Sergeants* by his preposterous dedication to the laundry service. The boy-girl story, so peripheral in the television script, becomes integrated on stage when Vidal turns it into specific sex, which to Kreton is just another primitive passion like the one that leads to war. In his Preface to the published play, Vidal regrets having been forced—by audience reaction during tryouts—to cut out the "heart of the play's argument," a scene between Kreton and the Secretary General of the United Nations. Vidal, who is something of a pedagogue, as he admits in the preface to the collected television plays, does not know when he is well off. The discarded scene, which is in the television script, is simply another example of playwright insecurity, that disease that makes our dramatists insist on explaining the obvious. Such a scene is bad enough when it forces its way into an Inge or Chayefsky family scene, but in a farce satire it might be fatal. There is much more satirical force in the scene in which Kreton tries to excite Conrad to a patriotic fury by quoting slogans and singing songs, the emotional trivia washed up from a half-dozen American wars.

The other two plays are quite like their television sources. *The Trip to Bountiful* is the same sentimental story of Mrs. Watts's need once more to get to Bountiful, her farm home, before she dies; in both versions the play has a few touching moments but fails ever to come to grips with the really interesting subject implicit in the situation: the disappearance of the small rural community and the human dislocation that follows on the transplantation to the city. In the stage version, Foote has greatly expanded the part of Jessie Mae, the daughter-in-law; he has made a rather grand caricature of her, a really horrifying nullity of language and action. *The Miracle Worker* is the same efficient machine in both versions, telling the familiar story, as Herbert Gans has said, of woman-meets-girl, woman-loses-girl, woman-gets-girl. The stage play is slicker in its telling of how Annie Sullivan wins Helen Keller's confidence and how the young Helen learns that her spelling game is an opening to the world outside her blindness; it is more sentimental as well, as in the call-for-tears curtain, Helen's offering the key to Annie.

The important differences in the two versions of Gibson's play— really the basic difference between any play and any television script—lie in the use of the camera. Since television is as much movie as it is play, the close-up can often do quickly what is unclear on stage. Early in the play, there is a scene in which Helen's aunt makes a rag doll for her and in which the child's pleasure gives way to bewilderment, even anger, as she finds that the doll has no eyes. If we put aside the problem about whether or not the blind Helen would have had a concept of eyes strong enough to make her tear buttons from her aunt's dress as substitutes, if we accept the scene as Gibson wants us to, as an indication that Helen is intelligent and is in some way aware of how she differs from everyone else, the scene on television does its work much more effectively than the scene on stage. Helen has to wander noisily, demandingly, around the room while the adults, not understanding, go on with their conversation; in the theater the audience could no more understand than could the other characters. From where I sat when I saw the play, too far away to follow the detailed action of the child's hands, I had no idea what Helen wanted until Mrs. Keller put the problem into words. Mine was a balcony seat, but no member of the audience, not even those in the front of the orchestra, could see what would be clear to the whole television audience when the camera moved in close and watched the child's hand feel for eyes on the face of the doll. In the same way, the scene in which Helen feels the talking lips of the two Negro children would have greater force and clarity in close-up.

Then, too, there is the business of the visual plant. In the last dinner scene of *The Miracle Worker,* Helen knocks over the water pitcher, an act that leads her to the pump in the yard and finally to the recognition that water is the *w-a-t-e-r* that Annie is spelling against her hand. Gibson suggests in the television version that the dinner be preceded by a close-up of the water pitcher in the hands of a servant. This shot not only prepares the audience for the dinner sequence but for the special significance of the pitcher in that scene. The visual shorthand of television was apparent a few years ago when Moss Hart's *The Climate of Eden* was presented by Play of the Week. Hart goes to some trouble in the play to establish the razor that belongs to the unbalanced protagonist; on television, a single shot of the razor, open in the man's hands, does the work of many lines. In transferring a television play to the stage, as most of the adaptations indicate, the playwright has to consider means rather than content. It is true that in the theater pantomimed action and planned groupings of the actors can often communicate directly to the audience. Yet, stage business is not really the business of the stage; the play in the theater is still much more a verbal medium than its brother dramatic forms—television and the film—that can use the camera. For this reason, perhaps, realism is less and less comfortable on stage. In television, the banality of language can often be masked, as it can be in the movies, by allowing the camera to make an intelligent, objective comment on the surroundings or by allowing the actor, through close-up, to suggest an emotion more complicated than the lines express. A play such as *Middle of the Night* may be no more bromidic on stage than it would be on television, but, trapped on stage, the clichés of language, character, and situation are more obvious.

Although the techniques of the two media are essentially different, television has had some influence on the staging of plays. This is most obvious in the adaptations, but original plays also use some of the borrowed methods. The multiple set and the use of lights for transition are the two techniques that owe much to television. For the most part, television plays are made up of brief scenes, often supposed to take place in different rooms of a house or different parts of a town. The sets, of course, may actually be no more than a chair or two and a piece of wall, but cribbed and cramped as they are they suggest space and movement impossible in a single-room stage set. When Robert Alan Aurthur turned *A Very Special Baby* into a stage play, for instance, he suggested that the set allow for several different playing areas—the living room, Joey's bedroom, the kitchen, the backyard. The second act of *The Trip to Bountiful* demands a set that places the Houston Bus Terminal on one side of the stage, the Harrison Bus Station on the other, and the bus itself, or the seat that Mrs. Watts shares with

Thelma, in the middle. With the proliferation of playing areas comes the need for quick transitions. Scenes no longer need to be formal divisions; within a single act the lights can go down on one area and up on another many times. The audience can move not only from one room to another in the Keller house in *The Miracle Worker,* but from Alabama to Boston without the old wait for a change of set. Lights, of course, are used not only for movement from place to place, but to indicate the passage of time.

It would be incorrect to overemphasize the influence of television on the fluidity of contemporary staging. Playwrights, particularly the expressionists, have been borrowing from the movies for forty years. Technical experimentalists have always been willing to use special devices even on material that was otherwise commonplace; Elmer Rice, for instance, has used nonrealistic staging—from the revolving stage of *On Trial* (1914) to the lighting plot of *Dream Girl* (1945)—even though his plays stick close to conventional Broadway forms. The postwar theater has made wide use of multiple sets and lighting transitions in plays that ape classic conventions, as in Maxwell Anderson's pseudo-Elizabethan chronicle play, *Anne of the Thousand Days,* and in plays that mix the present with the past or fact with fantasy, whether seriously, as in Sidney Kingsley's *Darkness at Noon,* or comically, as in George Axelrod's *The Seven Year Itch.* Musical comedy, in which one brief scene, built around a song or a dance, has to give way quickly to the next, early made use of shifting sets (an active variation on the multiple set) and lighting transitions; since musicals are no longer the specialist's activities that once they were, since playwrights and directors move between the musical and the straight play, it is safe to assume that the staging of musicals has had its effect on staging in general. More important, the younger playwrights, at the end of World War II, began to absorb (not simply to practice) expressionistic techniques, to mix them with realism in a way not unlike the television play. The most important examples are Tennessee Williams' *The Glass Menagerie* and Arthur Miller's *Death of a Salesman,* particularly the latter which uses the multiple set and an intricate lighting plot to cover wide jumps in time and space and, at the same time, to suggest that the events are all contemporaneous. Jo Mielziner, who designed the set for both of these plays, has made a large contribution to the neo-expressionism of the recent American theater; his more recent work—the set for *Sweet Bird of Youth,* for instance—suggests that fluidity can easily give way to chaos.

The influences, then, have been many, and they have almost certainly worked on one another. Ironically, although television drama is the most realistic of dramatic forms today,* its most important effect on the theater has been its contribution to the spread of nonrealistic staging and the concomitant shattering of the strict act structure. Still, whatever television drama offers comes in the cause of realism, the retaining of an old and restricting form that the expressionists, the chroniclers, the writers of musical comedies, the playwrights like Miller and Williams, would like to break open, to expand, to enrich. It is apparent with the influx of playwrights from television that what those dramatists want is the quick transitions that the camera allows them on television. One advantage of such changes is that the playwright who wishes to retain realism of motivation and action is spared the embarrassment of concocting reasons for getting unwanted characters off the stage so that an intimate scene may be played in comparative privacy. The cut and the dissolve, as the film at its best has indicated, are imaginative devices; their stage equivalents need not be simply hollow substitutes for the ringing phone, the dinner engagement, the business in the next room that have for years pulled the unnecessary third party off stage. Still, if only by accident, television has played its part in the new packaging on Broadway; sadly, it has not come up with any solid suggestions about what to put in those packages.

"Television is really an apprenticeship for the theatre," James Costigan told a New York *Times* interviewer (November 20, 1960), shortly before his unfortunate *Little Moon of Alban,* a noisy confusion of Irish politics and piety, opened and closed on Broadway. In the mid-fifties, judging by the comments of television dramatists on their place in the artistic fraternity, not many of them would have agreed with Costigan's statement. By now, for one

---

* The American film, perhaps because of wide-screen techniques, has moved away from the quasi-documentary form that flourished right after the war. Even those films that call for the intimacy of the living room or the bar stool share some of the visual bombast of the costume blockbusters.

reason or another, most of them have gone to work in the theater: to make more money, to acquire the prestige of being a playwright without the qualifying adjective of medium, to find a market in the face of changing habits of programming, to treat a subject that might not fit the time requirements of television. Gore Vidal followed *Visit to a Small Planet* (1957) with a political play, a *pièce à clef*, *The Best Man* (1960). Tad Mosel, who had tried off-Broadway (*The Lion Hunters,* 1952) before he made his television reputation, finally came to Broadway in 1960 with *All the Way Home,* an adaptation of James Agee's novel, *A Death in the Family.* Morton Wishengrad, a television and radio writer best known for his scripts for *The Eternal Light,* wrote *The Rope Dancers* (1957), an attempt at a parable on the destructive power of guilt, which succeeded, when it did, in grandly melodramatic moments that seemed to carry American drama back to those uncomplicated years before World War I. Horton Foote's *The Trip to Bountiful* (1953) was preceded by the one-act *Celebration* (1948) and *The Chase* (1952) and followed by *The Traveling Lady* (1954), none of which drew audiences; Foote has not been on Broadway since. *The Chase,* which he later turned into a novel, has a serious social intention, an examination of the culpability of the community in the making of a criminal, but it is so repetitive, so awash with fatuously realistic dialogue that it is killed by cliché; *The Traveling Lady* has all the faults of *The Chase* and not even the virtue of a discernible theme.

Of all the television dramatists who have worked on Broadway, N. Richard Nash has been the most persistent and Paddy Chayefsky the most successful, in a commercial if not in an aesthetic sense. Nash might well be identified simply as a theatrical playwright—he would not have been out of place with the new Pineros in the third chapter—for he began to publish plays in the early forties, when he was still N. Richard Nusbaum, and his Broadway career began with *The Young and Fair* (1948). Still, his best play and his only Broadway success is an expanded television script, *The Rainmaker* (1954). Nash, who has called himself "a playwright romanticist" in the production notes to *Handful of Fire* (1958), is attracted to nonrealistic stage effects and to fairly obvious symbolism, but his work has variety—at least on the surface. Still, whether he is writing a standard message melodrama, like *The Young and Fair,* or a pseudo-poetic attempt at romantic tragedy, like *See the Jaguar* (1952), an essay in the familiar analysis trade-last, like *Girls of Summer* (1956), or the book to a mediocre, star-vehicle musical, like *Wildcat* (1960), he is writing one of two plays that keep coming back in various forms. One is the story of integrity corrupted by compromise and regained through courage (*The Young and Fair*), through death (*See the Jaguar*), or through the recognition that man is a mixture of good and evil (*Handful of Fire*). This last is something of a change from the earlier treatments of the subject, in which Nash has usually differentiated carefully between what Patty in *The Young and Fair* calls "people of good heart and people of bad heart," but *Fire* has its own kind of myth, a peculiar concept of folk innocence. The other Nash story is about the awakening to life and love of a character —Lizzie in *The Rainmaker,* Hilda in *Girls of Summer,* and both sisters in *Wildcat*—when someone takes the trouble to break down the defenses that timidity and a sense of inferiority (Jane in *Wildcat* has a glass-menagerie limp) have built. "If somebody holds out his hand toward you," Lizzie tells File in *The Rainmaker,* a lesson she learns from Starbuck, "you've got to reach— and take it." Jules says the same thing to Hilda in *Girls of Summer*: "We gotta ask questions and give answers! We gotta look at each other—and reach!"

The Rainmaker is the only one of Nash's plays that comes close to succeeding. It has a number of faults that it shares with the rest of the playwright's work. There is clumsy exposition, as in the scene in which H. C. tells File that the town knows all about him, and a tendency to be explicit about what Starbuck represents: "You gotta take my deal because once in your life you gotta take a chance on a con man." Its characters speak the same stagey Western dialect that is so impossible in *See the Jaguar* where it tries to be verse:

> I keep drawin' beads on answers.
> I get one in my sights as clear as clear.
> I squeeze the trigger and the answer's gone,
> And Jann gone with it.
> In the end, it's hating counts.

But in *The Rainmaker,* the language—if it adds nothing—at least does not get in the way of the play. Nash's romantic comedy is stronger too for its rainmaker, who works as character and metaphor (probably because the con man is so indigenous to American life and literature) in a way that the cages in *Jaguar* and the plaza (out of *Camino Real*) in *Handful of Fire* do not work both as setting and symbol. There is some fun in Lizzie's clowning, when she acts the flirt she could never be, but the real attraction of the play is its simplicity, its willingness to be as obvious as a nursery story. Lizzie is the sleeping beauty. Starbuck, although he kisses her and awakens her, is not the prince; File is the prince with whom she will live happily ever after, the answer to her dream of a solid husband rather than a romantic lover. Starbuck, then, is the good fairy who defeats the black fairy, her brother Noah, who, in the name of truth (the enemy of dreams), would keep her ugly and alone. *The Rainmaker* would have worked better as the romantic comedy it is if Nash had been willing to offer his fairy story without explaining it.

Nash may use myth consciously, but Chayefsky is hip-deep in it without ever knowing it. It is hardly surprising that he should be the most successful of the television dramatists in the theater because his work is shot through with Broadway's most pervasive doctrine, the gospel according to William Inge, that love is the solution to all problems. Chayefsky's preoccupation was already evident in his television plays—in *The Bachelor Party,* in which a night on the town with the boys teaches Charlie that it is better to be married than bored, and in *Marty,* where the theme was treated most effectively, in the touching encounter of the lonely butcher with the lonely schoolteacher. In *Middle of the Night* (1956), Chayefsky's first play, an elaboration of a television script, the marriage of the principals, despite the difference in their ages, is presumably going to console The Girl for her loneliness and The Manufacturer for his aging. In *The Tenth Man* (1959), the despairing young man and the paranoid girl go off together to cure one another through love; as Gore Vidal said, quoting a probably mythical Broadway wit (*The Reporter,* December 10, 1959), "the rocks in his head fit the holes in hers." Yet, the apparent affirmation of these endings is riddled with despair. This is obvious not only in characters like Julie in *The Bachelor Party* and The Friend in *Middle of the Night,* who are put in as foils to the lovers who supposedly find a way in an unhappy world. Take as an example the declarations of love in *Night,* The Manufacturer's "Even a few years of happiness you don't throw away," and The

Girl's "maybe there's something wrong with loving an older man, but any love is better than none." Charlie's speech in *The Bachelor Party,* his assurance to himself and the troubled groom, must be one of the blackest positive speeches in contemporary drama:

Everybody's scared, Arnold. Everybody's got things in them they're ashamed of. That's what a wife's for. To make you feel you don't have to be ashamed of yourself. Then she tells you what makes her feel miserable. . . . Then, that's your job. It's your job to make her feel she's not as bad as everybody makes her think she is. That's what marriage is, Arnold. It's a job.

The bulk of Chayefsky's work displays this mixture of morose realism with the conventional happy ending; finally, in the preposterousness of *The Tenth Man* he has escaped into the completely artificial, prescribed marriage where all other forms of psychological therapy have failed.

Chayefsky's plays have other weaknesses that, in the context of current theatrical taste, may be commercial virtues. He is as relentless as any of his contemporaries in his use of pat psychological explanation of his characters. The Daughter offers pocket analyses of everyone in *Middle of the Night.* Both she and The Son-in-Law are comic characters, so far as I am concerned, but her kind of psychologizing becomes Chayefsky's own in his original film script, *The Goddess,* a case study stretched between two lines, the mother's "I didn't want her when she was born, and I don't want her now," and the ex-husband's "She never had a chance, honey. She never had a chance from the beginning." In *The Tenth Man,* the jargon is even more oppressive as the two young people exchange symptoms the way adolescents once exchanged identification bracelets. Another difficulty with the play, one that has its roots in the excess of psychology, lies in the dybbuk that supposedly possesses the girl and which, at the exorcism, is driven from the young man. The implication is that the dybbuk is metaphorical, an ancient name used to represent neurotic possession of the two young people. In the first act, however, the dybbuk speaks through the girl, identifies itself as the spirit of a woman whom the grandfather seduced years before in Europe. If Evelyn's dybbuk is simply a projection of her illness, the invention of a pious girl, as its end-of-play transference to Arthur suggests, then Foreman must have entertained his granddaughter with the details of his carnal youth.

If Chayefsky is a little uncertain about the nature of his dybbuk, he is straightforward about his broadly humorless comedy. The eight old men in *The Tenth Man* go through a number of Jewish-comedy turns, repetitive bits built around jokes that grow out of their age and their innocence. In his earlier work, Chayefsky has at least nodded at satire—the groom drunkenly singing the DeWitt Clinton alma mater in *The Bachelor Party*—but he is too sentimental really to be satirical; the tone at its best—the group of young men in *Marty*—is sweetly mocking. When Chayefsky moved from television to the stage, his comedy, like the rest of his occasionally effective devices, became distressingly obvious. The old men in *The Tenth Man,* then, are slapstick figures. In his first hour-long television script, *Holiday Song,* "a rather ponderous spiritual message," as he rightly calls it, he used the tiresome gag about the innocent old man and his confusion on the subway which he makes so much of in *The Tenth Man*—inappropriately, I think: a *babushka* who never left her neighborhood might get lost on the subway, but the old men, or so their lines indicate, have spent thirty-odd years working in and around New York (clothing business, journalism) and might be expected to have learned a little about the transit system. My first impulse, on seeing *The Tenth Man,* was to blame the comic excess on the director, Tyrone Guthrie, whose allegiance to theatricalism, so refreshing in his productions of *Tamburlaine* (1955) and *Mary Stuart* (1957), has occasionally, as in the Phoenix revival of *Six Characters in Search of an Author* (1955), let him sacrifice a play for an effect. But Chayefsky's note on *Holiday Song* ("Seen in the smallness of a living room, it may play with no more than a smile; but in front of a house audience it should get continual laughter") indicates that he shares his director's fondness for broadness. His notes indicate that he wanted the television play to be a folk comedy like those of Sholom Aleichem; it was more like a Jewish *Going My Way.* If Aleichem was still in his mind while he worked on *The Tenth Man,* the model must have been elbowed out by Anne Nichols, Sylvia Regan, and Milt Gross.

Television may be about ready for a new cycle of original scripts, about ready to discover another handful of talented playwrights, but if Paddy Chayefsky and his fellow dramatists are an indication, the American theater will be little the richer for it.

5 THE PLAYWRIGHTS OF THE TWENTIES AND THIRTIES

but that was in another country;
and besides, the wench is dead.
—BARABAS in *The Jew of Malta*

Commentators on the American theater have a passion or a need for time and genre labels. It is comforting, I suppose, to have set responses for particular stimulants. Push the button marked *S. N. Behrman* and get the answer—*twenties, high comedy;* push the *Lillian Hellman* button and get the information—*thirties, melodrama with a social conscience.* Playwrights are persistent, however; they refuse to operate within a single decade and, as often as not, they and their work are changed and colored by the years. Their generic badges are ordinarily no more useful than their decade designations. Sometimes, as with Behrman, the textbook descriptive phrase goes back to a first play; ever since *The Second Man* (1927), which *is* high comedy of a kind, Behrman has been writing comedies of ideas, but the reviewers have continued to search for wit in him and to ignore argument. Still, there is truth as well as confusion in the critic's tendency to put identifying boundaries around any playwright. There are fashions in the theater as obvious as those in dress and food, but an author who made his name in the twenties or thirties is likely to reflect such fashions differently from a playwright who has developed in the years since the war. It is, then, both artificial and inevitable that a book like this one should have a chapter on playwrights whose reputations (whose roots, perhaps) belong in another period.

Implicit in the making of time and type divisions is the assumption that the playwrights have ability or personality enough to make special consideration of them worth the trouble. Before I get to the serious dramatists of the earlier decades, perhaps a page or two might be offered to the playwrights of no time and no place. These are the Broadway regulars, the efficient hacks who turn out standard theatrical fare, who supposedly know how to mix the contemporary reference with the ancient sure-thing of show business. The team of Howard Lindsay and Russel Crouse is a case in point. Since the war they have played around with presidential politics (*State of the Union,* 1945), the United Nations (*The Prescott Proposals,* 1953), Communism in Czechoslovakia (*The Great Sebastians,* 1956), and the basketball scandals (*Tall Story,* 1959); in musicals, they have kidded Perle Mesta (*Call Me Madam,* 1950) and the Grace Kelly wedding (*Happy Hunting,* 1956) and have been reverent about the Trapp family (*The Sound of Music,* 1959). Although they appear to be in favor of clean politics and against tyranny, they are more obviously enthusiastic about pat gags, grandiloquent gestures, and teasing curtains than they are about the potentialities for seriousness or satire of their ostensible subject matter. They are as vulgarly casual in *The Great Sebastians,* for instance, as they are in their murder farce, *Remains to Be Seen* (1951), or in *Life with Mother* (1948), a blatant try at a repetition of their most lucrative success, *Life with Father* (1939). Although they know all the tricks that are supposed to insure popular success, Lindsay and Crouse have had no runaway hit—the musicals aside—since *State of the Union,* and it is at least arguable that the modest runs of *The Prescott Proposals* and *The Great Sebastians* would have been unlikely without the prestige of Katharine Cornell and the Lunts to keep the authors' trifles afloat.

Perhaps Elmer Rice's career in the postwar theater shows more surely than that of Lindsay and Crouse that, for all the fatuousness of contemporary drama, a certain kind of theatrical commonplace has become dated. There may be theater enthusiasts who would not approve of my placing Rice in the company of Lindsay and Crouse, but that is where he belongs. Although he wrote one of the best American expressionist plays, *The Adding Machine* (1923), and although he has a fondness for technical experimentation, the bulk of his work has been quite ordinary—melodrama or sentimental comedy. His best play since *The Adding Machine* and his last Broadway success was *Dream Girl* (1945). It is a fan-

tasy comedy in which the heroine regularly dreams herself into
the fame and adoration that she has not achieved in reality; its virtues lie in the inherent comedy of the dream sequences and an occasional sharpness of line, particularly in the mother's speeches.
Its weakness is its hero. A blunt, tough, anti-intellectual newspaperman (on stage that combination traditionally implies charm),
he is given to pedagogical speeches which the audience is supposed
to take seriously. The hero's message and the play's is that too
much dreaming is a dangerous thing, but since the heroine is interesting only in the fantasy sequences, the evidence of the eyes
and ears contradicts the lesson. After *Dream Girl* came the musical version of *Street Scene* (1947), with Kurt Weill's music and
Langston Hughes's lyrics, and after that a series of artistic and
commercial failures. *Not for Children* (1951), an occasionally
funny expressionist comedy, is a revision of a 1936 play. *The
Grand Tour* (1951) is sentimental hokum, a summer romance
between a schoolteacher and an embezzler, played against European guidebook backgrounds. *The Winner* (1954) clears the
good name of a tough-talking cigarette girl in one of the author's
too frequent assumptions that legal doings are necessarily dramatic. *Cue for Passion* (1958) is a retelling of *Hamlet,* a plod-
dingly explicit psychological study that makes the work of some
of our more obvious amateur psychologists—Arthur Laurents, for
instance—seem models of restraint and suggestion.

George S. Kaufman is a special case. From the beginning of his
theatrical career, his first attempts at collaboration in 1918, he
was always very much a part of the Broadway scene, completely
and frankly enmeshed in the manipulations of show business.
Even so, his work, at its best, outstrips the implications of his too-
often-quoted witticism about satire's being what closes on Saturday night. The comedies that he wrote with Marc Connelly in the
twenties and with Moss Hart in the thirties display an attitude—a
combination of sentimentality and self-mockery, an embracing and
a rejection of the obvious, a use of the wisecrack as weapon and defense—that most represents one image of the American—the
knowledgeable innocent. Whether Kaufman or the theatrical climate changed, however, it is apparent that the playwright, who
found the right tone and the right collaborators in earlier decades,
was lost in the years since the war. With Edna Ferber, his partner

for *Dinner at Eight* and *Stage Door,* he wrote *Bravo!* (1948);
with Nunnally Johnson, the book to the Arthur Schwartz musical
Park Avenue (1946); with Leueen MacGrath, *The Small Hours*
(1951) and *Fancy Meeting You Again* (1952); and with Miss
MacGrath and Abe Burrows, the book to Cole Porter's *Silk Stockings* (1955). None of them need comment. His one success in the
postwar years was *The Solid Gold Cadillac* (1953), a Howard
Teichmann play doctored for the considerable comic talents of
the late Josephine Hull. Although the play is built on a funny idea,
that a sweetly vague little woman could take over a corporation,
the play is haphazard in its plot and heavy-handed in its humor; a
typical line, alas, is this one, spoken by the narrator: "Little did she
think, as she sat there, that what she was going to get was not a
glass slipper, but *a good swift boot.*"

Neither of Kaufman's former chief collaborators has written
much for the stage in the postwar years. Marc Connelly, whose
output has always been small, had one unsuccessful play on Broadway—*A Story for Strangers* (1948). Moss Hart, who kept busy as
a director and who wrote an occasionally fictional autobiography,
Act One (1959), offered three plays—*Christopher Blake* (1946),
Light Up the Sky (1948), and *The Climate of Eden* (1952).
In the Foreword to the last, Hart mentions that after *Lady in the
Dark* (1941) he felt a "growing disaffection" with the kind of
work he had been doing on Broadway. *Christopher Blake* is not
quite the "abrupt departure from anything I had ever written before" that Hart thought it was, but it is unusual for him to be writing a problem play. Actually it is two plays—the fantasy of
Christopher Blake, who imagines himself in scenes that will keep
his parents from or punish them for divorcing, and the naturalistic
drama of the divorce hearings. At its best, when the audience is
inside Christopher's head, the play is reminiscent of *Lady in the
Dark.* The scene in which Christopher gets a medal for inventing
a super atom bomb and an infallible peace plan suggests Liza
Elliott's adoration fantasy in the first scene of *Lady,* and Christopher's imagined court scene, straight out of the movies, suggests
the circus-trial scene in the musical. The actual divorce drama is
ineffectively done. Since Hart wants to avoid the conventional
treatment in which a child holds the parents together, he sets up the
play as a series of conversations which finally teaches Christopher

to accept the separation of his parents; unfortunately, the play is full of entrances and exits that serve only to hold off complete revelation until the last big scene. This technical awkwardness and Hart's failure to make the parents either clear or interesting rob the play of any value outside the comic twists of Christopher's imagination. The play suffers most, as *Lady in the Dark* did, from Hart's inability to mix his earnestness with his sense of humor.

Light Up the Sky, a meager comedy that kids the affectations of theater people, is more like Hart's earlier plays with Kaufman; like *The Man Who Came to Dinner*, it tries to get comic mileage out of the dramatic equivalent of name-dropping, the use of characters who are supposed to suggest actual people—Billy Rose, say, or Guthrie McClintic. Hart's original intention, or so he says in the Foreword to *The Climate of Eden*, was "to say a number of things I wanted to say under the masquerade of hard-hitting comedy" and he admits that the play failed for him. As it stands, *Light Up the Sky* says nothing, except perhaps that only the combination of egotism and idealism can get a play on the stage. In his summary of the Boston season in *The Best Plays of 1948–1949*, Elliot Norton pointed out that Hart rewrote the last two acts, cut the "message" in favor of hilarity. Perhaps, then, the play itself, which is not all that hilarious, is an unfortunate example of the kind of compromise it advocates.

The Climate of Eden, an adaptation of Edgar Mittelhölzer's *Shadows Move Among Them*, is certainly not a play that one would expect from Moss Hart. Set in a strange religious community in British Guiana, it tells the double story of Olivia, a little girl who grows to maturity, and Gregory, a young man who is cured of his own guilt and the oppression of the European cities he left behind him. In both cases, the change involves the putting away of ghosts, shadows, spirits, although Hart does not (perhaps cannot on stage) dwell on the "local influences," the psychic phenomena, that are so important a part of Mittelhölzer's novel. Nor does Hart really establish "the climate of Eden" that Gregory speaks about, the novel's sense of the settlement as a civilization in healthy opposition to the demands of the world outside. The play is direct where the novel is evasive, dramatic where it is philosophic, even mystical. For all its limitations, *The Climate of Eden*, which failed on Broadway, is the most impressive of Hart's recent plays.

. . .

While the older Broadway professionals, the Rices and the Kaufmans, were trying and, as often as not, failing to find their footing in the postwar theater, Eugene O'Neill suddenly and posthumously became—once again—America's most important playwright. There are any number of reasons for the O'Neill vogue that marked the late fifties. For one thing, plays like *The Iceman Cometh* and *Long Day's Journey into Night* have so much more substance than the ordinary Broadway "serious" play. Still, quality is not reason enough, for if it were, *The Iceman Cometh* would have been more widely received in 1946 when it was first produced on Broadway, bringing O'Neill back into the theater after the absence of a dozen years. It was not until the off-Broadway revival of *Iceman* in 1956, followed later that year by the successful production of *Journey,* that the O'Neill boom became apparent. *A Moon for the Misbegotten,* which had died on the road in 1947, was produced in 1957 and *A Touch of the Poet* in 1958. In part, the popularity of these plays may have resulted from the fact that, *Iceman* aside, they are or may be taken for family plays, and they appeared in a decade in which domestic drama was big. In part, O'Neill's new success may lie quite outside his plays. By 1956, the first enthusiasm for Arthur Miller and Tennessee Williams had begun to die down and no new white hope for American drama had been found. Both newspaper reviewers and academic critics have a way of hopefully searching horizons and O'Neill may have been the only visible figure. Certainly his visibility was emphasized by the excitement of newly discovered manuscripts and lost plays refound, by the publicity given to events like Dr. Karl Gierow's dramatic flight to Stockholm with the manuscript of *More Stately Mansions,* which has yet to be produced or published in this country.

Whatever the reason for this sudden mushrooming of O'Neill productions, it is apparent that the plays themselves are not part of the postwar American theater. All of them were written in the late thirties and early forties. Here, much more than in his earlier plays in which he was consciously taking part in a theatrical revolution, he is working outside the theater, aware, as always, of the potentialities of the stage, but without thought of immediate production. For instance, when O'Neill wrote *Long Day's Journey* in 1940, he intended that no one should see it until after his death. This long autobiographical play, one of O'Neill's most important works, finds him—as so many of the later plays do—involved in the relationship of man to man rather than that of man to the universe which preoccupied him in his most ambitious early plays. Here, too, he has forsaken the elaborate use of myth and mask, the self-conscious literary posture that mars plays like *Mourning Becomes Electra* and *The Great God Brown*; he has returned to realism, accepting the statement of Edmond Tyrone (the portrait of the playwright as a young man) in *Journey*: "Stammering is the native eloquence of us fog people." The play is simply the depiction of the Tyrone family—the mother's addiction, the father's avarice, Jamie's alcoholism, Edmond's tuberculosis—and the slow descent of the four of them, crying shame and asking forgiveness, into the particular night that holds them and holds them together. The blackness of the play is lightened somewhat by the audience's extratheatrical knowledge, the awareness that beyond Edmond's sanitarium lay Eugene O'Neill's plays. The value of the play, however, has little to do with what the audience may think of it as autobiography. Its strength lies in the powerful depiction of the family, the abrasive interrelationships in which the love and guilt of each one helps to destroy all the others. Some of the play's force comes from its excessive length, the famous O'Neill repetitiveness that allows him to make his points again and again, piling them, like the stones in that old torture, on the chest of the listener or the reader. Sitting in the audience or reading the play, I have a feeling that O'Neill could have done his work effectively at less length, but if I were asked to cut the play I would have no idea where to aim the red pencil.

So, too, with *The Iceman Cometh,* O'Neill's long, argumentative excursion into man's need for illusions. The playwright could probably have managed with half the number of drunken dreamers, but he has so organized his play, letting the characters feed or poison one another's illusions, that no one can be removed without toppling the structure. For all its length and for all its discussion, the play is relatively simple in form. Into Harry Hope's saloon, where life is barely existence but where it is possible at all only because the regulars imagine that each new day promises a change, comes Hickey, half pitchman, half evangelist, trying to sell life without illusions. He needles the characters into trying to live up to their "pipe dreams" and, after they fail, he assures them that their new self-knowledge will bring them real peace. It turns out that Hickey's message is his own kind of illusion, his defensive invention to cover his real reason for murdering his wife. At the end of the play, as most of the characters drop back into their Act I dreams, Hickey is taken away by the police. He leaves behind only two converts to the truth: Parritt, the kid who betrayed his anarchist mother, and Larry Slade, the ex-anarchist whose pose has been that he is uninvolved, an observer who has rejected life. Parritt commits suicide and Larry, who does not have that kind of courage, is forced to wait for death, knowing that he is "a weak fool looking with pity at the two sides of everything. . . ." It is ironic that O'Neill's *Iceman* should have achieved success at a moment when so many playwrights were selling *maturity,* insisting that their characters and their audiences face the facts. O'Neill put that message into Hickey's mouth, showed the salesman's vaunted life without illusions as, to use Larry's words, "the peace of death." The play becomes a defense of "those damned tomorrow dreams" that Hickey on stage and less attractive men off stage would destroy, presumably for the sake of the dreamer.

O'Neill's other late plays also deal with illusion, the personalities that men put on to protect themselves or to hide themselves from the world. In *A Moon for the Misbegotten,* Josie pretends to be a slut to disguise the fact that she is a virgin who wishes she were a mother; Jamie covers the horrified child that he really is with the pose of the high-living playboy; Hogan acts the conniving father, allowing his schemes for Josie's happiness to pass for venality. The one effective scene in the play comes in the third act in which Josie and Jamie, masks down, play a love scene that is mother to son, not man to woman. *A Touch of the Poet,* one of an unfinished cycle of plays about an American family, is the account of Con Melody's fall, his recognition that he can no longer be the aristocratic English officer that he once was (or thought he was); in the last scene, the best in the play, he becomes the ignorant peasant that New England expects an immigrant Irish tavernkeeper to be. His daughter, who has been preaching Hickey's doctrine, discovers that, in exploding Major Melody, she has created not reality, but another and more frightening parody of truth. In *Hughie,* Erie Smith, who "is consciously a Broadway sport and a Wise Guy," brags to the new desk clerk, the dead Hughie's replacement, about his connections with gangsters and Follies girls; in the face of the listener's apparent indifference, he stumbles over his own fiction, begins to reveal the truth; then, as the clerk gets interested and becomes the Hughie that Erie needs, he starts to reconstruct his flashy self-image. An impressive short play, the only survivor apparently of a projected series of eight one-act monologue plays, *Hughie* has been published but not yet performed in this country. O'Neill in the fifties has many of the defects of O'Neill at any time. The infelicities of language, particularly the archaic slang of *The Iceman Cometh* and *A Moon for the Misbegotten,* continue to grate on sensitive ears. His comedy—Act I of *Moon,* for instance—is heavy-handed, grotesque without being very funny. His seriousness is sometimes portentous and sometimes—particularly in *Poet* and *Moon*—simply dull. He consistently falls short of what he wants to do—as Edmond says in *Long Day's Journey,* he has the habit of the poet without the makings—but in a period in which most attempts are small ones, this defect may be a virtue. Reading and, sometimes, seeing O'Neill alongside most of the rest of the American dramatists, I find myself sharing the yes-we-know-all-that-but respect that Joseph Wood Krutch and John Gassner have for his work. It may well be that O'Neill—especially the O'Neill of *Mourning Becomes Electra* and *Strange Interlude*—will become, like Thomas Wolfe, a writer for bright adolescents, but the literary historian of the future, looking for the O'Neill pigeonhole, may have to shave a little from *Long Day's Journey* and *Iceman* if he wants to fit the playwright into too small a space.

Although there is still argument about O'Neill's stature, I doubt if there is anyone around these days who wants to defend Maxwell Anderson as a major playwright. There is certainly nothing in his postwar career that would justify that label. Except for *Truckline Café* (1946), the plays from the late forties—*Joan of Lorraine* (1946), *Anne of the Thousand Days* (1948), and *Lost in the Stars* (1949)—were greeted respectfully and achieved a degree of popular success. The last of these, an occasionally effective sentimentalization of Alan Paton's *Cry, the Beloved Country,* has music by Kurt Weill, Anderson's partner in his earlier musical, *Knickerbocker Holiday* (1938); Weill, quite rightly, although too much of the score suggests the triumph of recitative, drew more attention from *Lost* than Anderson did. By the fifties, Anderson began to seem like a figure out of the past. His *Barefoot in Athens* (1951) managed only a short run. His one success of the decade was *Bad Seed* (1954), a meretricious little play, a dullish thriller, like the William March novel from which it was adapted. His last two plays—*The Day the Money Stopped,* an adaptation, with Brendan Gill, of the latter's novel, and *The Golden Six,* a play about Claudius—were produced in 1958 and both quickly disappeared. The fact that *The Golden Six* did not have a Broadway production but found its very temporary home at the off-Broadway York is probably as much an indication of the changed attitude toward the work of Anderson as it is evidence of the new ambitions of off-Broadway theater.

Although a number of these plays are special cases, three of them—*Joan of Lorraine, Anne of the Thousand Days,* and *Barefoot in Athens*—are typical Anderson. It is true that except for a few passages in *Anne,* the playwright has put aside the dreadful verse that he once felt serious plays demanded. He has, however, held on to the theme that has marked most of his work, that the world is a corrupting place and that idealism and innocence can only survive by dying. Esdras' words over the bodies of Mio and Miriamne—"this is the glory of earth-born men and women,/ not to cringe, never to yield, but standing,/ take defeat implacable and defiant,/ die unsubmitting"—are a benediction not only for the hero and heroine of *Winterset,* but for many of the leading characters in the early Anderson—Rudolph and Mary in *The Masque of Kings* and King in *Key Largo.* They will serve as well for Joan, for Anne, and for Socrates, who was *Barefoot in Athens.* There is a slight softening of Anderson's view of the world in the postwar plays, a willingness to admit that the world is a mixture of bad and good and that compromise is necessary, if not attractive. As Masters says, in *Joan of Lorraine,* "The human race is a mass of corruption tempered with high ideals. —You can't sacrifice your integrity, but short of that—." So, for that integrity—under whatever name—Joan goes to the fire, Anne to the chopping block, Socrates to the hemlock. Each of them, even a politician like Anne, discovers that there is a point beyond which compromise is impossible without the destruction of the self. The difficulty with Anderson's plays is not that they so consistently choose romantic death over practical life. Plays as good as Jean Anouilh's *Antigone* and John Millington Synge's *Deirdre of the Sorrows* make the same choice, but the romanticism of Anouilh and Synge is tough-minded; by comparison, Anderson is almost flaccid. His sponginess is technical, rather than ideational. He regularly fails to put flesh on his philosophic dilemma; too often—most obviously in *Joan of Lorraine* and *Barefoot in Athens*—his characters are abstractions.

Among the playwrights who first made their reputations in the twenties, S. N. Behrman is the only one besides Anderson who has worked regularly in the postwar theater. Not that any of his stage pieces of the last fifteen years add much to his reputation as a dramatist. Two of the plays—*Dunnigan's Daughter* (1945) and *Jane* (1952)—are reminiscent in theme and structure, if not in quality, of the earlier Behrman plays. Since *Jane,* a much rewritten adaptation of a Somerset Maugham short story, was first written in 1946, both plays come from the years immediately at the end of the war when the continuity of Behrman's career had not yet been interrupted by his successful and useful excursion into the historical journalism that produced his books on Duveen and Max Beerbohm. *Dunnigan's Daughter* is another Behrman study of a power-hungry egocentric (like *Meteor,* like *The Talley Method*) seen, as usual, in a personal and a public context; Clay Rainier is defeated by his wife, the lady of the title, and by the unrest among the Indians in his Mexican mines, both under the influence of the idealist Jim Baird. The latter, unlike the Behrman idealist of the thirties, a type that he distrusted as much as the autocratic rightists, is surprisingly sentimentalized. Behrman's plays have always carried heavy loads of discussion and argument, but at his best—in *No Time for Comedy,* for instance—his characters have ideas; at his worst—and *Dunnigan's Daughter* is an example —his ideas have characters. Here, after endless explanation, there is still no understanding of Clay and what makes him work; finally, there is no character at all. Although Zelda Rainier is the daughter of the title, she is only a weak version of the typical Behrman woman (Marion in *Biography,* Lael in *Rain from Heaven*), the embodiment of the humanistic values, particularly tolerance, that must struggle to stay alive in the face of ideational (and male) fanaticism. The heroine of *Jane*—the playwright gives substance to the eccentric he borrows from Maugham—is the Behrman woman at her best—plain-spoken, amusing, self-assured, and endlessly capable of seeing all round a person or an idea. It is difficult to understand why the dramatist, who had trouble finding the right time in which to place the action, chose to discard Maugham's 1915 setting for 1937; the subplot which involves getting a girl out of a concentration camp has nothing to do with the story of plain Jane whose bluntness captivates a society in which honesty passes for wit. Much lighter than Behrman's plays usually are, much nearer the high comedy that he is supposed to write, *Jane* is the best of his postwar plays.

His other recent works include *I Know My Love* (1949), a trying vehicle for the Lunts, carpentered out of *Auprès de ma blonde,* a tiresome work by Marcel Achard, one of the most fatuous of the *Boulevard* playwrights. His book for the Harold Rome musical, *Fanny* (1954), keeps the jokes low and the sentiment high and manages to miss the quality of the Marcel Pagnol trilogy on which it is based. His most recent work, *The Cold Wind and the Warm* (1958) is an unsuccessful attempt to use the characters and the material of *The Worcester Account,* one of the best books of reminiscence ever written. Although *Account* makes use of much anecdotal material, it is not a standard collection of amusing stories from the past; nor is it, like Alfred Kazin's *A Walker in the City,* an affectionate attempt to evoke the feel of an earlier time. It is a series of examinations of the past, in which the author, a man of the world, a successful playwright, moves back into his childhood in search of understanding, trying to find the connection between the boy on Providence Street and the man on Broadway. The material is essentially ruminative, not dramatic, and in transferring it to the stage, Behrman has had to invent a stock plot. The play is mainly the story of Willie Lavin, a bright boy who never understands Mr. Sacher's warning—"there must be limits—that's what sanity is—a sense of limitation"—and who, running from the world of fact and object, goes to a suicide's death. It is also a triangle play, in which the two girls represent the unattainable and the attainable (the horizon and the boundary) for Willie, and an account of Tobey Sacher's growing up. It is all these and none of them, for the characters are never successfully realized; the peripheral figures, including Aunt Ida, the wonderful daughter of the Ramaz, have been reduced to Yiddish-comedy stereotypes.

Most of Behrman's fellow playwrights from the twenties have been sparsely represented on Broadway. George Kelly's only play was *The Fatal Weakness* (1946), a confusing piece that falls somewhere between thesis drama and character comedy. It is an almost perfect illustration of Walter Kerr's complaint in *How Not*

to Write a Play about how dramatists waste time on trivia; half
the playing time is expended as the characters explain their unlikely entrances and exits, and stop, each time, to discuss the
weather with the maid. Philip Barry's only play was the posthumously produced *Second Threshold* (1951), in which Josiah
Bolton's recognition of his daughter's love for him gives him a
reason to go on living in a world that has become meaningless. The
play's chief weakness is the protagonist who is never realized as a
public figure, although we are to assume that his career is the result of his rejection of personal relationships, and who is singularly
charmless for a man who is supposed to be professionally charming. Three of the plays of Robert E. Sherwood, who revised *Second Threshold* before its production, have appeared on Broadway
since the end of the war: *The Rugged Path* (1945); *Miss Liberty*
(1949), an Irving Berlin musical; and a comedy that takes place
during the Revolutionary War, *Small War on Murray Hill,* which
was produced in 1957, after the author's death. None of them came
to much.

The best play from the older playwrights is Thornton Wilder's
period farce, *The Matchmaker* (1954), but it can hardly be called
a new play. It is a slightly revised version of *The Merchant
of Yonkers* (1938), which Wilder based on a nineteenth-century
comedy by Johann Nestroy which had in turn come from an English play by John Oxenford. It is difficult to understand why *The
Matchmaker* should have been a popular success where *Merchant*
failed, unless Max Reinhardt's earlier production lacked the exu-
berance and innocence that Tyrone Guthrie managed more recently. These qualities are Wilder's of course, and they are no
more contemporaneous in the mid-fifties than they were in the late
thirties, when, in *Our Town,* in quite a different theatrical form,
he successfully presented a play that celebrates the endless excitement of the ordinary. Using all the devices of standard farce—dis-
guises, artificial complications, surprise encounters, asides to the
audience—Wilder in *The Matchmaker* once again uses a nonrealistic theatrical form to praise the small pleasures of the real
world. As Barnaby says at the end of the play when asked to
point the moral, "Oh, I think it's about . . . I think it's about ad-
venture." Wilder, never a writer in a hurry, offered *A Life in the
Sun,* a play based on the Alcestis legend, at the Edinburgh Festival

in 1955, but it has yet to be seen or published in this country. *The Atlantic Monthly* (November 1957) did print *The Drunken Sisters,* the satyr play for Wilder's retelling of the story of Alcestis, a short, funny account of how Apollo got the Fates drunk, in which, for each of the sisters, drunkenness takes a different, but familiar, turn.

For the most part, the playwrights from the thirties have been as inactive on Broadway since the war as have the dramatists from the twenties. Clifford Odets, for instance, has had only three plays produced in fifteen years; Sidney Kingsley has had the same number. Even Lillian Hellman, the most active of the playwrights from the thirties, has had but three plays of her own. During this period, she did two adaptations—Emmanuel Roblès' *Montserrat* (1949) and *The Lark* (1955), from Jean Anouilh's *L'Alouette*—and wrote the book for Leonard Bernstein's *Candide* (1956), the best musical comedy to come out of the American theater. Only *Another Part of the Forest* (1946), *The Autumn Garden* (1951), and *Toys in the Attic* (1960) can be called Hellman plays. The first of these is a look at the Hubbard family about twenty years before *The Little Foxes,* when they were even littler foxes but had already learned to spoil the vines; *Garden* is a collection of Southern types, descendants of the Hubbards perhaps without their drive for power, who lead meaningless lives and who are forced, by the catalytic presence of Nick Denery, to recognize their failure and their responsibility for it; *Toys* is the story of two sisters who live on dreams unfulfilled and who—one of them at least—must destroy the brother whose new success threatens to remove his dependence on them.

In some ways, each of these plays reflects Hellman's early work. Since she is a playwright of the thirties, she has sometimes been taken simply as a social playwright. Although there is implicit anticapitalism in *The Little Foxes* and explicit antifascism in *Watch on the Rhine,* Miss Hellman has always been most concerned with personal morality, although, as both *Foxes* and *Rhine* indicate, personal action has public consequences. Any social content in the recent plays is far below the surface. One of General Griggs's speeches in *The Autumn Garden* suggests that the characters are failures because they belong to specific families, the decaying end of the post-Civil War money-makers, but the implication is not diagnostic; Miss Hellman makes quite clear that the problem is personal, not social, determinism. Something might be made once again of the Hubbards as budding capitalists, but in *Another Part of the Forest,* greed spreads to every character in the play (except perhaps Lavinia and Coralee) and the Hubbards have here become grotesques, their nastiness almost biological. If a character in any of these plays may be said to suggest social criticism it is the off-stage Cyrus Warkins in *Toys in the Attic,* the respectable businessman who uses thugs to beat up Julian Berniers and Mrs. Warkins, although even Cyrus' motivation may mix jealousy with outrage at being bested in a business deal. Despite her obvious concern with social evil, Miss Hellman more often seems preoccupied with abstract evil, even to the point of caricature, as in *Forest,* or she goes out of her way to provide acres of psychological motivation, as in *Toys.* For Miss Hellman, however, psychological determinism, as *Garden* shows, is never an excuse. Always the moralist, the playwright is usually intent on pointing a critical finger not only at the eaters of the earth, but at those who, in Addie's words from *The Little Foxes,* "stand and watch them do it."

There are structural as well as thematic consequences to Miss Hellman's morality. She points out in the Introduction to *Four Plays* (Modern Library) that the last scene of *The Children's Hour* is unnecessary, the result of her failure to avoid "that last summing-up." The same specificity marks the recent plays. The third act of *The Autumn Garden,* one recognition after another, hammers its point home with too great insistence; in *Toys in the Attic,* Anna has a chance to explain Carrie, and Albertine gets to point up the almost certain results of Julian's defeat. The melodramatist, like the moralist, is as apparent in the recent Hellman plays as in the early ones. Whatever Miss Hellman's thematic concern, her plays have always moved on events outside the characters, gratuitous devices and fortuitous circumstances, which give her work the feel of artificial efficiency for which she is famous. Artificiality is more obvious than efficiency in *Another Part of the Forest,* where the third-act discovery of Lavinia's confession of Marcus' crimes—written in a Bible, of course—gives Ben a weapon against Marcus, one that has nothing to do with the conflict between father and son. There is a certain amount of grandiloquent fun in the last scene, in which Regina transfers her allegiance to Ben, but it is difficult to take the play seriously. Much the same thing is true of *Toys in the Attic*. The third-act telephone call that finally puts Julian out of business is perhaps less gratuitous than Lavinia's Bible, but even if Carrie's cunning and Lily's feeble-mindedness make it possible the third act still suggests the end of a thriller. Besides, at least so far as I am concerned, all the characters in *Toys*—the incestuous Carrie, the bizarre Albertine, the infantile Lily—suggest parodies of Tennessee Williams instead of real people.

If Hellman's most recent play suggests Williams, *The Autumn Garden,* or so we have been told, suggests Chekhov. In *How Not to Write a Play,* Walter Kerr says of *Garden:* "the social kernel is almost obscured, the characterization is ruefully Chekhovian, the mood of the play is the principal guide to its meaning." It is the last point that has allowed critics to find a new Hellman in *Garden,* to see, as John Gassner says in *Best American Plays, Third Series,* "a considerable amount of tenderness in her writing." The tenderness is deceptive, I think. It is true that the characters in *Garden,* like those in many of the Chekhov plays, represent a society that is past its power, but Miss Hellman's attitude toward her characters can best be seen in a remark from her edition of Chekhov's letters (1955), one which says more about the editor than it does about her subject: "Chekhov makes it very clear that the lovable fools in *The Cherry Orchard* are not even worth the trees that are the symbol of their end." In one important way *Garden* is Chekhovian. Chekhov ordinarily built his plays on a single theme, letting each character present a variation on the main idea, as in *The Seagull,* where each, in his way, represents frustrated love. In *Garden,* of course, each character, with the possible exception of Sophie, is an example of the failure of inaction. By this definition, *Another Part of the Forest* is also Chekhovian, for in it, not only the Hubbards, but the other characters—Birdie and John Bagtry, Colonel Isham, the imported musicians, Oscar's whore—are given scenes which illustrate, in various degrees, the corruptive force of money. Although the influence of Chekhov may be apparent in *Garden* and *Forest* and although certain Williams mannerisms may have marked *Toys,* the plays are still obviously Hellman. Of the three, only *The Autumn Garden* is of more than passing

interest and even it suffers the faults of its form, becoming a kind
of psychological vaudeville in which each character does his turn
and temporarily vacates the stage for the next bit.

When *The Country Girl* (1950) was printed in *Theatre Arts*
(May 1952), Clifford Odets added a note in which he suggests
that this play is like his earlier ones, with a single exception: "The
only thing is that I usually verbalized the implications. It may be
that in *The Country Girl* I didn't verbalize them—things like
what makes a man like Frank Elgin a drunkard." Unless we are
to assume that Elgin has been victimized by his own past success,
like Charlie Castle in *The Big Knife* (1949), there is no possibility within the play of understanding why Elgin drinks. Since the
play ends with his new acting triumph and with a suggestion of
a cure as well, the corruption of success is hardly acceptable. It is
better to take Odets' statement as the nervous assertion of a writer
whose social conscience has been replaced by psychological concern, to take *Girl* for what it is. Extremely well structured (*slick* is
the word that comes to mind, but it would have to be used as a
compliment), the play is saved from being just another study of
an alcoholic by Odets' decision to focus on the wife, on Georgie's
distrust and her desire to help, both of which feed Frank's difficulties. The relationship between these two may call the end in
doubt—although Odets has wisely not made it a standard happy
curtain—but the skill with which their quarreling love is depicted
is the chief virtue of *The Country Girl*. The play's weakness is
Bernie. He is acceptable enough as a dictatorial director and as a
once-bitten ex-husband, but his love for Georgie is an unnecessary intrusion.

In one way, *The Country Girl* is like the early Odets plays.
Whatever their social or political message, their psychological or
mythical orientation, his plays—early and late—have the family
at their center. The conflict is usually between husband and wife
(*Rocket to the Moon*) or between children and parents (*Awake
and Sing*). In *The Big Knife,* Charlie Castle's difficulties are marital as well as moral, for he will lose his wife as well as his integrity if he signs a new Hollywood contract; in *The Flowering Peach*
(1954), Noah's pious conservatism is in continual conflict with
Japheth's practical idealism, a variation on the quarrel between
Ralph and Bessie Berger in *Awake and Sing*. The implications of
The Big Knife are certainly verbalized; Odets provides a periph-

eral character to make clear that Charlie Castle's problem belongs to America, not to Hollywood alone, that he represents a lush kind of success that destroys. It is Hank who speaks Odets' message, Charlie's epitaph: "He . . . killed himself . . . because that was the only way he could live." *The Big Knife* fails on three grounds. First, it never convinces us that Charlie Castle ever had any worth that could be corrupted; second, the portentous artificiality with which it reveals Marcus Hoff's hold on Charlie reduces it to hokum; third, the play, like Norman Mailer's novel *The Deer Park,* gets so involved in its lurid Hollywood surface that it loses its way as it wanders from one caricatured turn to another— the tearful vicious producer, the starlet-tart, the agent as father figure, the nonprofessional slut.

None of Odets' postwar work displays the optimism of the thirties, the naïve hope of Ralph in *Awake and Sing* and Cleo in *Rocket to the Moon.* After the pessimism of *The Big Knife* and the muted hope of *The Country Girl,* however, *The Flowering Peach* seems much closer to the earlier plays. At the final curtain, Noah cocks his head and gets his last message, "Yes, I hear You, God— Now it's in man's hands to make or destroy the world. . . . I'll tell you a mystery. . . ." *Peach* is less happy than what it has to say. It places Noah and his family in the Bronx of the lower middle class and gives them all the mannerisms and jokes that such a setting implies; it is *Awake and Sing* on an ark without that play's vitality.

The Flowering Peach was Odets' last play on Broadway. If Harold Clurman was right when he said, in *Lies Like Truth,* "The Big Knife represents Odets stewing in his own juices," then Odets has been happily stewing the last few years. Shortly before the release of *The Story on Page One* (1960), a film that he wrote and directed, Odets insisted, in an interview with Murray Schumach (New York *Times,* October 1, 1959), on the opportunities for creative work in Hollywood. Perhaps Charlie Castle drowned himself too soon. On second thought—since the movie is a relentlessly dull courtroom drama pieced out with helpings of soap opera —perhaps not.

Sidney Kingsley has been represented on Broadway since the war by the farce *Lunatics and Lovers* (1954) and by two plays— *Detective Story* (1949) and *Darkness at Noon* (1951)—which, for all their surface differences, share a common idea. In both cases, tyranny results when a desire for justice (legal, in one case; social, in the other) is carried to fanatical ends. In *Detective Story,* Captain McLeod is an implacable opponent of evil who learns, too late to save his marriage or his life, that mercy is necessary too and that, in rejecting it, he has become the thing he wanted to escape: "I built my whole life on hating my father—and all the time he was inside me, laughing—or maybe he was crying, the poor bastard, maybe he couldn't help himself, either." In *Darkness at Noon,* an adaptation of Arthur Koestler's novel, Rubashov learns, too late to save his life or his revolution, that the machinelike Gletkin is his spiritual son, that "The means have become the end; and darkness has come over the land."

Detective Story is weakened by the heavy weight of coincidence and psychological patness that it carries and by building to the tear-jerking end in which the dying McLeod forgives Arthur, the ex-hero good boy gone temporarily wrong. Kingsley often puts his moral tale aside to present the realistic comedy of a precinct station on an ordinary night, the parade of criminals and crackpots, detectives and accusers; most of these figures are stereotypes, but it is probable that the popularity of the play came as much from these details as it did from the melodramatic fall of McLeod. Kingsley's *Darkness at Noon* is less interesting than Koestler's because the playwright overemphasizes the sentimental, letting Rubashov's failure to help Luba (Arlova of the novel) finally break him; in the novel, he confesses to crimes that are the logical extension of his thought, even when they have no basis in actuality. The play is an attack on Stalinist Russia; the novel on the kind of thinking that made the dictatorship possible—"the running-amuck of pure reason." For the most part, the play is successful in making dramatic sense of a book that is as much philosophical discussion as it is novel; there are technical difficulties—such as the awkwardness of mouthing the messages tapped from cell to cell—and weaknesses in characterization, but these last are as much Koestler's as they are Kingsley's.

William Saroyan has had only one play, *The Cave Dwellers* (1957), on Broadway since the end of the war. It is a typical Saroyan play, in which some broken-down actors, an ex-boxer, a sweet girl, a trained bear and his human family huddle on the stage of a deserted theater ("all buildings are caves," says Saroyan, "and . . . the theatre is the cave at its best—the last arena in which *all is always possible*"); the play reaffirms the virtues of love, courtesy, and dignity, and says, as Saroyan has so often said before, "In the time of your life, live." *The Cave Dwellers* may have been Saroyan's only New York production, but it is certainly not his only postwar work. He has turned out a number of short plays, including some for television, and several full-length ones. *Don't Go Away Mad,* in which the affirmation of life takes place in the fatal-diseases ward of a San Francisco hospital, and *Sam Ego's House,* an allegory in which the house represents the United States and in which it is only as healthy as those who live in it, were published in 1949 in a volume that included an earlier play, *A Decent Birth, a Happy Funeral. The Slaughter of the Innocents,* published in *Theatre Arts* (November 1952), is about an undesignated government which, in the name of the people, kills the people; its point is that the victims and the victimizers are the same, that, in Rose's words, "*We* accuse and kill, and we *are* accused, and we are killed"; its setting, according to Saroyan, is "in our thinking, in our sleep, and in one degree or another . . . everywhere in the world, including our own country."

In his preface to *Don't Go Away Mad* Saroyan both accepts and defends himself against a criticism of Eric Bentley's:

I seem to insist that people are good, that living is good, that decency is right, that good is not only achievable but inevitable—and there does not appear to be any justification for this. At least, not in the terms of my own work. In short, the idea is all right but I don't know how to put it over.

He points out that an earlier version of *Don't Go Away Mad* ended with a stageful of corpses and displayed a pessimism that was false. The optimism of the printed version is just as false. The inescapable suspicion is that pessimism and optimism have no relation to objective reality for Saroyan, that they are simply projections of personal moods. The lightness of *My Heart's in the Highlands* and the blackness of *Hello, Out There* are simply the same view of the world on different days. My own inclination is to agree with Saroyan that pessimism has no more validity than optimism, but, like many other critics and playgoers, I resist sweetness and light, *and* sourness and dark when the dosage is too strong and its application too relentless. Saroyan is at his best in plays like *My Heart's in the Highlands* and *The Time of Your Life* in which the declaration is oblique, made through an eccentric character whose words and actions perform the work of a valid dramatic symbol without explaining it. There is still fine and funny invention in the late plays—the reading of the dictionary in *Don't Go Away Mad,* the moving of *Sam Ego's House,* the business with the mute milkman's son in *The Cave Dwellers*—but too often the eccentricity is demanding rather than endearing. More damning, all the late plays are weighed down with passages in which the characters philosophize pompously rather than amusingly, explain themselves instead of be themselves.

The American theater, perhaps more than that of any other nation, is dogged by the idea of the *right now,* the sense that a certain kind of play or a certain playwright goes at a particular moment. This is obvious when we look at the record that the dramatists of the twenties and thirties have made on Broadway in the years since the war. Except for the writers who make no pretense at serious drama, the older playwrights have appeared infrequently and, for the most part, unhappily. The younger ones, those from the thirties, have been no busier and only occasionally—Lillian Hellman's *The Autumn Garden* or Clifford Odets' *The Country Girl*—have they turned out a play that will stand comparison with the best of their early work. Ironically, the best plays to come from the playwrights of other decades, other eras, are Eugene O'Neill's *Long Day's Journey into Night* and *The Iceman Cometh* and Thornton Wilder's *The Matchmaker,* and these plays, like the reputation of their authors, were made in another period.

6 COMEDY

Only the honest hacks have a good time of it. Cannily,
they run up a banner: It's just us again, kids, trying to
make a buck.

—GORE VIDAL

To some comic writers—James Thurber, for instance—comedy
may be a philosophical stance, a way of viewing the world, of recognizing, satirically or fondly, that most human activities are as
ludicrous as they are important. To Broadway, *comedy* is a wonderfully imprecise generic label, supposedly attractive to audiences, which can be pasted on products as different as Neil Simon's
Come Blow Your Horn (1961), an often funny approximation of
prewar farce pieced out with standard bits of Jewish-family comedy, and William Gibson's *Two for the Seesaw* (1958), a bittersweet play that, for all its author's talk about psychological veracity
(in *The Seesaw Log*), is designed to be a little sad, a little funny,
and a great comfort to the matinee ladies. The designation covers
not only farce and sentimental comedy, but satire (an infrequent
visitor on Broadway), romantic comedy, high (or drawing-room)
comedy, the nostalgic period piece,* and any of a half-dozen other

* Liam O'Brien's *The Remarkable Mr. Pennypacker* (1953) is one of the
most unusual plays in this group. Its structure is farcical, the attempt to
hide the fact that the titular hero has a family in Philadelphia and another
in Wilmington; its quality is innocence—sweetness, if that word has retained any nonpejorative meaning. When I saw the play in New York, the
audience, between acts, behaved as I have never seen a New York audience behave before or since. There was none of the nervous, snickery repetition of gag lines, the attempt to hold on to an already disappearing
moment of pleasure. There was no attempt to discuss the play, for there
is really nothing in it to discuss. There was not even the usual bright, brittle

categories, all as difficult to define as the general term that encompasses them. The imprecision may be inevitable, since, as often as not, a particular play is two or three things at once. Take John Van Druten's *Bell, Book and Candle* (1950) as an example of the problem of choosing a label. Because it is about witches and their ways, it is a fantasy. Because Gillian, by falling in love with a mortal, loses her powers as a witch and learns to cry, it is a romantic comedy. Because the characters dress elegantly and speak correctly and the two leads were originally played by English performers (Rex Harrison and Lilli Palmer) with a reputation for sophistication, it might pass as a high comedy. Whatever it is, however, it is more neatly contrived, more restrained in making its comic and plot points, and more pleasant to see or read than many other Broadway comedies that hope for the same lightness.

Calling *Bell, Book and Candle* a high comedy on the basis of what its characters wear and how they speak (and I do not mean in epigrams) is not quite as flip as it appears. The genre, in so far as it exists, is a desiccated descendant of the Restoration comedy of manners, an English line that passes from Congreve to Wilde to Maugham to Coward and finally, one supposes, to Terence Rattigan. Even in England, the type is recognizable largely on the basis of setting and costume, for comedy of manners implies a tight society with fairly rigid patterns of correct behavior, and English high-comic writers, from Maugham on, have had to maneuver around decreasing rigidity. Understandably, the form never took in America. S. N. Behrman's *The Second Man* and Philip Barry's *The Philadelphia Story* are probably as close as we have come to high comedy, but I suspect that the tendency to hang that label on them comes not from a desire for accuracy but from an awareness that their work is not like George S. Kaufman's. It has become customary—particularly among the reviewers in the dailies—to call any comedy *high* or *drawing room* in which the characters are reasonably rich, well mannered and well dressed; and in which they face their problems in a civilized, by which we mean carefully modulated, tone of voice. In terms of

lobby chat that makes theater eavesdropping so unrewarding. Instead, there were a host of benign smiles, a general air of befuddled pleasure. It may have been the evening, the audience, the performance that was remarkable, rather than Mr. Pennypacker; in any case, the experience was too special to expand into a generalization about this kind of comedy.

bank account and tailor, any number of postwar comic characters might be said to belong in high comedy, but their failure to modulate ordinarily rules them out. The few attempts at this kind of comedy by Broadway regulars have been distressing. Norman Krasna's *Kind Sir* (1953) is a particularly tedious example; he attempts to mix the material of a French sex farce, which he refuses to treat farcically, with elegance and wit, for which he has no capacity.

Samuel Taylor is the only American playwright (Van Druten, after all, was an immigrant from the West End) since the war who has successfully written high comedy. His first postwar play—*The Happy Time* (1950)—does not belong in this category; it is a standard adolescent comedy carved out of Robert Fontaine's book of reminiscences with Fontaine's occasionally touching insights converted into sentimental stage gestures.* It is on *Sabrina Fair* (1953) and *The Pleasure of His Company** (1958) that Taylor's high-comic reputation rests. The plays have been praised for the elegance of their surroundings—the Long Island estate in *Sabrina,* the San Francisco house in *Pleasure,* both products of old and presumably disciplined wealth—and for the wit and charm with which they solve their problems: whether and whom Sabrina should marry, whether Jessica should not. These are superficial or, in the case of the wit, nonexistent virtues. There are very few witty lines in either play; the wit, if it exists—and I think it does—belongs to the author, not to the characters, and is dis-

---

* An example that may say something about the Broadway audience, or the professional's concept of the audience. In Fontaine's book, Bibi is accused by the school principal of having written dirty words; innocent, he refuses to say that he did it until Mama convinces him he should tell the "truth." In the play, the dirty words have become a dirty picture, but the situation is the same; this time, Papa and the two uncles, a posse of sorts, go to the principal and persuade him, through threats and wine, that violence does not make truth. Conventional justice triumphs and Fontaine's point—that in the world violence and misunderstanding do sometimes make truth—is lost.

** This play was written "with Cornelia Otis Skinner," whatever that means; presumably something the unproductive side of co-authorship. More productive, one assumes, than the telling side of "as told to" and more active, perhaps, than the kind of credit that turns up on *West Side Story:* "based on a conception of Jerome Robbins." These nice distinctions may be setting up future problems like those that face Elizabethan scholars: which lines belong to Chapman, which to Jonson, and which to Marston.

played in the changes he rings on conventional situations. Both plays involve households that have accepted a particular pattern of living as best, even necessary, and both are disrupted by the appearance of characters who call the assumptions in doubt: Sabrina, the chauffeur's daughter, who "shall keep my place as soon as I know it," and Pogo Poole, the playboy-sportsman, who doubts that marriage is every young girl's dream. Perhaps Taylor really is approaching the comedy of manners; at least, he is edging toward social comment. In *Sabrina Fair,* it is largely irrelevant, for if there are really families as isolated as the Larrabees, they are too insignificant (in number) to use for comic generalization on society at large. *The Pleasure of His Company* is not so limited. It is Pogo, the invader, who is the refugee of an earlier period, the "sybarite in a sober world," as he says, and his presence discountenances the value of what Grandfather Savage, his Thoreau-quoting ally, calls "the security of marriage, the dull comfort of marriage, the sanctuary of marriage." Taylor is fair enough (and playwright enough) to show the attractions of Roger and marriage and the emptiness of Pogo's busyness ("One may be trivial about things, but never about pleasure"), but in the end he lets Jessica choose her father and fun (there are mildly incestuous overtones throughout) over Roger and security. He manages a small irony, however, for her choice is essentially anti-Pogo, an instinct to do the right, not the pleasing thing—"To give you substance!" *Sabrina Fair* is a more conventional romantic comedy; the heroine identifies herself with Cinderella, but Taylor saves the play from being the standard marriage-across-the-classes comedy (a 1913 play in 1953) and saves her from being a stage Cinderella by letting the stock exchange be her fairy godmother, revealing that her chauffeur father, on the basis of tips picked up while driving, is worth a million dollars. It is the substance of these plays (if I may use the word about such light comedies) and not their surface that makes them work as well as they do. For proof go to the deadly movie version of *The Pleasure of His Company,* also written by Taylor, in which the surface elegance is drowned in twin sentimental conventions —father as father rather than lover, and boy gets girl.

It is the tone of the Taylor plays that differentiates them from the kind of comedy that is more typically American—the tough, fast, loud, vulgar play that had George S. Kaufman (with Marc Connelly or Moss Hart) as its most typical practitioner. Its structure is often farcical; its lines are usually wisecracks. It is cynical without being seriously concerned about much of human activity, which means that its satire is oblique, almost accidental; at the same time, it is sentimental, which means that it cannot escape the serious American playwright's tendency to point lessons. At its best, it reflects one image of the American—the knowledgeable innocent. At its worst it becomes mechanical horseplay or sentimental bosh. In the years since the war, the comedies have been more often sentimental than tough, have been both safe and sorry. They have lost much of the vitality of the twenties and thirties (watch even a mediocre thirties movie comedy on television and then go see a contemporary one at your neighborhood theater). Perhaps the pace has slowed down because we like to think of ourselves as a more genteel nation. The wisecracks are still around, but they are seldom funny (take a line from Harry Kurnitz's *Reclining Figure*: "I could stand poverty . . . but I couldn't bear not to have money"), perhaps because they are trying to become epigrams without knowing that the good epigram, like the good wisecrack, depends on irreverence, not on acceptability. As a result, gags have been dwindling in Broadway comedies and playwrights either depend on the laugh of recognition (the stage equivalent of the cartoon caption) or on no laugh at all—the happy ending of the romance, the saving of the hero or the heroine from a loss of money, reputation, prestige, what have you. When a playwright comes along who wants to be funny, as Jean Kerr does in *Mary, Mary* (1961), she becomes an anomaly. Mrs. Kerr sins in the other direction, for if every line is a laugh line (particularly if the actors know it) the play refuses to operate; besides she is not as funny as all that (maybe one laugh out of ten tries), and she is such a moral little woman. At times, *Mary, Mary* seems like a production of "The Ugly Duckling," doctored by six of Bob Hope's writers.

For the most part, the hard-boiled sentimentalists are never more than talented hacks, reacting to the tastes—or the imagined tastes—of their audience. There was a time, shortly after the war, when Garson Kanin looked as though he might be something special, a comic writer who would use the form for his own purposes. He had worked, as an actor and assistant director, with George Abbott in the mid-thirties and then gone on to Hollywood, where, among other things, he directed a comic morality play in

the Frank Capra tradition, *The Great Man Votes* (1939).* His
first play and his only success was *Born Yesterday* (1946), a
combination of *Pygmalion* and liberal platitudes. Plainly a fable,
it tells the story of Billie Dawn, an ex-chorus girl ("In *Anything
Goes* I spoke lines"), who is educated by Paul Verrall, a *New Republic* correspondent (*New Republic* could never have afforded
him), until she is able to understand that Harry Brock, the junk-
man tycoon who keeps her, is a danger to the country. With the
help of a drunken lawyer and a captive Senator (Norval Hedges),
Brock is trying to buy laws that will let him set up an international
scrap combine and cash in on the wreckage left behind by the
war. A personal and a public bully, he is finally defeated by Billie
and Paul. The pleasure of the plot is that of the good guys winning over the bad guys, and even though the black-and-white simplicity about political matters, so characteristic of the forties, has
given way to complication, I still take an innocent pleasure in the
triumphant exit of Billie and Paul and the benediction spoken over
them by the lawyer:

To all the dumb chumps and all the crazy broads, past, present, and
future—who thirst for knowledge—and search for truth—who fight for
justice—and civilize each other—and make it so tough for sons-of-
bitches like you—(*To* Hedges)—and you—(*To* Brock)—and me.

In admitting that I am touched by so obvious a romantic speech,
I am violating a conspiratorial silence among critics who prefer
not to publicize their susceptibility to any kind of hokum—although none of us is immune. There are extenuating circumstances. I doubt that the plot or even the speech would have
worked if Kanin had not created a comic character as vital as
Billie Dawn, a variation on the standard dumb blonde, but one
with individuality enough to get up and walk out of her play, with
strength enough to rob Dulcy of the archetypical honors that
she had held in the American theater. Harry Brock is almost as
impressive; in his way as innocent as Billie, he makes the aver-
age Broadway businessman blusterer (the father, for instance, in
Tennessee Williams' *Period of Adjustment*) seem an obvious
construction of mannerisms.

* I remember this film with great fondness, but I was only fourteen years
old when I saw it.

The three Kanin plays that followed—*The Smile of the World*
(1949), *The Rat Race* (1949), and *The Live Wire* (1950)—
failed to attract audiences. *The Live Wire,* the best of them, is
an American myth pulled inside out, the success story of a heel
who makes it big in show business by taking advantage of nine
good guys, including his own brother. Much of the incidental
comedy is not very funny, the civilian equivalent of barracks gags
since the ten men live communally, and Sol's "so what is success?"
speech, which is supposed to be taken at its face value, never
achieves the flamboyance of the lawyer's toast in *Born Yesterday*
because it smacks of rationalization. The play is most effective
when Kanin manages to get the audience to identify with the good
boys, to regard their unfulfilled hopes as better than Leo Mack's
success, without softening Mack, without letting him ever doubt
that he is right and they are fools. Alfred Harbage once said, an
incidental remark during a lecture on Elizabethan comedy, that,
after seeing *The Rat Race,* he felt as though he had swung home
through the sewers. Kanin's story of a beaten dancer and a hope-
ful saxophone player in New York does have a general air, of
sleaziness, but the playwright tries to modify it with some little-
people sweetness; the result is reluctant Saroyan. By the time these
plays appeared, Kanin was already working again in Hollywood,
on *Adam's Rib* (1949) and *The Marrying Kind* (1952), both written with Ruth Gordon, and *It Should Happen to You* (1953), all
of which were directed by George Cukor and had Judy Holliday
in the cast. This group of films, even more than Kanin's plays,
seemed to hold out hope that he would develop into a comic writer
who was tough rather than simply hard-boiled, who was willing
to be affectionately satirical about contemporary mores. The
hope was deceptive. Kanin left both the theater and films for narrative fiction of a sort (if "Who to Who" in the January 1961
McCall's is an example, he should not have bothered) and has
been back on Broadway only twice—as the adapter of Felicien
Marceau's *The Good Soup* (1960), a softhearted business about
a French whore, and as book writer for Jule Styne's *Do Re Mi*
(1960). An undistinguished musical based on a Kanin novella,
Do Re Mi begins broadly and somehow edges into *Death of a
Salesman* as Hubie sings about choosing the wrong dream.
. . .

Norman Krasna, Harry Kurnitz, Joseph Fields, Jerome Chodorov, F. Hugh Herbert, Howard Teichmann, George Axelrod—
these are much more typical comic writers. Their plays never
have, as Kanin's seem to, any hint of ulterior motive, any suggestion that their authors ever considered them more than marketable products. This is a fact, not a judgment. The best intentions
in the world will not insure a good play, and the crassest motive,
as the history of literature illustrates, has sometimes done what
sincere ambition has failed to do. Not that these playwrights illustrate my somewhat pompous dictum. Take Axelrod, for instance.
He is probably the most imaginative playwright in the group (in
a Broadway comedy such an assertion would elicit, "What kind of
crack is that?"), but he always hedges his invention as though he
lacked the courage or the talent (or perhaps the patience) to develop a comic idea fully. Having hacked for radio and television
before his first Broadway success—*The Seven Year Itch* (1952)
—he may have picked up the habit of working fast and casually;
that, at least, is the impression his work gives. *Itch* is the most
successful, actually and commercially, of his three plays; the other
two are *Will Success Spoil Rock Hunter?* (1955) and *Goodbye,
Charlie* (1959). The plot of *Itch* is simple enough; the hero, with
his family out of town, sleeps with the girl upstairs, feels guilty
about it, feels relieved when she makes no demands on him, and
goes off, his hat "at a rakish angle," to join his wife in the country.
The main joke is Richard's reluctance, his ineptness, his remorse,
contrasted to his vision of himself as the suave seducer; this characterization is illustrated through a number of devices (expressionism thoroughly domesticated)—fantasy sequences, flashbacks,
soliloquies. The appeal, I should think, is that the hero is gauche
enough to be acceptable to the men and likable to the women, and
he is still successful. Besides, in the best fifties tradition, the experience is educational. Richard returns, refreshed, to his wife, and
his partner for the evening, who has accepted him only because he
is not likely to ask her to marry him, decides that maybe, after all,
marriage might not be a bad thing. *Will Success Spoil Rock
Hunter?* has the same pedagogical quality. George MacCauley,
who sells his soul, ten per cent at a time, for money, sex, prestige,
physical prowess, etc., learns at last that the world of splashy success is not for him. Since a friend saves him from the devil in the
end, George manages to have it both ways, to have his fantasy ful-

filled and still not to lose his soul, just as Richard in *Itch,* to put it crudely, manages to get laid and cured at the same time.

Axelrod, then, plays safe in his comedies as though he wanted to titillate his audience without offending it. His verbal and visual jokes display the same tendency; in technique, as well as in idea, his work suggests imagination, but rests on the acceptable. Some of the fantasy sequences in *Itch* are funny—particularly the one in which a very domestic Helen shoots Richard for infidelity—but they represent the kind of parody that is at least as old as the melodrama it kids. *Rock Hunter* starts out with a basically funny idea and a potentially satirical one, that the devil should be an agent; but the possibilities are wasted when the diabolical agent remains simply a device, like Applegate in *Damn Yankees,* which had introduced the devil to Broadway five months before the opening of Axelrod's play. The gag lines in the plays also suggest assumptions that Axelrod has made about his audience. In *Itch,* he assumes that it will recognize fairly obvious topical and locality references—Mickey Spillane, Marilyn Monroe, the Easter show at Radio City, *Pal Joey* (it had been revived early that year); by *Rock Hunter,* he is going in for the kind of Broadway name-droppery— which only became possible after show-business chatter on television made everyone an insider—that demands mention of particular writers, actors, restaurants, hotels, agencies, even plane flights. These references seem to imply that Axelrod's audience is at least as sophisticated as the one that used to understand Lorenz Hart lyrics; but other Axelrod usages suggest that he considers his hearers knowledgeable, but not bright. For instance, he often repeats a joke—the one about the paperback edition of *The Scarlet Letter* in *Itch,* the one about making love on sand in *Rock Hunter*—and he sometimes feels that he has to explain: when Richard points out the stairs, "They just go up to the ceiling and stop. They give the joint a kind of Jean Paul Sartre quality," The Girl says, "I see what you mean. No exit." Even the satire, which is more indulgent than it is pointed, aims at targets that are regularly riddled, not only on Broadway, but on television, in the movies and in popular magazines: in *Itch,* psychiatry, rental-novel sex, paperback books (in 1952 the quality paperbacks were not yet a consideration); in *Rock Hunter,* Hollywood, fan magazines, decadence in the drama, the Monroe-type sex image (Jayne Mansfield played the part). If Axelrod is a fair example of the popular Broadway comic writer, and I think that he is, it is evident that commercial comedy is designed to seem outrageous and to be comforting.

One of the difficulties in discussing any of the popular arts is that assumptions are necessarily assumptions at second hand, that writers, producers, directors, and actors decide what the audience will take before observers have a chance to build generalizations on the taking. Another difficulty is deciding what it is in a particular play that makes it popular. Take Anita Loos's *Happy Birthday* (1946) as an example. The story of Addie Bemis, a spinsterish librarian, who gets drunk in the Jersey Mecca Cocktail Bar and becomes an exciting woman, the play is a combination of *The Playboy of the Western World* and *The Time of Your Life*. The appeal may lie in its being still another ugly-duckling story, in its use of the old farce device of drinking as a release of inhibitions, in the incidental comedy of the bar's patrons, in the mechanical tricks—the bottles that light up, the musical cash register, the growing bar stool—that accompany Addie's alcoholic fantasy. Its popularity may have had little to do with Addie and her play, but rather with the star, Helen Hayes, who was being sold as a theatrical lady with her hair down, like Helen Traubel singing with Jimmy Durante. Despite these complications, it is fair to assume that writers of popular comedy do, in some ways, reflect the taste of their audience and that, in exchange, contemporary attitudes help shape the comedies.

Since sex, in some form or other, is likely to turn up in most comedies, it might be well to begin with that subject. In Broadway comedies, sex is ordinarily either intentionally innocent or unintentionally prurient. It is almost never a matter-of-fact device, as it is in French farce,* or if it is—as in F. Hugh Herbert's *The Moon Is Blue* (1951)—it turns out to be nonexistent sex. The heroine of that play is a familiar Broadway type, the cute American girl, Herbert's Corliss Archer a few years older. She is, as the off-stage other woman says, "a professional virgin," and, in actuality, she would probably be charmingly unpleasant or coldly pleasant, what the boys in the barracks call a cock-teaser. Only

* Carolyn Green's *Janus* (1955) is one of the few recent American comedies that treats sex casually—at the end, the heroine decides to keep both her husband and her lover—but not even entrances through a dumb waiter can enliven a very dull play.

occasionally, and then I suspect by accident, does her less attractive side show on stage—as in Lindsay and Crouse's *Tall Story,* in which June is obviously aware of the economic value of her virginity. In *The Moon Is Blue,* Patty O'Neill is supposed to be sweet. After having been provocatively innocent for three acts, she is rewarded with a young, handsome, successful husband. There is a scene, in the last act, where she almost—but not quite—gives herself to the young man; this bit, I assume, is designed to assure the audience that her inclinations are correct, whatever her capabilities, and to let them know that the last-scene proposal is a happy ending, not likely to lead to any of the incompatibility that is the making of so many current serious plays. The author's business in a play like this is to keep the heroine intact and at the same time to keep the conversation about sex going. Sometimes it is a young man, not a young woman, who has to be kept virginal. Waldo Walton in Lindsay and Crouse's *Remains to Be Seen* is a stereotyped male innocent, and Buddy Baker in *Come Blow Your Horn* is the inept adolescent trying, and failing, to be a man of the world. These are standard farce figures, but Wormy in Mary Chase's *Bernardine* (1952) is the same character, drawn more realistically, but protected by sentiment. Wormy hopes to turn the gang's fantasy land ("Every girl is Bernardine, and the word 'no' is never spoken") into fact, and Mrs. Chase provides him with the opportunity; although she has prepared the audience to accept a young man-older woman relationship, she keeps Wormy comic and saves him at the last minute. To be fair to Mrs. Chase, her play is primarily about the fantasies and defenses of adolescence (although those boys could not be eighteen) and not an attempt to make use of sex; still Wormy's escape owes something to the Broadway necessity to protect the innocent. In plays like Norman Krasna's *John Loves Mary* (1947) and Gore Vidal's *Visit to a Small Planet,* where both the boy and the girl want to get to bed, the playwright provides complications that keep them apart.

Even when the escape is not made, the innocence can be sustained. The description of *The Seven Year Itch* above indicates how this is possible for the man, but The Girl in that play is an even better illustration. Although technically she is not a virgin, she is essentially the same character as Patty O'Neill; both are probably descendants of Sally Middleton in John Van Druten's *The*

Voice of the Turtle (1943), but Van Druten makes the type more attractive. Axelrod insists on his heroine's sexual status so that there will be no hint of violated innocence, which would injure the purity of the hero as much as of the heroine, but he also takes the trouble to indicate that she is not promiscuous; before she meets Richard, she has been had only once, by a boy who became hysterical and wanted to marry her; she is, in short, a good girl with a good body. Her declarations of her wildness—"I drink like a fish"; "I smoke like a chimney"—place her with all the other Broadway adolescents who want to L-I-V-E; her remarks are as indicative as Patty O'Neill's "I think it's sort of high school to drink and smoke when you don't actually crave it." If her characterization and her decision to look around for a husband sustain the purity of Axelrod's heroine, her sisters in error are ordinarily cleansed by marriage, even when they are ostensibly women of the world, as in *Bell, Book and Candle* and *Kind Sir.* The condition is best summarized in *Anniversary Waltz* (1954), by Jerome Chodorov and Joseph Fields, in which Bud Walters comments on his premarital affair with his wife: "Look—it's history—nothing happened. I married the girl. She's got a diploma." *Nothing happened* is the operative phrase. The symbolic type of the comic heroine on Broadway is apparently Esmeralda in Tennessee Williams' *Camino Real,* the gypsy girl who becomes virginal again with each full moon.

Such innocence is aggressively infectious. In an extreme case— Eileen Sherwood in the Leonard Bernstein musical *Wonderful Town* (1953), the book of which Joseph Fields and Jerome Chodorov made from their *My Sister Eileen*—the beautiful and pure takes on mythic proportions; Eileen collects admirers, including a precinct station full of policemen, without doing more than smiling and looking helpless. Her sisters under the skin do not work in such numbers, but they as effectively tame the beast in man. Patty O'Neill not only gets her architect in *The Moon Is Blue,* she gets a proposal—not a proposition—from an older man who is supposed to be an efficient and dedicated rake. Similarly, Alan Baker in *Come Blow Your Horn,* with a reputation for conquests, is upset that his pure girl should try to move in; he marries her, of course. It is to be expected, in farce, that the seducer be outwitted, but it is characteristic of Broadway comedy of all types that the only acceptable rakes are reformed ones or foiled ones. Seduction scenes are ordinarily designed, like the parody ones in *The Seven Year Itch,* as broadly comic. It is typical of Broadway that Ensign Pulver, in *Mister Roberts* (1948), by Thomas Heggen and Joshua Logan, should be the most famous operator on the ship. Heggen, whose stories were more knowledgeable than the romantic farce that he and Logan made out of them, was apparently aware that the face of a boy—the harmless lure—can be used effectively in the game of love, but Pulver, in the play, becomes a standard stage adolescent, clean in deed if not in thought. Although Tennessee Williams obviously never set out to provide convenient symbols for Broadway comedy types, the perfect Broadway sexual man, like the representative heroine, can be found in his work: George Haverstick in *Period of Adjustment,* the army make-artist who turns out to be a virginal little boy lost.

Despite—perhaps because of—the emphasis on technical and spiritual purity, the comedies tend to get their laughs through a snickery preoccupation with sex. The audience is continually in the position of the crew in *Mister Roberts* in the scene in which the sailors watch the nurses' shower room through binoculars, titillated but untouched. Never does American comedy say anything really biting about contemporary sexual mores, a fair subject for satire as the best of the Restoration dramatists have shown. Instead, the comic writers escape into sentiment, or, as in *Anniversary Waltz,* use an incredible problem. Chodorov and Fields have constructed their farce on the assumption that someone might care that a man and his wife had had premarital sex, as we call it in the courses, fifteen years earlier. Someone must have cared because the play ran for a year and a half, a fact that should be of interest not only to amateur sociologists, but to incipient satirists. Where *Anniversary Waltz* is tiresomely simple, *The Tunnel of Love* (1957) is openly offensive. There is real satiric potential in the central situation of the Peter DeVries novel from which he and Joseph Fields made the play—that a man should be in danger of adopting his own illegitimate child. The novel loses its possibilities, as so often with DeVries, in a wealth of puns, but the play sacrifices any possible substance to easy laughs, particularly about ways of inducing pregnancy. One of the most embarrassingly disgusting scenes that I can recall seeing on stage is the one in *Tunnel* in which the wife tries to seduce the husband. "That is not very pleasant," says Algernon in *The Importance of Being*

Earnest. "Indeed, it is not even decent. . . . It is simply washing one's clean linen in public." I can admire straightforward bawdy and I can understand Victorian circumlocution, but prurience is as annoying as it is boring. The suppressed titter, the elbow in the ribs, the leer that accompanies the slightest reference to the human anatomy—these are characteristics of both writers and recipients of contemporary comedy; and if they are not prurient, I have no idea what name to give them.

As with sex, so with politics. Broadway comedy writers tend to treat the subject sentimentally, or to be obliquely cute about it, a chance phrase that is a gag, not an attitude. In neither case is seriousness possible. In the late forties there were a number of plays, of which *Born Yesterday* is an example, that were almost pietistic in their liberalism. My quarrel with them is not on political grounds —usually they advocate the most benign kind of generalized good—but on technique. A political comedy that operates like an ordinary boy-gets-girl play (in this case boy-with-principle gets girl-with-principle) tends to reduce its ideas to mush. Lindsay and Crouse's hero in *State of the Union* (1945), a liberal Republican businessman, wants to run for President on his beliefs; in the course of the play, he gives up not only his Presidential ambitions, but his mistress (who is an advocate of political compromise), and returns to his wife, proving that political integrity and marital fidelity dwell in the same house. The heroine of Fay Kanin's *Goodbye, My Fancy* (1948), a liberal Congresswoman, returns to her alma mater to make a speech and stays to defeat the reactionary trustee and to inspire the college president, an old love of hers, with new courage; her reward, self-satisfaction and a *Life* photographer for a husband. The hero of Allan Scott's *Joy to the World* (1948), needled by a good-looking lady Ph.D., defies the New York office of his movie studio, whose reactionary representative wants him to disown an attack on would-be censors "whether they be individual reformers, economic associations, cowards within our own industry, pressure groups of a political or religious nature"; although the action takes place at the time when Hollywood had panicked in the face of the investigations of the House Un-American Activities Committee, Alex is not put on the black list ("The little one they pretend doesn't exist," as he calls it), but he is given another studio to head, by a *deus ex machina* named Sam Blumenfeld, and a chance to cripple the villainous studio by swiping most of its technical personnel.

All of these plays are constructed on the same principle; in each case the hero (or heroine) almost gives in to the reactionary powers but saves himself and his ideals at the crucial moment, capping his triumph with a speech and an embrace. The plot, then, is out of sentimental melodrama; the comedy is only incidental. In each of the plays, there are peripheral characters who are supposed to be comic, perhaps even satiric—the party regulars in *State of the Union,* particularly the sazerac-drinking Southern lady; the giggling schoolgirls and the faculty eccentrics in *Goodbye, My Fancy*; the studio personnel in *Joy to the World.* None of them are particularly funny. Nor are there many comic lines. The bulk of them, in each play, goes to a standard type from American comedy, the lovable cynic—the newspaperman in *State,* the secretary in *Fancy,* the publicity man in *Joy*—who is, of course, an idealist with a hard shell, a built-in salve of characterization to take the sting out of any harsh lines. The audience knows instinctively of each of these characters what the hero of *Fiorello!* (1959) says of Morris, the same stereotype with music, "Under the melon he calls a face, he's got a kind heart." Occasionally the idealism pushes through the hard exterior, and wisecrack gives way to moral or political apothegm, like Spike's remark in *State*: "Mary, lazy people and ignorant people and prejudiced people are not free."

The tough guys can barely find space in which to deliver their aphorisms because the stage is ordinarily littered with finesounding speeches, usually from the protagonist or his sexual-spiritual partner. Within the sentimental context of the plays, the speeches are seriously intended and, at the time they were written, were as happily received. If these were satirical instead of sweet political comedies, if the authors had not chosen sides so obviously, the lines might cut up the speaker that they are supposed to build up. In *State of the Union,* for instance, Mary, just back from a swing around the country with her nomination-hungry husband, says to the political boss, "I'd forgotten how good it was to be with people. . . . They're so eager to do whatever is the best thing to do—and they're so quick—they're so intelligent." Taken straight, her line makes sense only within the context of the period, a holdover from the thirties when the people were not a

fact, but an abstraction, and an endearing one at that. Unless the
line is read against such a background, it becomes a little horrifying, turning Mary into a kind of political den mother who knows a
"they" when she sees one, or potentially satirical, if her remarks
about the people are placed against political and civic performance in this country. In *Joy to the World,* Alex says of the picture
that he wants to make, a life of Samuel Gompers: "Some might
say this is not the time to make it. This is exactly the time. Labor
is here to stay. An adroit and honest dramatization of the human
problems involved is in the best tradition of American thinking."
Unless Allan Scott is up to something very subtle, and the play as
a whole suggests not, he means us to accept Alex's speech at its
face value; yet an old Hollywood hand like Scott (he worked on
the scripts of most of the Astaire-Rogers musicals) must know a
publicity release when he hears one.

This kind of comedy almost disappeared in the fifties. It is
customary to blame its death on the excess of investigation and
accusation that disrupted the early years of that decade. Certainly
the climate of fear must have had its effect, especially on the timid,
and nothing is more timid than money, a necessity for any production. More important, I suspect, was the change in the cultural
climate of which the investigations were only a virulent symp-
tom, the move toward personal comfort and security which—as
the recent history of serious drama shows—decreed that the reign-
ing popular clichés should be psychological rather than political.
Although John Patrick's *The Teahouse of the August Moon*
(1953), an adaptation of Vern Sneider's novel, is several things
at once (an unrealized satire, an ineffectual farce, a character
comedy), its pervading atmosphere suggests that it belongs, in
spirit, with the comedy dramas of the forties. The big change is
that the villain has disappeared. Instead of a struggle with a sentimental victory, we have a series of farce complications designed to
show that there are only degrees of sweetness. The Okinawans
are funny foreign people, cute and quaint, but they are basically
sweeter than Captain Frisby, who is a humanities professor from
Muncie, Indiana (he is a druggist in the novel, but the Broadway
anti-intellectual does not think a druggist as pathetic as a professor), and, hence, terribly ineffectual, but he is basically sweeter
than Captain McLean, who is a comic psychiatrist, but he wants
to be an organic farmer which makes him basically sweeter than

Colonel Purdy, who is stupid and blustering and self-seeking, but even he is basically sweet, and anyway he cannot beat the Okinawans who are funny foreign people, cute and quaint, but basically . . . East happily meets West again in Leonard Spigelgass' *A Majority of One* (1959), a saccharine lesson play in which it becomes clear that kreplach and kindness will solve most of the world's problems.

By 1960, the villain was back. Gore Vidal's *The Best Man* is a political comedy, vintage *State of the Union*. Once again, a man of integrity (a politician, not a businessman) has a chance to get a Presidential nomination that he wants, but he refuses to use a secret scandal (homosexuality, a 1960 touch) against his villainous opponent; at the curtain, it looks as if the Russells, like the Matthewses in *State,* will be reconciled, that Bill will get Alice even if he does not get the nomination. As is customary in plays of this kind, the principals are allowed to give short lectures on the nature of the Presidency, on the function of the ego in the political arena, on any other subject that touches the teacher in Vidal. The play is even less a comedy than its late-forties equivalents, but to do Vidal justice he calls it simply "A Play about Politics"; Bill Russell does make a few literate jokes in the play and this fact, plus the playwright's reputation as a wit, explains its reception as a comedy. Vidal, who can be funny and even satiric, as *Visit to a Small Planet* shows, obviously had something else in mind. As a political melodrama *The Best Man* is as dull as it is standard; as a political document, it is a little more interesting. In an interview in the New York *Times* (March 27, 1960), Vidal was coy about his characters and their resemblance to living politicians, but it is fairly obvious that Harry Truman, Adlai Stevenson, and Richard Nixon are the models for the three leading characters. Wendell Willkie presumably was the original of Grant Matthews in *State of the Union,* but Lindsay and Crouse only used Willkie as a starting point. Vidal's play is an obvious attack on Nixon as the kind of politician for whom personal ambition is the only political motive.

Even so uncommitted a committed man as Gore Vidal could not write satire in a play like *The Best Man,* in which his political allegiances so obviously show. He is safer in *Visit to a Small Planet* in which he attacks the human predisposition for war and the incidental forms it takes with several specific American types—the military man, the newscaster, the pacifist. *Visit* is a farce, of course, and it is typical of American drama since the war—perhaps of American drama at any time—that satire, if it is to get to Broadway at all, comes buried in a farce or slips in for the length of a single line. The central idea of Samuel Spewack's *Two Blind Mice* (1949) is a sound one for satirical farce: that two elderly ladies should continue to operate a government office that has been abolished, and that a friend of theirs, a practical joker, should protect them by inventing a secret agency that enlists the aid of the Army, Navy, Air Force, and State Department, the curiosity of the President, the opposition of a Senator, and the attention of the press. Spewack is reacting against the same political phenomena that moved the writers of the sentimental comedies of that period, as this mock oath of his hero indicates:

> I hereby pledge allegiance to the United States Government and swear I have never read the New Republic, The Nation or the Sioux City Bugle, and will defend the Office of Medicinal Herbs against all enemies, including the Pure Food Act, so help me, Hannah!

I am not quoting the line as an example of rich satirical humor, for Spewack's pointed gags, like those of Fred Saidy and E. Y. Harburg in *Finian's Rainbow* (1947), are as naïve in their way as the curtain solutions to *Goodbye, My Fancy* or *Joy to the World*. The line, however, is indicative of the whole tendency of Spewack's play. The immediate target of the gag, the people who thought there was something subversive about reading the liberal weeklies, gets lost in the generalized fun at the expense of government oaths, just as the satirical attitude toward bureaucracy that lies behind the plot of *Mice* is often dissolved in the mechanical horseplay of what is actually and often funnily an old-fashioned newspaper farce. It is this free-wheeling quality, the farce form itself, that saves Spewack from the sentimentality of Fay Kanin, say, and that allows his play to retain some of its bite.

There is some satirical intention, obviously, in the Howard Teichmann farces—*The Solid Gold Cadillac* (1953) and *The Girls in 509* (1958)—but the playwright seems unable to implement his comic ideas, even with the help of George S. Kaufman, his collaborator on *Cadillac*. His lines, for one thing, are not very funny, and his situations quickly lose their vitality. The plot of *509,* that two staunch Republican ladies should shut themselves

in a hotel room on the night of Franklin D. Roosevelt's first elec-
tion and stay there until 1958, is potentially funny, but after a
series of reference gags—to *The Literary Digest,* for instance—the
satirical potential is exhausted in trivia. Teichmann's one first-rate
satirical idea in the play is that the national chairman of the Republican and the Democratic parties should be played by one actor,
using identical mannerisms and speaking almost the same lines.
Cadillac is not political at all; its target is big business. Unfortunately, the hero goes to Washington where he becomes softly
pious about the workings of the government ("I've made a discovery, here in Washington, and I'll tell you what it is. Honesty!") and the play suffers as a result; it is difficult for a single
work to be Red Riding Hood in Washington and the Big Bad Wolf
on Wall Street.

Occasional tough lines stand out in *The Teahouse of the August
Moon* (Sakini's "Explain what is democracy. They know what
rice is"), indicating what that play might have become if its author
had not been intent on a lovable Sakini and a collection of stupidly
sure jokes, like the endless confusion between a geisha and a prostitute. Vaguely political lines in other comedies do not have even
the point that Sakini's few good ones in *Teahouse* do. "You have
a genius for doing the wrong thing at the wrong time," says David
in *The Moon Is Blue.* "You should be in the State Department."
Edgerton, the art-collecting soft-drink tycoon of Harry Kurnitz's
Reclining Figure (1954), says of the reception of his product in
France: "You'd think our State Department would do something
about that. In the old days, T. R. would have shoved it down their
throats." Howard Carol, the hero of Ronald Alexander's nause-
atingly wholesome *Time Out for Ginger* (1952), says—and notice
the year—"In my twenty years of married life I have confused
more issues than a liberal. . . ." The quotations could be continued, but there would be no more point in such a list than there
is in most of the lines in context. This kind of line has no real
satirical intention. It is introduced as casually as Axelrod's name-
dropped celebrities and with much the same idea in mind. The
listener presumably gets the same satisfaction from a mention of
currently acceptable targets* as he gets from the topical references

* Shortly after the unfortunate and unsuccessful Cuban invasion a mention
of the Central Intelligence Agency was a sure laugh in Arnold Weinstein's
Red Eye of Love (1961), an off-Broadway comedy that had laughs enough
without having to reach for an extra easy one.

in a patter song. This kind of casual allusion only emphasizes what is implicit in the political comedies—that the Broadway comic writers are really no more serious about politics than they are about sex.

So it is with the other possible satiric targets. Any number of postwar comedies—*The Teahouse of the August Moon, Visit to a Small Planet, John Loves Mary, No Time for Sergeants, Mister Roberts*—has had one or more stupid, blustering military men. The stuffy businessman (sometimes dishonest) has turned up not only in *The Solid Gold Cadillac,* but in *Period of Adjustment, Reclining Figure, Born Yesterday,* and *Auntie Mame.* This last play, a watered-down adaptation by Jerome Lawrence and Robert E. Lee of Patrick Dennis' already watery novel, attacked the stupidity and self-righteousness of the suburbs, but suburbia was already a conventional target and has continued to be one in comedies as different as *Period of Adjustment, Invitation to a March,* and, in the formation of the Ladies' League for Democratic Action, *The Teahouse of the August Moon.* The movie industry has had it from *Will Success Spoil Rock Hunter?,* television from *Anniversary Waltz,* the theater from *Light Up the Sky. Janus* stuck a blunt pin into historical novels and *The Seven Year Itch* did the same service to paperbacks. Psychiatrists got it from almost everyone—*The Seven Year Itch, The Teahouse of the August Moon, No Time for Sergeants, Oh, Men! Oh, Women!*—and children got it from absolutely no one. Even though occasionally comedies like *Anniversary Waltz* needled the products of progressive education, audiences persisted in accepting stage children as cunning and cute, which meant that in plays like *Waltz* and *Time Out for Ginger* the family fell into the pattern of the television domestic comedy that makes the father a fool and the mother a patient and understanding woman, but gives all the gags to the kids. Canny commercial types often cash in on this peculiar addiction of contemporary audiences by providing scenes in which children are given adult chores, as Lawrence and Lee do in *Auntie Mame* when they let Patrick prepare a Martini for the stuffy banker. This jumble of plays is not meant to suggest that the comedies all have the same value. *Born Yesterday* and *Visit to a Small Planet,* for instance, despite their faults, are good plays of their type, while *Auntie Mame* and *Time Out for Ginger* are remarkably bad. Some of the plays and some of the characters and lines within particular plays are more obviously successful as satire than most of the others, but all of the plays, even the best of them, operate within a theatrical context where serious satire is hardly possible.

The context is more than theatrical, of course; it is societal. Some comic writers—James Thurber, most notably—have insisted that it was the political climate of the early fifties that dried up satire in this country. In his speech accepting the Ohioana Sesquicentennial Medal awarded by the Library Association of that state (*The Library Journal,* February 15, 1954), he says that political satire, like that of Peter Finley Dunne, "sickens in the weather of intimidation and suppression, and such a sickness could infect a whole nation." However genuine Thurber's distress at enforced political conformism and however courageous his statements during that troubled period, it is now clear that his diagnosis was too superficial. Not only political satire, but all satire seems to have disappeared. The obvious reason is that the critic of society has no place to stand. There are no beliefs and no values that a satirist can attack because, particularly during the fifties, we have become a nation that prefers a high moral tone to a high moral position. When values are largely verbal, the ground shifts too quickly for the satirist. Any man who lifts his voice to criticize our society today is in danger of becoming a popular idol. Thus, writers like Vance Packard achieve conventional success by attacking conventions, and more serious critics like John Kenneth Galbraith become the vogue, get on the best-seller lists. Such economic facts might be taken as an indication that we Americans are seriously involved in an examination of ourselves and our society. At some levels of enquiry we may be, but it is safer to assume that our permissiveness has become our weapon against criticism. Our society, largely through the activity of the mass media, has learned to absorb any criticism by celebrating the critic. If Socrates were in operation in this country today, it is doubtful that he would be forced to drink the contemporary equivalent of hemlock (that is, be deprived of an audience); instead, he would get a spot on the Jack Paar show and, alas, turn into Alexander King.

Lionel Trilling, in quite a different context, has commented on the contemporary tendency to make all things acceptable. He describes (*Partisan Review,* January-February 1961) how his students absorb the horrors of modern literature by a mental process that knocks the ideational and emotional sharp edges off the works they study: "One response I have already described—the readiness of the students to engage in the process that we might call the socialization of the anti-social, or the acculturation of the anti-cultural, or the legitimization of the subversive." It is hardly surprising that the process that Trilling describes, and that he himself illustrates in having adapted his critical apparatus to the book-club business, should be operative in the theater where popular success is not simply a desideratum, but an economic necessity. With most of the Broadway practitioners of comedy there are no sharp edges to be knocked off. For the most part, the playwrights embrace the world that they are ostensibly attacking. This is particularly obvious in the case of George Axelrod. He says of *Will Success Spoil Rock Hunter?* "there is not a character in this play who would be caught dead in a hotel room that cost less than fifty bucks a day"; in other contexts, this might be a criticism, but, for all the vaguely satirical gags in that play, it is apparent that Axelrod is happily in and of the group he is kidding.

Somewhere, under the very soft skin of our society, there is an itch for real satire. A group of performers, the vaguely named "sick comedians," turned up in the second half of the last decade, an answer to an obvious need. As soon as they appeared, however, the process of softening began; the mechanics of success went into operation and the venom that was apparent in their early work became a national drink—a soft one at that. Primarily, these performers worked out of night clubs, but since Mort Sahl tried Broadway unsuccessfully (1958) and Mike Nichols and Elaine May with phenomenal success (1960), they are part of the contemporary theatrical scene. Certainly, what has happened to them as satirists in the face of popular success is another indication of the state of recent comedy. As soon as every national magazine began to quote Sahl's best lines, they became fashionable rather than outrageous. The success of Nichols and May gave them a place on the television spectacular *The Fabulous Fifties* (CBS, January 31, 1961) where, among other things, they did a commercial; it was a funny commercial, it is true, but they were still selling refrigerators, and once the satirist gets lost in the pitchman, he becomes a dart thrower who, incongruously, is standing where his target is supposed to be. That Nichols and May have become one with the rest of Broadway comedy is apparent in numbers like

"Adultery" in *An Evening with Mike Nichols and Elaine May,* in which their supposed kidding of English and French mores sounds like standard revue parody of movies of those countries, and in photographic essays like the pointless bowling one that they did for *Good Housekeeping* (May 1961). The work of these comedians, particularly of Nichols and May and Bob Newhart, is funnier and has better comic characterization than a good deal of what passes for comedy on Broadway today, but their satire is increasingly incidental, like the occasional sharp line that stands out in the softness of the usual Broadway product. Instead of infecting contemporary comedy, they seem to have been infected by it. Their work, like most of the comedy since the war, is becoming an illustration of William Gibson's contention, in *The Seesaw Log,* that "the theater, in this country, in this decade, was primarily a place not in which to be serious, but in which to be likeable. . . ."

7 MUSICAL THEATER

Bernard Shaw was, as usual, more than half serious in a complaining letter he wrote to J. E. Vedrenne in April 1907 in which he explained the small success of the Court Theatre: "I have given you a series of first-rate music hall entertainments, thinly disguised as plays, but really offering the public a unique string of turns by comics and serio-comics of every popular type." Although Shaw knew that all works of art, including his own plays, move toward unity, an integration of all parts through plot or theme, color or symbol, implicit in his remark is the recognition that there is a distance between the conception and the reception of any work. The idealized aesthetic experience may be the perception of unity, but in actuality audiences tend to split any work into fragments, and critics, unless they indulge themselves in the old-fashioned generalization of the appreciative essay, necessarily take a work to pieces. The individual reader or listener—even those of us who give lip service to aesthetic unity—cheerfully quotes a favorite line of poetry, hums a particular musical phrase, turns to a specific scene in a novel, illustrating in his enthusiasm that the part is more than a fragment of the whole.

If the audience for any art displays a tendency to disintegrate the work in front of it, how much greater that inclination must be in the theater where the details of performance, of setting, of costume, offer that many more opportunities for incidental enchantment. Of all the theatrical forms, the American musical theater offers the most obvious chance for fragmented appreciation, because the musical comedy, related on one hand to vaudeville and the revue, and on the other to opera, is in a continual struggle between its desire to become an art form and its need, economic and visceral, to see that the chief comic has at least one show-stopping number. This dichotomy is nowhere more evident than in *My Fair Lady* (1956), the musical play (the authors' label) that Alan Jay Lerner and Frederick Loewe made from Bernard Shaw's *Pygmalion*. It has been widely praised as an example of the movement of musical comedy toward a form in which all of the elements contribute to the work's unique impression, and there is justice in the praise. Still, as though the composer and lyricist (the song writers, as we used to call them) had unconsciously followed the lead of the Shaw quote above, the main songs are basically star or comic turns. There are plot songs in *My Fair Lady* ("You Did It" is fairly obvious exposition), but ordinarily the action stops to allow Professor Higgins to deliver "Why Can't the English?," "I'm an Ordinary Man," and "A Hymn to Him" and to let Eliza do "Wouldn't It Be Loverly?," "Just You Wait," and "Without You." The interruption is more obvious with Mr. Doolittle, for "With a Little Bit of Luck" and "Get Me to the Church on Time" resemble standard music-hall numbers in which the popular comic (significantly, Stanley Holloway was the first Doolittle) takes the spotlight as part of a trio or as a single with chorus. The songs, however, are not gratuitous. All of them contain lines that tie them into the plot of the play, that refer to characters, situations, ideas, that the book or earlier songs have suggested, but connection by reference is hardly genuine integration. "Think of the Time I Save" from the Richard Adler-Jerry Ross *The Pajama Game* (1954) and "More I Cannot Wish You" from Frank Loesser's *Guys and Dolls* (1950) are good examples of songs that have apparent connection to character or situation, but which are more clearly used, in the first instance, to give the lead comic a second-act number, and, in the second, to provide a specialty for a performer who had a way with sentimental Irish songs. By comparison, the *My Fair Lady* songs are functional. If they do not develop character, they at least define it; through these numbers, the audience comes to know that Eliza, whether she speaks Cockney or not, is always the spirited flower girl, that Higgins is both irascible and witty, that Doolittle is the "original moralist" that Higgins calls him. Staging, of course, plays a large part in the apparent integration of these numbers. When the transition from dialogue to song fails to seem natural, whether the fault is in the writing or the staging, the total effect of the musical is splintered and the listener senses it even if he takes pleasure in the splinters. This was particularly noticeable in the staging of the lugubrious Lerner-Loewe *Camelot* (1960), in which each of the principals, like opera singers in the days before Rudolph Bing, moved to the front of the stage to deliver his number.

In *Theatre at the Crossroads,* John Gassner, ordinarily a gentle critic, manages a mild explosion at musical comedy. Goaded by what he calls "the bromide that the American theatre's greatest achievements, its justification and glory, have been musical comedy and music-drama," he complains: "The fact is that Broadway musicals are and must remain a makeshift species of showmanship under present conditions of inflated production costs and the need to please a public that brings only its own flabby spirit of accommodation to the theatre." In any season, there is ample proof of the truth in Gassner's remarks. The Richard Rodgers-Oscar Hammerstein 2nd *Flower Drum Song* (1958), for all that it makes the customary nod toward a serious book, is a pastiche of all the elements that went into their earlier successes, a perfect example of Gassner's "makeshift species." Later in the same season, however, came Jule Styne's *Gypsy* (1959), evidence for Leonard Bernstein's remark in "American Musical Comedy," his Omnibus show: "In a way, the whole growth of our musical comedy can be seen through the growth of integration." Although the elements that go into musical comedy—music, book, lyrics, dance, costume, setting, performers with and without specialties—are often at war, it is clear that the tendency of musical comedy, perhaps since *The Black Crook* (1866), certainly since *Oklahoma!* (1943), has been toward integration.

The development may not be as neat as Bernstein makes it in his television lecture on the subject, a capsule account that suggests that of Cecil Smith in *Musical Comedy in America,* but it is evident in any number of ways. The increasing importance of the book can be seen in the attraction to the form of a large number of serious writers—Maxwell Anderson, Lillian Hellman, Robert E. Sherwood, Truman Capote, S. N. Behrman, Arthur Laurents, Elmer Rice—and in the increasing insistence that the book be an adaptation from a novel, a play, a collection of essays, or even a comic strip (*Li'l Abner,* 1956), from which—it is fondly hoped —a controlling plot, character, or attitude may be borrowed. The addiction to adaptation is not always as happy as producers, backers, and some practitioners seem to think; any number of ponderous, pompous, mock-serious shows—*Camelot,* Frank Loesser's *Greenwillow* (1960), Harold Arlen's *Saratoga* (1959)—have resulted from the attempt to transfer intractable material to the musical stage. *Saratoga,* which was swallowed by Cecil Beaton's sets and costumes, and *Camelot,* which was crippled by, among other things, Hanya Holm's pointless choreography, are examples of what happens when a musical's sense of its own importance expands until each element is treated not professionally, but reverently. Still, the importance of the designer and the costumer and, even more, of the choreographer in any musical's conception is a further testimonial to Bernstein's view of the course of musical comedy. So, too, and sadly perhaps, is what has happened to the musical-comedy performer in the last fifteen years. There may be no loss in the replacement of the stick-figure tenor by the talk-a-song actor, for in the absence of the singer-actor, the straight actor who can work his way through a song may be preferable to the singer who freezes in every scene, especially in those musicals where plot and character make a difference. It is the disappearing comic who may finally be regretted. With the advent of the sweet book, starting with *Oklahoma!,* Nancy Walker observed when I interviewed her, work for comics began to decline in American musicals. Increasingly, with the dwindling of revues, comedians with a personal style have had to work in night clubs or adapt themselves to book shows in which they do not fit comfortably. In the long run, a group of musical-comedy character actors may be developed; although, in the abstract, I may prefer the comedian who can play a particular part instead of one who does his familiar hat trick, it would be unfortunate if the development of musical comedy displaced comedians as special as the Marx Brothers, W. C. Fields, Bert Lahr, and Miss Walker.

In his discussion of musical theater, Bernstein lists the species within the genus, in what he calls a continuum, with the variety show at one end of the line and opera at the other. For the most part Broadway operates toward the center of the list, but occasionally the ends are made welcome. With vaudeville gone, the variety show appears only when a performer with personal drawing power decides to mask a one-man show by hiring a dancer, a juggler, a comedian, by way of complement. The variety show, in its purest, its most chaotic, form has generally been considered entertainment for the hinterlands and, in its most recent manifesation on television, is still so considered. On Broadway, particularly since the twenties, the variety show has undergone a transformation into the revue; material has been specially prepared so that the old variety has edged toward unity—of tone, of theme, of satiric attitude. Revue fanciers tend to look back fondly to the sophisticated revues of the twenties, the satirical ones of the thirties. The backward glance, however, is more than the customary essay at nostalgia; it is almost a necessity. The years since the end of World War II have offered few revues to remember. There was a time, in the late forties, when the form did flourish, when Harold Rome's *Call Me Mister* (1946), Charles Gaynor's *Lend an Ear* (1948), Richard Lewine's *Make Mine Manhattan* (1948), and Arthur Schwartz's *Inside USA* (1948) were extremely successful. Much of *Lend an Ear* kids the oddities of the entertainment business (its most famous number is "The Gladiola Girl," a lampoon of a mid-twenties road company), but not so relentlessly as Gaynor's later *Show Girl* (1961), a weak vehicle for Carol Channing. The other three revues mentioned above—all with sketches by Arnold B. Horwitt, two with sketches by Arnold Auerbach—have their share of entertainment parodies, but—particularly in *Call Me Mister*—both sketch writers and song writers act as though there is a world outside the theatrical one. It may be that *Call Me Mister* was able to break out of the professional provincialism in which most revues—even very funny ones—operate because its creators, with the war just over their shoulders, had not yet settled into the restricting milieu of the entertainment industries. During this period, other revues, less flamboyantly successful, lasted for respectable runs, and some of them—*Angel in the Wings* (1947), *Small Wonder* (1948), and *Touch and Go* (1949)—had a high percentage of effective material, often by writers such as Walter and Jean Kerr and George Axelrod, who were to go on to other kinds of theater in the fifties.

By that decade, the revue had practically disappeared from Broadway. A few shows tried each year to buck the change in fashion, but only the two editions of *New Faces* (1952, 1956) made any real showing. There are ample reasons—societal, economic, aesthetic—to explain the decline of the revue. The fifties, as the chapter on comedy indicates, was a period in which, whether out of fear or out of complacency, the taste for satire and irreverence dried up. This general attitude, which pushed both the serious drama and straight comedy toward the therapeutic, probably made its contribution toward the increasing popularity of the heavy or the sweet book. Whether one says that tastes in musical comedy had changed or that tastes had changed musical comedy, it is obvious that the revue had become decidedly peripheral. Aside from the general problem of social climate, the form had a very specific problem, an economic one. Although there are revues that have achieved a large degree of popular success (*Call Me Mister* is the best example since the war), the form usually has a limited appeal. With increasing production costs in the fifties, the possibility of commercial success for a revue on Broadway became more and more unlikely. The potential revue audience did not disappear completely. In search of that audience, producers moved the revue off Broadway, most notably in the two *Shoestring Revues* (1955, 1957) and in *Phoenix '55*. When even these proved economically unfeasible, the revue—down now to a handful of performers—retreated to the coffeehouse and the night club.

If one end of Bernstein's continuum has been withering on Broadway, the other—the opera end—has never really flourished there. It is true that for a time shortly after the war there was much talk about American opera and its growth in the commercial theater. One reason for such longing conjecture was that *Oklahoma!* had turned out to be seminal, as *Porgy and Bess* had not, and there were any number of musicals that were trying to make integrated use of ballet and recitative, that were trying to elevate the reprise to a theme. It was a simple step from the serious musical to opera, assumed those optimists who prefer the latter over the former, and they were wrongly certain that Broadway audiences would happily watch while that step was taken. As evidence, they could offer Gian-Carlo Menotti and his success on Broadway.

Menotti came first to Broadway in 1947 with *The Medium,* which he called a tragedy, on a double bill with the *opera buffa, The Telephone, or L'Amour à trois.* Both had been written, as operas ordinarily are, on commission, the one for the Alice M. Ditson Fund of Columbia University, the other for the Ballet Society. It was almost an accident that enterprising producers (Chandler Cowles and Efrem Zimbalist, Jr.) brought them to Broadway and it was a surprise that they should run for more than six months. After the success of *The Medium* (*The Telephone* was an amusing trifle, but it was the other half of the bill that drew the audiences), the appearance of Menotti's next musical drama (his designation), *The Consul* (1950), was considered an occasion; it became a critical and a popular success. Since then, Menotti has offered two works—*The Saint of Bleecker Street* (1954) and *Maria Golovin* (1958)—neither of which has attracted audiences. The success of *The Medium* and *The Consul* depended, I suspect, on extramusical considerations—the excessive theatricalism of the first, the theme (in a literary not a musical sense) of the second. Although the two later operas give evidence of Menotti's preoccupation with romantic and sentimental drama, neither of them manages the dramatic clarity of the two early successes. Even in *The Consul* there is an indication that Menotti is not able to avoid the dramatic anticlimax; neither the spy-melodrama business of Act III, Scene 1, nor the dream sequence of the last scene can mask the fact that Magda's "Papers! Papers! Papers!" aria at the end of the second act is the culmination of the really important conflict in the drama.

If it appears that my discussion is too obviously about the play and not about the music, I can only plead that it is the drama—the musical drama—that interests Menotti and that I am unwilling (and unable) to discuss the music outside the complete effect of the work. In "A Note on the Lyric Theatre," written for the New York *Herald Tribune* and published in the libretto that accompanies the recorded version of *The Consul* (Decca DX-101), Menotti writes:

Our theatre relies almost entirely on dialogue of action, and the contemporary lyric work must appeal to its audiences in equivalent terms. A composer today can not hope to build an opera by stringing together a series of brilliant arias. He will simply fail to provoke excitement in any but the most effete of his listeners. For the contemporary composer the exciting challenge is the recitative. . . . With a single, well-written musical phrase, he can convey the most delicate relationships of character and establish the most elusive abstract emotions.

I can think of no set piece from any of the Menotti operas—except Monica's song "O Black Swan" from *The Medium,* and it suggests a folk ballad—that I would care to listen to outside of its dramatic context. The chief difficulty with the Menotti music in its dramatic usage is that the composer has a tendency toward a rhetorical style that makes his music flamboyantly descriptive at times instead of emotionally effective—for instance, when the orchestra scurries flutteringly near the beginning of *The Medium* as Monica and Toby try to put away Baba's belongings before she makes her first entrance. The nature of *The Medium* makes almost any kind of hokum, musical or dramatic, forgivable, but it is difficult to put up with the finger-pointing absurdity of the music under Magda's "And they shot at you!" at the beginning of *The Consul,* or the ridiculous orchestral hammering in of the spikes that Menotti uses toward the end of Annina's vision-of-Calvary aria in *The Saint.*

Although *The Medium* is the least ambitious of Menotti's serious musical dramas, it is easily the most effective theatrically. If one were to accept his designation of the work as a tragedy, it might provide difficulties, but if we take it for what it is—a musical melodrama with luridly grotesque surfaces—the work is exciting. A good case could probably be made for the psychological soundness of the drama—for Baba's increasing loss of control, particularly in the face of the trio in Act II, and for Toby's paralyzing fear at the end—but acceptable psychology is not even necessary for an appreciation of a drama in which the developing line of action is clear and logical within the work's own context. Both the bully and the charlatan in Baba prepare us for her collapse in the face of her self-induced fears (whether the induction comes from her imagination or the psychic powers that her profession mocks), while the mute Toby's helplessness and the sweet impossibility of his love for Monica set him up as the natural victim of Baba's panic. Although *The Medium* could not have managed without so clean a plot line and such simple characterization, it is the theatricality that feeds the tone of the complete work, that gives the opera its special quality.

By giving Toby's role to a dancer, by making the boy a mute, Menotti provides himself with an opportunity to write scenes in which the child in the character is emphasized, scenes in which he and Monica play, she the voice, he the movement, in a loving approximation of children's-book splendor ("Behold the King of

Babylon . . ."); the transition, in Act II, from child's game to
love game, which never gets a chance to move from recognition
to implementation, is all the more touching because Monica must
sing both parts. If Monica is mother-lover-playmate to Toby,
she is mother-child to Baba. Her first singing of "O Black Swan"
in which she "begins gently to rock Baba" is an attempt to comfort a frightened child. Her repetition of the song at the end of
Act II, against Baba's panic-stricken recitation of *"Ave Maria,
gratia plena . . . ,"* is one of the most outrageous tricks in contemporary theater; it is also one of the most effective, not only because the gesture is disarmingly grand compared to the ordinary
search for an effective first curtain, but because the contrast of
Monica at song with Baba at prayer does what the whole drama
does, compares the assurance of innocence to the uncertainty of
experience. These are imaginative inventions, but the play has its
share of splashy effects that indicate Menotti's fondness for clap-
trap: Baba clutching her bottle, her tearing off Toby's shirt, the
use of the bullwhip, the Grand Guignol blood stain that spreads
slowly across the curtain after she shoots Toby. These effects
might be ludicrous in another context, but here they do not seem
out of place. One reason is that the drama operates in a world in
which the mixture of the supernatural and the fraudulent prepares
us for anything. Another is that Menotti's language leads us easily
to an acceptance of incidental horror. I am not thinking only of
the aria in which Baba, half in defiance, half in prayer, sings "I
have seen many terrible things," but of Monica's songs as well;
sweet though they may be, the opening number is about a queen
who, having lost her golden spindle, fears the king will kill her,
and "O Black Swan" is about a girl whose lover is dead and who
is contemplating suicide. "The sun has fallen and it lies in blood,"
she sings. "The stars stitch a shroud for the dying sun."

The Medium, then, is all of a piece. So much cannot be said for
the other works—not even *The Consul.* The drama opens with a
record playing in the café across the street from the Sorel apartment. *"Tu reviendras,"* sings the voice of the chanteuse, in one of
those hope-deferred popular songs that the French seem to dote
on, but it ends, *"Ah, pauvre toi, la vérité tu ne sauras jamais."* This
opening may be preparation for the romantic side of *The Consul,*
the parting of Magda and John Sorel, and her suicide, which is
meant to keep him safe in another country. The thing that gives

The Consul whatever stature it has, however, lies not in this story, but in the opposition that Magda must confront in trying to get away to rejoin her husband. She and the other would-be refugees face an almost mechanically efficient secretary (the humanization of her in Act III, Scene 1, is a mistake, I think) who fronts for a faceless, perhaps nonexistent, authority in whom their hopes of safety rest. One of the bromides of contemporary discussions of tragedy is that the genre is impossible because, the gods having been discountenanced, the universe provides no force that the tragic hero can oppose; Menotti has solved that problem in a Kafka-like way by offering an amorphous authority figure with which his heroine must struggle and whom she must defy, not only in her angry second-act aria, but in her suicide itself. In the context of the love story, her death may be a romantic gesture, a standard sacrifice of self for the beloved, but, in relation to the Consul, it is a rejection of the whole process of deindividualization implicit in the secretary's "Your name is a number. Your story's a case. Your need a request. Your hopes will be filed." The impact of *The Consul* when it first appeared was strong enough to make some of us suspect that Menotti had found the form of contemporary tragedy. Whether or not that is true—and the problem of whether or not a work is tragic seems increasingly pointless to me—it is apparent that his conception of the Consul, the bureaucratic bogey of questionnaires and official papers, touched a nerve in his audiences. There, I suspect, is the chief cause for *The Consul's* success.

The other two operas have neither the dramatic focus of *The Medium* nor the contemporary appropriateness of *The Consul*. Presumably, *The Saint of Bleecker Street* is not about Annina and her faith, but about the incestuous love of her brother. The central line of action gets lost in peripheral themes: the struggle between Annina's faith and Michele's disbelief; Michele's sense of not belonging, his feeling that he is neither Italian nor American, which is evident only in his aria in Act II in which he sings about being "the rebel and the cursed one." The best dramatic scene is in that act, the stabbing of Desideria, but it is weakened by the fact that the victim, introduced so abruptly at the end of Act I, is never more than a mechanical device. *Maria Golovin* may be "an unrelenting, an almost clinical examination of the progression of sexual jealousy" that Samuel Chotzinoff calls it in his essay in the libretto that accompanies the recorded work (RCA Victor

LM-6142), but much of it, particularly the whole business of the rose at the end, is sentimental melodrama. That genre only works, however, when the hero and heroine can incite audience sympathy; for me at least, Menotti's blind hero is a tiresome young man who can sing his heart out without ever touching mine. The author makes much of the cage metaphor, introduced in his description of the set and in the bird cages that the hero makes, but it is difficult to accept Chotzinoff's elaborate explanation that makes of every character a trapped figure. The comic tenor, the schoolmaster, seems much less "a prisoner of his aesthetic preferences in art" than he does a gratuitous satiric figure; his third-act aria on his tastes, a dropping of the names—Vivaldi, Mondrian, Kafka—fashionable among intellectuals, has both humor and point, but it is about as integral as "Zip" in *Pal Joey.*

Most of the Broadway composers, even those of serious musicals, operate at a distance from what Menotti was trying to do, but, at the time of his greatest success, there were a few attempts at opera or the near-opera of his musical drama. Jan Meyerowitz's *The Barrier* (1950), with a libretto by Langston Hughes, moved, like *The Medium,* from Columbia University to Broadway, but it stayed only a few days. Marc Blitzstein's *Regina* (1949), based on Lillian Hellman's *The Little Foxes,* after a brief Broadway run was added to the New York City Opera Company repertory. So, too, was Kurt Weill's *Lost in the Stars* (1949), but this "musical tragedy" with a book by Maxwell Anderson, based on Alan Paton's *Cry, the Beloved Country,* had already had a successful Broadway run. Menotti aside, Weill was probably the composer making the most conscientious attempt to find a form of musical drama that would wed opera to musical comedy. *Love Life* (1948), an amusing episodic look at marriage in America, with a book by Alan Jay Lerner, was his only musical comedy in the postwar years. His *Street Scene* (1947), with book by Elmer Rice and lyrics by Langston Hughes, plainly belongs with *Lost in the Stars.* Although it was billed as "a folk play with music," Weill wrote in his notes on the record jacket (Columbia OL-4139):

The integration of music and drama has been carried so far in the case of *Street Scene* that the work has been regarded as an "operatic" event ever since it opened in New York, because "opera" is the form of the theatre in which the dramatic action is expressed through music, and the emotional power of the original play is heightened and intensi-fied through the use of singing voices and orchestra.

If we are to come again to integration as a criterion, *Street Scene* may be nearer what Weill had in mind than *Lost in the Stars,* for the latter has several numbers—notably "Big Mole" and "Who'll Buy" that are plainly gratuitous. Still, the music does try both to forward the plot and to set the mood of tension (only the number "Fear" really succeeds) that the drama needs. Since *Down in the Valley* (1948) is "mainly conceived for production by non-pro-fessional groups," it can hardly be considered with either Weill's musical comedies or his "operatic" events; a pastiche of traditional folks songs and Weill recitatives, it shows again the deep involve-ment with America and American themes that marked his last years, but it is no less dull for that.

Leonard Bernstein's short opera *Trouble in Tahiti* (1952) was not written for Broadway, but it finally got there in 1955 on an incredible triple bill with Tennessee Williams' *27 Wagons Full of Cotton* and Paul Draper. Bernstein's satiric use of the pop-music trio with its nauseously cheerful song about "the little white house" in Scarsdale, Ozone Park, Wellesley Hills, Elkins Park, Beverly Hills, shows the same kind of wit that he uses in a musical comedy such as *Wonderful Town*; so, too, does Dinah's song, in which she describes the movie "Trouble in Tahiti," at first deri-sively and then with deep involvement. The main difficulty with the opera is that Bernstein seems to imply, through his satire, that suburbia is in some way responsible for the rather standard mari-tal problems of Sam and Dinah, but the implication is never sub-stantiated dramatically.

Between the disappearing revue and the occasional opera lies the bulk of American musical comedy. It is difficult to talk of the genre as a single unit because there is such a spread within the form. Frank Loesser's *The Most Happy Fella* (1956), on the one hand, approaches the kind of musical drama that Weill was attempting in *Street Scene.* According to David Ewen, in *Com-plete Book of the American Musical Theater,* Loesser thinks of his adaptation of Sidney Howard's *They Knew What They Wanted* not as an opera, but as an "extended musical comedy." Since there is much more music than dialogue in *Fella* and since the action and its motivation move on that music, the listener might be tempted to doubt Loesser's designation until numbers like "Big D" and "Standin' on the Corner" come along to remind him that Loesser is very much a Broadway song writer. On the other hand, there is Jule Styne's *Bells Are Ringing* (1956). Although Betty Comden and Adolph Green provide a book with the hint of a plot, the story is only an excuse for a group of numbers that, like those in a revue, kid fads in entertainment. The difference between *The Most Happy Fella* and *Bells Are Ringing* is essentially the one put forward by Bernstein in "American Musical Comedy," in which he divides Broadway musical theater into two main types: the operetta and the musical comedy. The basis of his division can be found in his reasons for considering George Gershwin's *Of Thee I Sing,* which is more intricate musically than most 1931 shows, a musical comedy: "it has a super-American theme, the characters are not remote or exotic—although the situation is pretty wild—and it is, both verbally and musically, in the vernacular." The musical vernacular, he says in another context, is "urban jazz, which is the essence of American popular music." The difficulty in holding to workable designations is immediately apparent. Loesser uses the vernacular in some of the tunes from *Fella,* the theme is as American as Sidney Howard, and the characters are not remote in time or space. They are remote, so far as the musical-comedy audience is concerned, only in the relative seriousness of the story they tell, but if seriousness were a final consideration, Bernstein's *West Side Story,* which makes impressive use of the musical vernacular, would have to be considered an operetta. Since I am much more interested in individual works than I am in labels and since the original intention of this generic discussion was to find a convenient way of sorting out the musicals that I want to talk about, I shall be reasonably arbitrary about my division. So far as this chapter is concerned, Rodgers and Hammerstein and Lerner and Loewe will be considered as the chief practitioners of the Americanized operetta, the "musical play" as both book writers usually call it, and Jule Styne, along with such institutions as Cole Porter and Irving Berlin, will represent musical comedy.

"It was a continuous battle," Richard Rodgers told a New York *Times* interviewer (November 20, 1960), "but you can manage, with a little care, not to repeat yourself too much." He was talking about the background music he was doing for a television series on Winston Churchill, but, had his subject been his work with Oscar Hammerstein, he might have been talking about a battle lost. By now, despite the variety of places and times in which they take place, the Rodgers and Hammerstein musicals all seem alike. It is not simply that the later Rodgers tunes suggest the earlier ones, but that Hammerstein's books display a continuing preoccupation with the same characters and situations, the same ideas and attitudes. The distance from *Oklahoma!* (1943) to *The Sound of Music* (1959), in which Howard Lindsay and Russell Crouse provide what is essentially a Hammerstein book, is a temporal one, never an emotional or an ideational one. The cloying sweetness, the cockeyed optimism, the high-school humor, that are characteristic of Rodgers and Hammerstein have been apparent since their first musical, but in the early work—*Oklahoma!, Carousel* (1945), *South Pacific* (1949), and *The King and I* (1951)—it had not yet been reduced to formula. The apparent seriousness of plot and theme and the comparatively sophisticated use of dance and musical bridging* in these early works give them a permanent place in the history of the American musical theater. More important, at least to Rodgers and Hammerstein, these shows became hits. One reason, obviously, is that the shows provide the pleasure of the musical comedy with the suggestion that the listener is involved in some more serious pursuit, an examination of racial relations, say, at the level of "You've Got to Be Taught," in *South Pacific.* Another reason—the main one probably—is the immediate attractiveness of the Rodgers songs. Deems Taylor, trying to explain the wide appeal of Rodgers' music, says in *Some Enchanted Evenings,* "There is a conversational quality about it that makes it easy to sing." The same singability is apparent in the later Rodgers scores ("Do Re Mi" has, alas, become a nursery-school classic) and the same mock-seriousness is evident in the more recent books—*Pipe Dream* (1955), *Flower Drum Song,*

---

* Robert Russell Bennett, who did the orchestrations for so many of the Rodgers and Hammerstein shows, should be credited for some of this sophistication. In "American Musical Comedy," Bernstein points out that most Broadway composers are still song writers, and he praises the orchestrators and the arrangers "who are responsible for writing all the in-betweenies, the connective tissue, the ballets, musical links for scene changes, overtures, interludes—in other words, everything but the tunes themselves."

and *The Sound of Music.* Yet, these shows are, at once, so mechanical and so pietistic (Cole Porter has been quoted as saying, "I can spot one of Dick Rodgers' tunes anywhere. There's a sort of holiness about them") that approaching them, on stage or on records, has become difficult for me. Since there are so many theatergoers who have overcome that difficulty, it might be well to look at some of the common elements of the Rodgers and Hammerstein canon.

Although Lindsay and Crouse wrote the book to *The Sound of Music* and Joshua Logan and Joseph Fields served as co-author with Hammerstein on, respectively, *South Pacific* and *Flower Drum Song,* the musicals are all recognizably Rodgers and Hammerstein; it will be convenient, and spiritually, if not technically, accurate, to think of Hammerstein as the author of all of them. Except for *Allegro* (1947), a medical-musical celebration of idealism over materialism, and *Me and Juliet* (1953), a backstage romance that the authors called a musical comedy, all of the Rodgers and Hammerstein shows have been based on, adapted from, suggested by, literary sources—plays, novels, short stories, biography, and autobiography. Although Hammerstein got much of his material from his sources, particularly in his early adaptations (there is as much Lynn Riggs as Hammerstein in *Oklahoma!*), his own imprint is on all the work. The chief characteristic of all the Hammerstein books is wholesomeness. This is apparent, first of all, in his heroines. There are two basic types, both of which come from *Oklahoma!,* the palely gentle girl (the Laurey type) and the supposedly lovable hoyden (the Ado Annie type); sometimes—Nellie in *South Pacific,* Suzy in *Pipe Dream,* Maria in *The Sound of Music*—the two types are embodied in one person. The innocence of the Laureys and the coltishness of the Ado Annies allows Hammerstein to play his love stories in an atmosphere of sweetness. Although there are hints in his plays of adultery (*Allegro*), lust (*Oklahoma!*), prostitution (*Pipe Dream*), these possibly sharp edges are bedded in the cotton wool of the central love story that, following the Laurey-Curly romance of *Oklahoma!,* allows the young lovers (hello, wherever you are) to surmount outside or self-imposed difficulties, more often the latter, and to achieve a final chaste embrace as the curtain descends. Hammerstein imposes this pattern, however inappropriate, on all his

lovers, even though the nature of his heroine means that characters such as Billy Bigelow in *Carousel,* Emile in *South Pacific,* and
Doc in *Pipe Dream* are forced to renounce their age and experience and become soda-fountain lovers.

Radiating from the central story in every play is an atmosphere
that colors all else. There is an inescapable air of innocence about
the sailors in *South Pacific,* as in the frustration made funny in
"There Is Nothing Like a Dame"; about Fauna's brothel in *Pipe
Dream,* so genteel that the singing of "The Happiest House on
the Block" seems less entertaining than definitional; about the
supposedly sleazy night club in *Flower Drum Song.* All of Hammerstein's attitudes are of a piece with the treatment of his lovers.
His comedy, for instance, is broad and bumptious, completely de-
void of wit. Think of Aunt Eller's playing with the garters in *Oklahoma!,* Luther Billis' female impersonation in *South Pacific,* the
scene in *Pipe Dream* in which "The dainty lingerie in the wash
baskets is tossed around and displayed in amusing fashion by the
gang." With Hammerstein, the absence of wit is almost a principle. His distaste for the intellectual is evident in his celebration
of the homely virtues of good simple folk, from Oklahoma to Aus-
tria, and in his reduction of complicated characters, like the King
in *The King and I,* to good but mixed-up guys: "Is a puzzlement!"
His renowned optimism is not so much a positive outlook in a frequently bleak world, like that of George Bernard Shaw or Thornton Wilder, as it is an ideational mannerism that transforms, if you
"whistle a happy tune," all serious problems into disappearing
plot devices. The attitude is expressed in two ways: the spunky
and the prayerful. Nellie's "A Cockeyed Optimist" in *South Pacific* is the best example of the first, one so popular that Hammerstein varied "But I'm stuck / (Like a dope!) / With a thing called
hope" only slightly when he gave the message to Hazel in *Pipe
Dream*: "And our hearts get lousy with hope!" The paean of
affirmation that ends *Carousel*—"You'll Never Walk Alone"—is
the type of the second, and its last manifestation closes both the
first and second acts of *The Sound of Music*:

> Climb every mountain,
> Ford every stream,
> Follow every rainbow
> Till you find your dream.

What Rodgers and Hammerstein have managed to do in their musicals is to make quite clear what has been implicit about Broadway, at least since George M. Cohan took the spotlight, that the street is as sentimental as it is tough. In his days with Lorenz Hart, Rodgers was in the tough-tears school of music purveyors, but with Hammerstein the cynical cover has been removed; the sentiment is an open wound. This is particularly obvious in their use of stage children. Having discovered moppets in *South Pacific,* where Ngana and Jerome sing the rather charming "Dites-Moi Pourquoi," the authors went in for numbers in *The King and I* and flooded the stage with children ("Getting to Know You"); after marking time for a show or two, the children returned— cheeky adolescents in *Flower Drum Song* and incipient professionals in *The Sound of Music.* By this time, however, they were little more than devices, part of the repetitive pattern that spelled success for Rodgers and Hammerstein. By this time, too, there was another contender for the sweetness honors on Broadway. Meredith Willson's *The Music Man* (1957) and *The Unsinkable Molly Brown* (1960) display the kind of prim vulgarity and strident wholesomeness that mark the work of Rodgers and Hammerstein; it is typical of Willson that in the first of these shows he softens the familiar American con man, and, in the second, he bowdlerizes an extremely colorful woman by insisting that Mrs. Brown return to her Leadville Johnny. Willson's shows do, at least, have a stamp of individuality. Albert Hague's *Plain and Fancy* (1955) is the best example of Rodgers and Hammerstein at second hand. Not only does the music suggest Rodgers at his most innocuous, but the plot also provides a love story that triumphs over the restrictions of a melodrama father and presents an opportunity for several phoney Amish local-color comedy songs ("Plenty of Pennsylvania," "City Mouse, Country Mouse") and a hymnlike end to Act I: "Plain we live / For plain is good. . . ."

Although Frederick Loewe, the son of a Viennese tenor, grew up in the atmosphere of European operetta, his first Broadway success—*Brigadoon* (1947)—is firmly in the Rodgers-and-Hammerstein American operetta school. On two counts, at least, Alan Jay Lerner's book is very reminiscent of Hammerstein. In setting up the contrast between the confusion and cynicism of contemporary urban life (represented by Tommy and, comically, by Jeff) and the charm of the village of Brigadoon, Lerner seems to share

Hammerstein's longing for the simple life; in fairness to Lerner, it should be pointed out that, although Hammerstein's attitude is implicit in *Oklahoma!* and *Carousel,* its first clear statement comes in *Allegro,* which followed *Brigadoon.* Since Lerner's chief comic character, the lusty Meg Brockie, is so obviously an Ado Annie, one of far too many that crowded Broadway after *Oklahoma!,* his comedy plainly derives from Hammerstein even if the controlling idea for the musical stems from some Broadway *Zeitgeist.* The book is most unusual in its use of fantasy, a rarity in the American musical theater (although this was the year of *Finian's Rainbow*), and is most effective in the opportunity that it provides for the integration of dances. There are two faces to the music: the Scotch, or bagpipe, one of numbers such as "I'll Go Home with Bonnie Jean" and the pop-ballad one of the songs ("Almost Like Being in Love," "There But for You Go I") that became hits; as a whole the score is sweetly and successfully romantic. Although *Paint Your Wagon* (1951) has a score that suggests *Brigadoon* in the ballads and American folk music (in exchange for the Scottishness of the earlier show) in the plot and comic numbers, it failed, probably because it is so plot-heavy. There is an interesting idea in the chaotic book, that the musical should present a panoramic view of the California gold fields, and musical numbers like "I'm on My Way," which mixed the singing chorus with an almost montagelike shifting from one brief introduction-of-character scene to another, attempt to implement that idea. Unfortunately, most of the sentiment and the comedy is embarrassingly obvious, and the dialogue is in the Hammerstein school of musical regionalism.

"So start off on the right foot," Lerner warned aspiring book writers in his Introduction to the published *Paint Your Wagon,* "and select a story that is all prepared for you." *My Fair Lady* marked not only his conversion to adaptation, but a change in style for the team of Lerner and Loewe. Although the show does have standard ballads like "On the Street Where You Live," the score, the lyrics, and the book display a brittle quality and a wit that is not to be found in their earlier musicals. Although the tone is the correct one for the characters, whom Lerner has kept close to Shaw's originals, the manner of *My Fair Lady* quickly became a mannerism as Lerner and Loewe retained it for their movie *Gigi* (1958) and for *Camelot.* The scores for these last two are extremely reminiscent of *My Fair Lady,* particularly since so many

of the numbers have been orchestrated for nonsingers. The dullness of the later shows, however, cannot be blamed on the music
alone; Lerner's books are also at fault. This is particularly
obvious in *Camelot,* where excess of plot—the bogey of *Paint
Your Wagon*—again confronts Lerner, and where he allows himself (and Loewe) to be caught in an inconsistency of tone. For
most of the first act, Lerner's book and the songs ask the audience
to accept Arthur and his court almost in the spirit of lampoon
(consider the self-mockery of "The Simple Joys of Maiden-
hood" and "C'est Moi"), but suddenly, in Scene 8, Lancelot prays
a dead knight back to life and, on this miracle, we are to shift to a
serious concern with the love of Lancelot and Guenevere, and the
danger that that love brings to Camelot. By this time, Camelot is
an idea not a city, an early version of the United Nations, which
provides Arthur with a chance for message rhetoric not available
on Broadway since the thirties. By this time, too, the more sensitive members of the audience have begun to think fondly of the
old-fashioned musical comedy.

Richard Rogers was not the only Broadway composer from
the twenties and thirties to move toward operetta, but—thanks
probably to Oscar Hammerstein's influence—he was, to borrow a
lyric from Leonard Bernstein, "so easily assimilated." If *Bloomer
Girl* (1944), for all its period setting, remains a musical comedy,
Harold Arlen did try, with *Saratoga* (1959), to provide the score
for an elaborate musical play. His music for *St. Louis Woman*
(1946), *House of Flowers* (1954), and *Jamaica* (1957), even with
the Caribbean affectations of the last two shows, is plainly Arlen
and plainly Broadway. Arthur Schwartz's *A Tree Grows in Brooklyn* (1951), with a book by Betty Smith and George Abbott, attempts to catch the sentimental seriousness of Miss Smith's novel,
but Schwartz's other postwar work, including the period (and
lamentable) *By the Beautiful Sea* (1954), makes no pretense at
the serious musical play. Harold Rome's *Fanny* (1954), with a
book by S. N. Behrman, belongs in the operetta tradition, but
most of his work since the war has been in revues or in obvious—
in every sense of the word—musical comedies, such as *Wish You
Were Here* (1952) and *Destry Rides Again* (1959). If their musical brothers and competitors made gestures toward operetta, both
Cole Porter and Irving Berlin keep their feet firmly in musical

comedy, even when the former was involved in the Paris of the
nineties in *Can Can* (1953), and the latter, with Robert E. Sherwood's help, was investigating, in *Miss Liberty* (1949), a newspaper war in New York in 1885. If Berlin's hymnlike setting of
Emma Lazarus' "Give Me Your Tired, Your Poor" in *Miss Liberty*
owes something to the affirmative bleat at the end of *Carousel,* it
owes just as much to "God Bless America." Berlin's only other
two postwar works have been the Ethel Merman vehicles, *Annie
Get Your Gun* (1946) and *Call Me Madam* (1950). Porter has
been a little busier—*Around the World* (1946), *Out of This
World* (1950), *Silk Stockings* (1955)—but *Kiss Me Kate*
(1948) is his only outstanding score. With a book by Bella and
Samuel Spewack, *Kate* mixes a standard backstage romance with
The Taming of the Shrew and gives Porter a chance to provide
amusing material for his contemporary actors ("Always True to
You") and—with anachronistic but typical Porter *double-
entendre* in the lyrics—for their Shakespearean counterparts
("Where Is the Life That Late I Led?"). Although the composers
mentioned in the paragraph above are among Broadway's most
distinguished, very few of the shows are of more than routine interest and many of them are surprisingly vacuous. For the most
part they are remembered, as the musicals for the twenties and
thirties are, for an occasional song, a single bit of business. A defense might be made for a few of the shows as complete units
(*House of Flowers,* with a book by Truman Capote, has its true
believers), but defenses crumble easily around all but *Bloomer
Girl, Annie Get Your Gun,* and *Kiss Me Kate.*

Good or bad, however, almost all of these shows illustrate that
the popularity of the Americanized operetta has been at work on
them; only two of them—*Wish You Were Here* and *Call Me
Madam*—are consistently contemporary and unexotic (ruling out
the Arlen shows) in setting. In the years since the war, in fact,
only a handful of musicals have touched the topicality that was
once the mainstay of musical comedy. One of the best of these is
Frank Loesser's *Guys and Dolls.* Loesser, a lyrics writer for pop-
music publishers and for Hollywood, began doing his own music
during World War II. His first Broadway show was *Where's
Charley?* (1948), a musical version of *Charley's Aunt,* which is
remembered chiefly for the fine soft-shoe number "Once in Love
with Amy." A case might be made for *Guys and Dolls* as a kind

of nostalgic gesture since the Damon Runyan characters that Jo Swerling and Abe Burrows borrow are the product of a kind of comic writing that belongs to the years before the war. Still, the music makes no attempt to re-create an earlier time and the show, as a whole, displays a contemporary concern for the integration of book and music. The carefully plotted book is close kin to the kind of comedy that mixes sentiment and farce,* the multiplication of exterior and interior obstacles that keep the two leading couples (the juveniles and the comics) from getting together until the last scene, which in *Guys and Dolls* is played tongue in cheek. The musical numbers are in character, but many of them—the night-club parodies, for instance—have little to do with the action. Although the trip to Havana is part of the plot, the bet that Sky makes with Nathan, it is probably in the show as an excuse for the introduction of the Spanish number that was once mandatory in the American musical. If most of the musical numbers do not forward the plot, they do help to provide the texture that makes *Guys and Dolls* distinctive: the feel of the world of bookies and crap games, cheap night clubs and mission houses, that Loesser, Swerling, and Burrows, like Runyan before them, offer audiences as vulgar and vital, funny and a little romantic. With the brassy opening, a choreographed look at the characters who people Runyan's Broadway, followed by "A Fugue for Tin Horns," the most interesting song in the show, Loesser sets the tone that he will sustain throughout. Occasionally, as when he forces Sky to sing about the chemistry of love, Loesser strains at his lyrics, but for the most part he is inventive in this show, particularly when one considers how lyrically fatuous he can be, as in "My Darling" from *Where's Charley?*. After his success with *Guys and Dolls,* Loesser went over to the musical play—with some success in *The Most Happy Fella,* with none at all in *Greenwillow*—but with *How to Succeed in Business Without Really Trying* (1961) he returned to musical comedy.

Most of the other musicals in contemporary setting are less successful than *Guys and Dolls* in communicating a complete impression. The two shows by Richard Adler and Jerry Ross—*The Pa-*

---

* One of the ways of distinguishing operetta from musical comedy that Bernstein might have used, since it is consistent with his division, is that the book of the former is allied with sentimental melodrama, of the latter with sentimental farce.

jama Game (1954) and *Damn Yankees* (1955)—do have books with plot ideas that stem from the novels on which they are based: the settling of a labor dispute in a pajama factory in the first, the winning of the pennant through diabolic machinations in the second; in both cases, George Abbott served as co-author with the originating novelist—Richard Bissell, Douglass Wallop. The music, in both shows, is simply a collection of popular standards, although Adler and Ross do occasionally—as in "A New Town Is a Blue Town" in *The Pajama Game*—try to write a characterization piece. *The Pajama Game* is the more imaginative of the two shows, making sensible use of music and dance in the slowdown in the factory, and its tunes are much more attractive. In *Damn Yankees,* Adler and Ross seem to have been trying to emulate their success in the first show, even to the point of providing comparable numbers; "Whatever Lola Wants" is the "Hernando's Hideaway" of *Yankees,* and "Who's Got the Pain?" is a mambo variation on "Steam Heat." In economic terms they succeeded, but the length of the run cannot change the fact that *Damn Yankees* is a sad carbon of *The Pajama Game.*

The topicality of musical comedy has ordinarily been apparent in two ways: in the kinds of character and attitude that are presented, and in the lyrics. In *Guys and Dolls,* for instance, Adelaide and Sarah sing, in "Marry the Man Today": "Slowly introduce him to the better things / Respectable, conservative, and clean / Reader's Digest / Guy Lombardo / Rogers Peet / Golf / Galoshes / Ovaltine." Golf and galoshes, and perhaps *Reader's Digest,* are respectability identifications that are not tied to a particular year; Ovaltine was already out of its time when this lyric was written—put in for the rhyme—and Guy Lombardo, still possible in 1950, would need to be replaced by Lawrence Welk in 1961. Most of the lyrics in *Guys and Dolls* and in other recent contemporary musicals do not have the kind of topicality that you get in revue lyrics which are supposed to be as up-to-date as this morning's gossip column. With the movement toward the tightly plotted musical, the immediate reference has to give way because it dates a book more quickly than do the manners and attitudes of a show even when they, too, are current. In *Bells are Ringing,* in a scene that kids the mannerisms of actors who imitate the Marlon Brando of *The Wild One* and *On the Waterfront,* everyone in a chorus of miniature Brandos pulls on a white mitten in a moment of inarticularity; the gag is funny, of course, only as long as audiences recall the playground scene from *Waterfront* that gives it point. "Adelaide's Lament" in *Guys and Dolls* is a topical song, but its reference is more than momentary; its target is the popularity of psychological jargon, and its wit is as pointed in 1961 as it was in 1950.

The topicality of the musical, like that of an Axelrod comedy, is seldom satirical; its function seems to be to prove that the authors are as up-to-date as the audience. Potentially satirical lines operate in a context that robs them of real sting. *The Pajama Game* opens with Hines speaking directly to the audience:

This is a very serious drama. It's kind of a problem play. It's about Capital and Labor. I wouldn't bother to make such a point of all this except later on, if you happen to see a lot of naked women being chased through the woods, I don't want you to get the wrong impression.

If this speech seems to imply that the musical is going to make serious fun of its announced subject (there are a few blunted barbs thrown at both labor and management) or of the solemnity of recent musicals, the implication is only a possibility for those members of the audience who do not correctly translate the speech: We know, and you know, that musicals are taking themselves seriously these days, but we plan to enjoy ourselves. If *The Pajama Game* has no intention of kidding serious musicals, the songs that Adelaide and the Hot Box Girls sing in *Guys and Dolls* ("A Bushel and a Peck," "Take Back Your Mink"), funny though they are, and "The Midas Touch" in *Bells Are Ringing* are only secondarily satirical comments on flashy night-club shows; they are primarily acts of homage to *Pal Joey,* in which numbers like "That Terrific Rainbow" and "Chicago" do the night-club parody so much more effectively and in a context that helps define the heel-hero of the musical. "The Midas Touch" number, like so much else in *Bells Are Ringing,* loses even its small point because Comden and Green never give it focus; it spreads itself in an effort to nod smilingly at targets as separate as adagio dancers and Elvis Presley. The satirical possibilities in the rock-and-roll singer—not simply another comic imitation of Presley's hip movements—are the origin of Charles Strouse's *Bye Bye Birdie* (1960). The book, by Michael Stewart, takes swipes at a number of subjects—the teen-ager, the dominating mother, television, the record business —but it finally backs away from the harsh and funny idea with which it began. Conrad Birdie, the play's rock-and-roll star, the ideal of the American adolescent, is presented at first as a venal and lecherous little monster, but before the musical has ended he has become one with the cliché of the fifties, another misunderstood boy. Abe Burrows and Frank Loesser are more consistent in *How to Succeed in Business Without Really Trying*; their hero remains a baby-faced shark from the opening number to the finale, although there is more fun than venom in the portrait. One of the virtues of the Leon Pober-Bud Freeman *Beg, Borrow or Steal* (1960), a failure on Broadway, is that it, too, stuck to its satirical point; through its con man, the same in gray flannel as he is in beat beard, the author insists that the takers and the taken do not vary according to their acceptance of, or contempt for, bourgeois society.

If satire on the surface of American life is rare in musicals, political satire and attacks on societal prejudices are almost nonexistent. In *Damn Yankees,* when the Devil complains that he is overworked, Lola says, "I know, poor dear, elections coming up." So generalized a gag certainly implies no conviction about politics; it is as meaningless as a casual reference to the State Department in *The Moon Is Blue.* The fun poked at Perle Mesta by *Call Me Madam* is no more serious; it has no real quarrel to pick with the way American ambassadors are chosen. Burton Lane's *Finian's Rainbow* (1947) is the only postwar musical that has social purpose; coming as it did right after the war, it still carries the look of the thirties about it. The satire is as broad as it is blunt—as when Buzz tries to teach the Negro college boy to shuffle. In the long run, the attack on bigotry loses its force because Fred Saidy and E. Y. Harburg, who did the book, make cartoons of their characters—particularly Senator Rawkins, who says of the Constitution, "I haven't got time to read it! I'm too busy defendin' it!"— and thus keep the satire as obvious as it is virtuous. They do kid their union-organizer hero a little by letting him speak in "Talking Union Blues" rhythm when he first appears and by having him announce, "I've got to take some guitar lessons from a folklore teacher on Fifty-second Street," but, for the most part, the division between the good and the bad is as obvious as it is in a fairy tale. Of course, *Finian's Rainbow* is a fairy tale of sorts. The fantasy involving the leprechaun, the professional Irish-ness of Finian, the romance of Woody and Sharon—all these belong to another order of musical than that suggested by the antiracism of the Rawkins story. In the long run, the sweet elements seem to have triumphed over the satirical—and Lane's score had much to do with the tipping of the balance—for *Finian's Rainbow* is remembered for "How Are Things in Glocca Morra?," not for its moral intentions.

In the absence of topicality and satire, nostalgia has become one of the main ingredients of the musical comedy. The list of shows by popular composers mentioned a few pages back indicates that most musical comedies take place in another time, and there is no point, in the fifties, in being satirical about the nineties, the twenties, or the thirties, the favorite decades for musical revisiting; one can only be affectionate. Leonard Bernstein's *Wonderful Town* (1953) is a good example of the nostalgic musical; even the "moderately satiric atmosphere" that Harold Clurman (in *Lies Like Truth*) finds in it is a reflection of Greenwich Village in the mid-thirties, not a comment in retrospect. The book by Joseph Fields and Jerome Chodorov sticks closely to their play *My Sister Eileen* (1940), on which it is based, and the play, in its turn, tries to retain some of the flavor of the Ruth McKenney stories from which it was derived. Bernstein provides numbers—"Conga!," "Swing!," the dance sequence that opens the last scene—that recall the music of the period, and Betty Comden and Adolph Green give his songs lyrics that would have been topical in 1935, but which are popular history in 1953; "Swing!," with its quotations from actual lyrics of the time and its scat-singing, is the best example. The period feel of the show is broken in only one number, "Wrong Note Rag," which is 1913 rather than 1935; there is no reason why Eileen and Ruth should be doing a pre-World War I sister act, but it is typical of fifties musicals that even the anachronisms are exercises in reminiscence. Jerry Bock's *Fiorello!* (1959) is also a nostalgic show, but this time the focus is not a decade, but a man. The book, by Jerome Weidman and George Abbott, for all that it seems to be about the political and marital adventures of its hero, is not seriously concerned with the real La Guardia. For New Yorkers, La Guardia has become a kind of mythical figure, and his name, like that of Jimmy Walker, induces a nostalgia that has nothing to do with his actual political accomplishments. With such

a figure at the center of the drama, *Fiorello!* needs no revelation
of character; suggestion will do the work. The spread of his hero's
career gives Bock a chance to write numbers that are reminiscent
of World War I ("Till Tomorrow," "Home Again") and the late
twenties ("Gentleman Jimmy": for me, the tap dance that accompanies this number recalls the movie musicals of the thirties);
the songs of the politicians ("Politics and Poker," "Little Tin
Box") and the strike song of the girls ("Unfair") are plot numbers
to some extent, but even they work nostalgically by suggesting the
era of the old-time political boss toward which most of us feel
affectionate although reason decrees that we deplore. The Robert
Merrill scores for *New Girl in Town* (1957), by George Abbott
out of *Anna Christie,* and for *Take Me Along* (1959), by Joseph
Stein and Robert Russell out of *Ah, Wilderness!,* are certainly—
for all that Eugene O'Neill is the source of the books—not designed to enrich complicated drama; they are fond backward
glances, appropriate in the second case, for in *Ah, Wilderness!*
O'Neill was consciously trying to step away from the cosmic problems that nagged at him and to take a touching look at a past that
was never his.

Perhaps the best, certainly the most prolific of the nostalgia
composers, is Jule Styne, a Hollywood song writer, who came to
Broadway in 1947 with *High Button Shoes.* With Styne, the nostalgia is never taken straight; there is an overtone of parody that
seems to insist that the audience be amused as often as it is
touched. "I Still Get Jealous," for instance, is a sentimental number, but it is also a standard soft shoe that builds to "still get jealous 'cause it pleases Y-O-U," a touch of period corn. Much of the
success of the show depended on the Jerome Robbins dances, not
only on the famous Mack Sennett ballet, which successfully re-
created some of the chaos of the silent-movie chase, but on smaller
effects, such as the tango that recalled and kidded not only Valen-
tino but a whole era's attitude toward him; that era, though no
one watching the Robbins tango seemed to mind, belonged not to
1914 but to the early twenties. In his next show, *Gentlemen Prefer Blondes* (1949), Styne moved into the twenties, and this
time, not by accident. *Blondes* is a kind of animated John Held,
Jr., cartoon, a projection of the wild and wonderful twenties that
all of us remember, particularly those of us who were on mother's
milk rather than bathtub gin at the time. Everything about the

show contributes to its general tone—the book Anita Loos and
Joseph Fields adapted from her novel; the music, particularly the
Charleston finale, "Keeping Cool with Coolidge"; Leo Robin's lyrics, when, as in "Homesick Blues," they turn into a catalogue of
celebrities of the decade. After *Blondes,* Styne wrote the music
for a revue, *Two on the Aisle* (1951), and an unfortunate musical, *Hazel Flagg* (1953). This last is a completely unsuccessful
attempt to catch the mockery of the thirties movie *Nothing Sacred,*
and the book by Ben Hecht, who wrote the film, does no more
than the music toward rescuing the show from innocuousness; typically, the only song worth remembering is "Every Street's a Boulevard in Old New York," a parody of the kind of sentimental talk-
song that is associated with performers like Ted Lewis. Aside
from some incidental songs that he contributed to the Mary Martin *Peter Pan* (1954), Styne's other shows are *Bells Are Ringing*
(1956), *Say, Darling* (1958), *Gypsy* (1959), and *Do Re Mi*
(1960). Much of *Bells Are Ringing,* as I indicated earlier, is almost revuelike in its parody and the best things in *Do Re Mi*—
aside from "Take a Job," a very effective plot song—are Styne's
approximations of jukebox successes.

If it were not for *Gypsy,* Styne might be dismissed as a composer with a sharp-enough ear to recapture, in fondness or in fun,
the popular music of an earlier period and to capture, in the spirit
of parody, the same kind of music in his own time. If it were not
for *Gypsy,* he might be simply a man who had once written a
bright and lively show—*Gentlemen Prefer Blondes*—but whose
work as a whole indicates industry rather than invention. But
there is *Gypsy.* It is one of the most carefully integrated musicals in the American theater, a virtue it owes to the librettist Arthur Laurents and the lyricist Stephen Sondheim, as well as to
Styne. Its attention to plot and to mood, but, more important,
to the psychological veracity of its leading character puts to shame
some of our ostensibly well-organized operettas, and it does so
without ever ceasing to be a musical comedy in the noisiest, most
vulgar sense of the term. For one thing, the backstage setting and
the spread of years that the plot covers allow Styne to work with
the combination of nostalgia and parody that he has used so often
before, but, for the first time, that kind of number exists for a purpose outside itself. The wonderfully ghastly vaudeville routines
that show Baby June and then Dainty June performing with her

troupe are funny as parody, are incidentally effective to those members of the audience (and to that quality in every member of the audience) who once supported flag-waving child acts, and at the same time illustrate the tasteless vitality of Rose. Tulsa's single, "All I Need Is the Girl," is a sophisticated tap, the kind of pseudo-Astaire routine that was endemic to the thirties, and it is so well done that I, for one, am drawn in sentimentally as the musical build begins; it is extremely effective corn and that effectiveness lets the audience know why Tulsa, whom the book has little time to characterize, is attractive to Louise and to June. The multiple use of "Let Me Entertain You"—in the amateur act at the beginning, in ragtime for Baby June, as a strip song for Gypsy—is not simply a display of cute inventiveness; it underlines the vacuity of that kind of song. Sondheim's lyrics, apparently innocuous when we first hear them, are clever enough to turn the harmless tune into good strip accompaniment for Gypsy, whose act depends on ladylike, almost prim, obscenity.

The strength of *Gypsy,* however, is the characterization of Rose, through the music as much as through the words. She is a stage mother who pushes her children relentlessly toward fame so that she may share it vicariously; she even forces her name on Louise. All of the songs contribute to the plot of the show, but most of Rose's numbers do much more than that. The vigor of the woman, the quality that keeps her going, is apparent in "Mr. Goldstone, I Love You"; her ruthlessness looks out through "Some People"; her naïveté, the quality that colors her sense of what success will be like, is clear in "Everything's Coming Up Roses." The implication throughout the play is that Rose's drive comes, in part, from a sense of inferiority, from a fear that without a spotlight on her she is not worthy of being loved; Laurents' book hints at this in the brief exposition at the beginning in which we learn that Rose has had three husbands and that her mother walked out on the household when she was a child. It is in the song "If Momma Was Married" that we learn most about the defenses that Rose has built up against her self-doubt, for June and Louise insist, "But Momma gets married— / And— / Married— / And— / Married / And never gets carried away." The climax of the play comes with Gypsy's stardom and her apparent rejection of her mother that leads to "Rose's Lament," a musical unmasking of everything that has been eating the character throughout the play. The midsong

breakdown may be a bit too pat, a suggestion that all Rose has
wanted all this time was her missing mother's love. In a play of
his own, Laurents might have pushed this idea; here it is simply
suggested and the tough Rose regains control of herself, the defenses go back up. The show should probably have ended with
Rose's last song, but there is an almost sentimental afterthought,
a reconciliation between Gypsy and Rose, which is saved from
saccharinity by the fact that Rose is still talking and is still pushing
herself in front of her successful daughter. The virtue of *Gypsy*—
and particularly of Styne's score—is that it lets us admire Rose's
gusto without our admiration making her any less a monster.

The two most recent Leonard Bernstein musicals—*Candide*
(1956) and *West Side Story* (1957)—are special cases; they do
not fit conveniently even in the somewhat amorphous categories in
which I have been separating American musicals. In one sense,
Candide is the "comic operetta" that its creators call it, but it is
much more than that; even if it were simply the genre it pretends
to be, it would be out of place in a theater in which the operetta
has become so completely Americanized. The jazz-based music
of *West Side Story* and its remarkable sense of contemporary idiom
place it with the musical comedies, although not in the way that
earlier Bernstein musicals—*On the Town, Wonderful Town*—
belong in that genre; its romantic story—Arthur Laurents' borrowing of *Romeo and Juliet*—might make it an operetta; its sociologi-
cal undertones, a problem play. It is simpler to consider the two
works in no context but their own.

The parallels between *West Side Story* and *Romeo and Juliet*
are so many and often so foolish that it is easy to be distracted
from the significant debt that Laurents owes to Shakespeare; the
musical, like the play, is built on the assumption that the lovers
are trapped by the conventions and prejudices of their society,
and that their desire to live beyond that society—in the community of love—is not strong enough to free them. One of the interesting things about *West Side Story* is its depiction of that society.
Laurents' book and Bernstein's music (with lyrics by Stephen
Sondheim) suggest that there are two forces, one psychological,
the other social, pushing the two street gangs toward the explosion
that kills Riff and Bernardo, and finally Tony (the Romeo of the
play). The two forces are intertwined, of course; it is the environ-

mental situation—the slums of the upper West Side in Manhattan, the opposition of authority, the complete isolation from the adult world—that creates the state of tension in which the boys exist. The need for explosive outlet is put into words by Anita: "You saw how they dance: like they have to get rid of something quick. That's how they fight." This explicitness, to be expected from Laurents, is hardly necessary in the face of musical numbers like "Cool" in which both lyrics and music depict the interior excitement hidden behind the mask of casualness, a mask that is removed as the boys reach the end of the song and go into a dance that gives them a momentary release, makes them, for the time being, "cooly cool, boy." The mambo duel in the dance at the gym does much the same thing, but it also restates the rivalry between the gangs, made clear—more forcefully than lines could do it—in the opening dance of the show, and does so in a context that suggests that the rivalry is really less important than the shared contempt for the adult world, represented here by Glad Hand and Krupke. Bernstein has used jazz joyously in the past—in *On the Town* and the ballet *Fancy Free*—but the jazz undertones of the opening dance are ominous. This quality, one of ugly expectation, is apparent under "Cool" and "The Dance at the Gym," and is finally realized in "The Rumble." Since this ugliness is to be fatal to the love of Tony and Maria, it is used effectively in the ensemble reprise of "Tonight," a number that is first introduced as a duet between the lovers. Most of their songs—"One Hand, One Heart," "Maria"—are almost hymnlike, an attempt to suggest the innocence of their love in contrast to the fierceness around them; although it is easy to see how Bernstein uses them, these are the least effective songs in the show, perhaps because Sondheim, who is most awkward with an affirmative or sentimental lyric ("Little Lamb" in *Gypsy*) cannot allow himself to be as clever as most of his lyrics indicate he is. "Tonight" shares some of the almost pious innocence of "One Hand, One Heart," but it is really a love-triumphant song, an operetta standard; in either case, it is in no way related to the frightening quality implicit in the gang numbers. In the reprise Maria and Tony continue to sing it as they had before, but the romanticism of their duet is mixed with the gangs' expectant preparations for the rumble.

The same kind of musical conflict is apparent in "Somewhere," the one number that makes an explicit statement about the

surroundings in which the gangs flourish. Tony sings it to Maria
shortly after the rumble, after he has killed her brother; there is
desperation in his voice and in the music as he insists that "Somewhere there must be a place we can feel we're free." The music
changes tone, finally—by the time the off-stage voice begins to
sing—becomes gentle, comforting, peaceful; at the same time the
scenery shifts, the enclosing walls of the city lift and let in space
and light, like the visionary scene in Sean O'Casey's *Red Roses for
Me*; the violent movement of the gang figures slows and a dance
begins that shows "no sides, no hostility now; just joy and pleasure
and warmth." Toward the end of the number, Tony again picks
up the song, singing it sweetly, as the disembodied voice had
done, but there is both irony and longing in his singing because,
just before he begins, a jagged quality creeps back into the music.
"Somewhere" is followed, after only a few lines of dialogue, by
the comic number, "Gee, Officer Krupke!," a juxtaposition that is
not as odd as it at first seems. If this were an ordinary musical comedy, the explanation would be simple: the show-biz bromide that
a slow, serious number must always be followed by a fast, funny
one. This is a consideration that Bernstein probably did not ignore,
but "Krupke" has its social function, too. Where "Somewhere"
expresses a yearning for an Arcadian escape for Jet and Shark
alike, an impossibility within the context of the plot, the comic
song satirizes and dismisses most of the diagnoses of, and solutions for, the problems of juvenile delinquency. This is another, a
comic, way of setting up the dichotomy between the adolescents
and the adults that is emphasized in the "Finale" in the proces-
sion with Tony's body, the two gangs intermingled, which leaves
the adults "bowed, alone, useless." There are accusations enough
within the play, insistence on the part of the boys or by the kindly
Doc or the vicious Schrank, to show that everyone has an idea
where the blame lies; certainly never with the accuser. The virtue
of *West Side Story* is that it is neither apologetics nor protest. It is
a romantic play in which the villain is the setting; no Prince of
Verona appears at the end to point the moral; the social implications are left to the audience.

More often than not, in the paragraphs above, I have used the
word *dance* to indicate a particular musical number; there are vocal numbers, of course, but for the most part the *dance* designation
is the correct one. With the increased popularity of the integrated

musical show, dances have been made to do plot work, to express character, to indicate the nature of a particular conflict; but *West Side Story* is the first musical to be conceived as a dance show. It is not so much a musical comedy with dances added as it is a ballet expanded into a musical play. The show, which, according to the credits, was "based on a conception by Jerome Robbins," owes its final effectiveness as much to the choreographer as it does to the composer or the librettist. Robbins had done imaginative work on Broadway before—the chase ballet in *High Button Shoes,* "The Small House of Uncle Thomas" in *The King and I*—but most of it was little more than decoration. In *West Side Story,* he shows how dance can cease to be simply a contribution to the musical and can become a necessary, an informing, element in it.

Candide is as different from *West Side Story* as it is from the rest of American musicals. A great many Broadway shows are sprinkled with musical jokes, as well as with ordinary sight or sound gags, but *Candide* is the only one that I can think of in which the musical and verbal wit is so demandingly intellectual. This fact, plus the tone of the show as a whole—a cynicism that is satirical, even moral, rather than conventionally sentimental—may explain its failure on Broadway. Many of those involved in the show have accepted its commercial failure as an artistic one and have made excuses. Tyrone Guthrie in *A Life in the Theatre* blames himself, Lillian Hellman (the book), Oliver Smith (scenery), and Irene Sharaff (costumes) for losing "whatever share of lightness and gaiety and dash we might possibly have been able to contribute"; this, despite the fact that *Candide* was one of the most handsomely staged and dressed shows that I can remember having seen on Broadway. John Briggs, in his biography of Leonard Bernstein, quotes Richard Wilbur, the chief lyricist:

I can see that everyone fell down. . . . Lenny's music got more and more pretentious and smashy—the audience forgot what was happening to the characters. Lillian's book got to be mere connective tissue. And I was inclined to be too literary and stubborn.

Guthrie exempts Bernstein from his accusations ("Only Bernstein's mercurial, allusive score emerged with credit"), but Briggs suggests, although he gives no evidence, that Bernstein himself feels that *Candide* was a mistake. No comment on American theater could be as acid as this picture of a group of creative people, having chosen to do an imaginative musical, backing away from their creation in horror on discovering that the audience that made hits of *Happy Hunting* and *Li'l Abner* had failed to take their baby to its bosom.

Lillian Hellman's book, which came in for heavy criticism when the show opened, does its job well. It sets up the situations in which the musical numbers can do their satirical work and, through occasionally strong lines and dramatic juxtapositions (the contrast of beggary and wealth in the Paris scene), contributes to the satirical effect of the operetta as a whole. She manages to do what most musical adaptations never even attempt to do, retain the artistic intention of the original work in the new form. Her *Candide,* like Voltaire's, is the story of an incredibly naïve young man whose nastily funny travels test the optimism that he has learned from Dr. Pangloss. "The heart of mankind is a generous heart," the golden rules begin; "the honor of man is all he needs on life's journey. . . ." Candide's lovely song, "It Must Be So," is painfully ironic in the context in which he must sing it. My chief doubt about the musical lies in its ending, in the "Make Your Garden Grow" number that brings the curtain down. The fault here is probably more Bernstein's than Hellman's. The selfish squabbling of the last scene leads first to the outburst of the no-longer-innocent Candide and then to the shy, hesitant offering of each principal to try to do his work. This is not preparation enough, however, for the transition from the brittle tone of so much of the show to the massed determination of the whole cast as they sing the hymnlike finale. Perhaps the effect should have been less grand, nearer that of Voltaire, a smaller garden. Still, Bernstein has prepared musically for "Make Your Garden Grow"; it reworks the theme from Candide's ballad "Eldorado" and, in tone at least, suggests "It Must Be So."

The cleverness of Richard Wilbur's lyrics (and of those of Dorothy Parker, John Latouche, and Bernstein himself) is immediately apparent to anyone who listens to the songs, but it is only when they are considered in relationship to the music and the placing within the book that the extent of their ingeniousness is clear. The song "You Were Dead, You Know" that Candide and Cunegonde sing when they meet again in Paris is ostensibly a sentimental lovers' duet, but its lyrics completely demolish it. Candide sings:

Dearest, how can this be so?
You were dead, you know,
You were shot and bayoneted, too.

and Cunegonde goes on: "That is very true. / Ah, but love will
find a way." This song will do as well as any to illustrate the way
in which the operetta works. It is apparent that Bernstein and his
lyricists (Latouche and Wilbur, in this case, if the copyright indicates authorship) are not only kidding a particular kind of operetta, but are satirizing the whole attitude that lies behind the line,
"Ah, but love will find a way." Bernstein makes use of standard
operetta numbers—gavotte, waltz, schottische—in a context or
with lyrics that insist on a far from standard reception. He takes
some incidental thrusts at opera, but, once again, the satire is more
deadly than simple parody; the vocal flourishes of Cunegonde's
coloratura aria, "Glitter and Be Gay," are ironic comments on her
high-minded apologia for her prostitution, and Martin's line in
the middle of the quartet that ends Act I is more than a comment
on the face-forward disconnection that parodies the grand-opera
curtain: "Well, they all believe what they are screaming. We'll
see." Without Bernstein's music, of course, the good intentions of
all the other participants would come to nothing. The triumph of
Candide is that the music is magnificently what it pretends to be
(find a mazurka as lovely as the one that opens the Paris scene),
but every number contains a hint of mockery that welcomes the
contradicting lyrics. Bernstein has written a delightful operetta
that at the same time, thanks to his ability to work with his associates, is an almost brutal satire.

An evening with *Can Can* or *Camelot* might convince me of the
justice of Gassner's complaint about the current tendency to over-
rate the American musical comedy. Still, it is difficult to escape
the fact that *Candide* is not only the most sophisticated product of
the American musical stage, but probably the most imaginative
American play to reach Broadway since the war.

8 THE VAGARIES OF ADAPTATION

Over somebody else's shoulder,
I fell in love with you!
—AL LEWIS and AL SHERMAN

Anyone who looks at the theater advertisements in the Sunday New York *Times* is likely to come away with the impression that there are more carpenters writing plays than building sets for Broadway. During the 1960-61 season, for example, more than a third of the new American plays were adaptations. This is hardly a new phenomenon; the nineteenth-century theater, particularly in the United States and England, leaned heavily on adaptations, the turning of popular fictional characters into vehicles for matinee idols. The good-natured venality of those days has, however, given way to artistic pretensions. Not that economic motivation has disappeared; producers still scramble for best sellers or for books with built-in publicity value and still assign professional adapters (playwrights of reputation if they can find them) to make the necessary alterations. Yet, the general attitude has changed. As though the celebration of adaptation were not one of the reasons for the flabbiness of contemporary American drama, reviewers tend to join theater professionals in treating adaptation not as the respectable hack work that it is, but as an act of creativity. No one takes the Pulitzer Prize very seriously any longer, but it is a comment on recent American theater that five of the last twelve awards, set up for the best "original American play," should have gone to adaptations: *South Pacific* in 1950, *The Teahouse of the August Moon* in 1954, *The Diary of Anne Frank* in 1956, *Look Homeward, Angel* in 1958, and *All the Way Home* in 1961. The New York Drama Critics awards have gone just as frequently to adaptations.

One of the difficulties in discussing adaptation is that it is often impossible to decide why a particular novel—especially one not immediately in demand—should be adapted at all. In their Introduction to the published *The Immoralist,* Ruth and Augustus Goetz, in describing their visit to André Gide for permission, recall their attempts to convey their intense conviction that there was a play in the novel; Moss Hart in the Foreword to *The Climate of Eden* explains that Edgar Mittelhölzer's *Shadows Move Among Them* so impressed him when he read it that, after two years, he finally gave in and did an adaptation of it. In both cases, the remarks are reprinted from preopening essays in the New York *Times,* a literary form that, since it is a kind of genteel advertisement, is not designed to inspire confidence in the reader. Still, there is no reason why Hart and the Goetzes should not have been telling the truth; certainly an adapter must often be motivated by his admiration for a particular novel or by his attraction to what he considers its dramatic possibilities. A producer or an actor, similarly moved, must often go in search of a writer.

In the pages that follow, I shall occasionally suggest why a particular book attracted an adapter; my reasons, of course, are only informed guesses, based on a look at the play and the novel; I am privy to no adapter's unpublished secrets. It is safe to assume, however, that many adaptations, particularly those that turn light comic novels into even lighter stage comedies, are attempted because the novelist has created an eccentric vivid enough to catch the adapter's or an actor's eye. Ira Levin's *No Time for Sergeants* (1955) is an obvious example. It is true that it came to Broadway only after a successful television production, but on stage or on screen it is simply a series of farce scenes that capitalize on the hero of Mac Hyman's novel, a hillbilly variation on a standard comic type, the innocent who takes every statement at face value. Vern Sneider's Sakini in *The Teahouse of the August Moon* is the comic antithesis of Hyman's Will Stockdale; he is the knowledgeable manipulator who wears the mask of naïveté. Sakini figures largely in the early chapters of the novel, but as the author becomes involved in the education of Captain Fisby, he pushes Sakini onto the periphery of the action. In John Patrick's adaptation (1953), Sakini takes center stage and keeps it, a position that

suggests that Patrick is more interested in his chief comic character
than he is in making Sneider's mildly satiric point about the cultural contribution of American military government. *Auntie Mame*
(1956), by Jerome Lawrence and Robert E. Lee, is an attempt—a
successful one in financial terms—to cash in on the popularity of
a book whose leading character has a marketable flamboyance.
The play, like Patrick Dennis' novel, is a series of disconnected
episodes, although the adapters have tried to hold them together
with a semblance of plot. Dennis' heroine is supposed to be an
exotic and exciting woman, full of glamor and good fun, at once
down-to-earth and head-in-the-clouds; it is impossible, however,
to distinguish between her enthusiasms and the affectations of others—for instance, the Maddox sisters, whom Dennis treats satirically. There is so much that is phoney and stupid about Mame that
it is a kind of victory that she does finally emerge from the novel
as a symbol of the healthy noncomformist. Lawrence and Lee drain
the character of even the whiff of substance that Dennis has allowed her; they retain her most obvious mannerisms and broaden
them—an operation, in the face of the original, that is rather like
irrigating the Mississippi River.

The danger for adapters lies in those fictional works that have
an immediately attractive character at their center, but that, unlike
Auntie Mame, are more than display cases for that character. John
Van Druten's *I Am a Camera* (1951), based on some of the stories in Christopher Isherwood's *Goodbye to Berlin,* is a case in
point. Van Druten's heroine is Isherwood's Sally Bowles, particularly in the early scenes of the play where the playwright's invented
dialogue sounds exactly right for a character whose actions and
affectations have been taken almost intact from the original. Before the play ends, however, several intrusive forces manage to
mar the Van Druten copy. Both a heavy moral tone and conventional sentiment creep in. The first is most evident in Chris's frequent harping on reform (at the end, he is heading back to England
to write his book), and the second is apparent in his offer to marry
the pregnant Sally, a gesture that turns him into the "loyal friend"
who used to inhabit seduction melodramas. One of the points
about Isherwood's characters (the unwritten novel of which these
stories are fragments was going to be called *The Lost*) is that they
are floaters, without roots and without ties, somehow representative of the Berlin of the early thirties. The slow dissolution of the

friendship of Sally and Chris is, then, as important as its accidental beginning. Unfortunately for the adapter, such an ending is tied to no incident, is not climactic in an ordinary way; so Van Druten has had to invent his way to a curtain and in doing so he has introduced Sally's mother, as surface as a cartoon, and has let her break up the nonexistent romance between the two principals. For a subplot, Van Druten brings together two Isherwood characters who never meet in his stories and provides them with a romance that allows him to make explicit the growing Nazism and the anti-Semitism that is the somber background to Isherwood's work. The tendency toward explicitness, the playwright's traditional distrust of his audience, is one of the annoying characteristics of the Van Druten play. The playwright's title comes from one of the novelist's lines, one which, slightly changed, appears in the play: "I am a camera, with its shutter open, quite passive. Some day all of this will have to be developed, printed, fixed." There is an accidental irony in the fact that although the adapter borrows Isherwood's camera metaphor, he ignores it. The play does not simply record actions and people and leave the implications to the audience; everything is too consciously spelled out.

The Ponder Heart (1956), which Joseph Fields and Jerome Chodorov made from Eudora Welty's short novel, is an even better example of a play in which the adapters see a character without a context. Their Uncle Daniel Ponder is a loving and lovable eccentric, like Miss Welty's, but they are unable or unwilling to accept the implications of his story. Miss Welty's comedy is an extremely funny one—as much the result of her narrator's style as of the incidents—but it is a harsh one. Uncle Daniel is a man who basks in the attention and the affection of others, one who likes both to give and to give pleasure. His trial marriage to Bonnie Dee Peacock comes to an end when he tickles her to distract her from her fear of a storm and discovers that "she'd died laughing." His trial for the murder of Bonnie Dee comes to an end (if not to a decision) when he walks through the court, passing out his money, and goes to the seclusion of a room that shuts him off from the town. The Ponder heart, we discover from Edna Earle, is not only the affectionate heart of Daniel but a fragile mechanism, one likely to stop at any moment. Bonnie Dee only really becomes a Ponder, finally laughs for Daniel, at the moment of death. As Daniel's gift

of laughter kills Bonnie Dee, his gift of money turns the town
against him. His small favors have been welcome, but the human
heart dare not be the Ponder heart; the ordinary world is not
ready to accept so much giving. Miss Welty's Uncle Daniel is more
than a sweet, odd Southern gentleman; he is a kind of fool-in-
Christ. Fields and Chodorov, indulging in Broadway's fondness
for the nice, the smooth, the right, let Daniel's innocence triumph;
he makes a speech giving everything away and goes out for an ice-
cream cone with Bonnie Dee's little sister. One might make a case
for the sweet curtain by insisting that audiences prefer a warm
heart to a cold truth, but there is no excuse—economic or artistic
—for the adapter's decision to substitute a long speech for so fine
a piece of business as Daniel's distribution of the money. The Daniel of the play is not only not Miss Welty's character, he is not
quite believably daft and touching in the play's own terms. He
comes off better than most of the other characters, it is true; Bonnie Dee is little more than a vaudeville hillbilly and Edna Earle,
who, as narrator, pervades the novel, loses all her vividness, although she hangs on to a few of her original lines. The quality of
the play is implicit in the way the adapters treat one such line:

The Peacocks are the kind of people keep the mirror outside on the
front porch, and go out and pick railroad lilies to bring inside the
house, and wave at trains till the day they die.

The Edna Earle of the play keeps the last two items in this catalogue of the Peacocks, but as soon as the description is out of her
mouth, she adds, "Shiftless trash," an appositional assertion that
not only takes the edge off the Welty line, but is out of character
for Edna Earle. There are a few nice inventions in the play, like
Bonnie Dee's passion for electrical appliances (although this turns
out to be a device not an idea), but the play as a whole is as unsure
in tone—part Welty, part Broadway Southern—as it is hedging in
spirit.

Sometimes it is an obvious situation rather than an unusual
central character that marks a book for adaptation. Perhaps it
was both in the case of William March's *The Bad Seed*. Since, for
all the genetics talk, it is little more than a standard mystery melodrama, an adapter could hardly do the novel a disservice. Suspense, I suspect, like beauty, is in the eye of the beholder, but
for me neither March's book nor Maxwell Anderson's adaptation,

Bad Seed (1954), bates the breath as a good thriller should. Anderson is incredibly clumsy at times; for instance, to establish the excelsior bed that will become Leroy's pyre, he lets Rhoda receive a present—a jigsaw puzzle, of all nonfragile items—packed heavily in excelsior. It must have been the fixing of the football game in Howard Nemerov's *The Homecoming Game* that made Howard Lindsay and Russel Crouse decide to make a play out of it. *Tall Story* (1959) retains nothing of the original except the name of an occasional character; in the interests of contemporaneousness, even the scandal has been transferred to basketball. Nemerov's novel is a sardonic comedy in which his hero, trying to do the right thing, finds himself involved in a series of situations— reflecting a variety of kinds of dishonesty, viciousness, callousness —which, to his worried surprise, work out comfortably for everyone involved. The play is a standard sports comedy, c. 1934, in which the campus hero clears his name, wins the game, gets the girl. *Tall Story* is not, as *The Ponder Heart* is, an illustration of what happens when adapters see the surface of a novel but not below it; obviously Lindsay and Crouse never intended their play to have any relation to its ostensible source, unless an ironic relationship is implied in the fact that so benignly an anti-intellectual play is supposed to be based on what is, after its fashion, a philosophical novel.

The serious problems in adaptation arise when a playwright tries to be faithful, in spirit or in letter, to a work for which he has, or suspects that his audience has, deep admiration. In the Foreword to his collected television plays, Gore Vidal, whose remarks on adapting for television should be valid for any kind of adaptation, makes the process sound simpler than it is: "One must get the idea, the fundamental *donnée,* of the work clearly established in one's own mind—the rest is simply a matter of taking the characters given and re-creating them in scenes of one's own fashioning." Whether the failure is intellectual or mechanical, whether the idea is never grasped or is lost in re-creation, adapters—faced with classics or with contemporary works that have a strong individual tone—frequently kill the work that they hope to make live in a new form. There are almost as many reasons for failure as there are adaptations, but a few of the causes recur so often that they might almost be called occupational hazards—genuine intractability, because of the scope or the introspective quality, of the material to be adapted; a conflict between the adapter's idea of what the professional theater demands and his sense of the original work; a difference in sensibility between the adapter and his source. Frequently, several of these handicaps are at work on a single adaptation.

John Hersey's *The Wall* is a good example of the kind of novel that defies adaptation to the stage. Although there are central characters in the book, it is primarily a portrait of the Warsaw ghetto, a depiction of the ideational and emotional stratifications within a society that, to the world outside, had been converted by destruction into a single entity. Although Millard Lampell's adaptation (1960) is by current standards a large-cast play, he can still do no more than suggest the ghetto by using a handful of bit players whose stereotypes come and go on the periphery of the main action, that involving the Apts and the Bersons. Such a device is a respectable stage convention, like doing the battle of Shrewsbury with six soldiers. The important difference is that *Henry IV* is not about the battle of Shrewsbury and *The Wall* is, or ought to be, about the ghetto.

Tad Mosel's *All the Way Home* (1960) indicates the difficulties inherent in an attempt to adapt a novel in which most of the action is interior. Mosel retains the characters and many of the incidents from James Agee's *A Death in the Family*; he does make Mary pregnant, presumably so that he can get life to balance against the death of Jay, but even this is not invented material, just a shift from Agee's fragments to his main story. Although the play is mechanically true to the original, it is spiritually quite dead—an exercise not a creation. The probable reason is that Agee's novel is a record of feelings, and we come to understand incidents and characters only after we have seen multiple reactions to them. Mosel has to offer the incident directly or force the characters to verbalize their feelings about it, a process that, in the context of Agee's method, necessarily means falsification since his characters are so often careful not to say what they feel. There is a wealth of external detail in Agee's book, too, but it is used by the characters; Jay's early-morning breakfast before his trip to his parents' place is a collection of images colored by the reactions of Jay and Mary to them, to each other, and to the possibility that Jay's father is dying. It is during this breakfast that Agee speaks of "the neces-

sity for action and its interruptive minutiae," a phrase that suggests
the whole texture of the novel: Agee's recognition that Mary's grief
and the feel of a cup of warm milk in her hands are both real to
her—not different orders of reality, but part of a single reality.
The stage business in Mosel's play seems to indicate that he hopes
to retain some of this quality from the novel, but he cannot in-
spirit his props as the novelist does. The intimacy of the movie
camera (Agee, after all, understood how film images work) might
be able to invest an inanimate object with the feeling that a character has toward it, but distance in the theater makes such investi-
ture impossible. Words would have to be spoken over the object
and, in Agee, it is what is not spoken that tells most about the
character. In the face of such obstacles, it is not surprising that
Mosel's play never even approaches the quality of Agee's novel.

Some of Mosel's problem with Agee faces Frances Goodrich and
Albert Hackett in their adaptation of *The Diary of Anne Frank*
(1955); they solve it by sacrificing the quality of Anne Frank's
diary to the demands of conventional theater. One of the controlling ideas in the diary is Anne's sense of isolation from everyone
in the Secret Annexe—even from Peter about whom she has hopes
—and her need to talk to the imaginary Kitty of the diary in the
absence of a flesh-and-blood friend. It is typical of the adapters
that they use her self-analysis directly, as in Act I, Scene 4, in
which, incredibly, she tells her father, ". . . I have a nicer side,
Father . . . a sweeter, nicer side. But I'm scared to show it. I'm
afraid that people are going to laugh at me if I'm serious." This is
a mandatory scene from the play of troubled adolescence, the one
in which the child finds that at least one adult understands. The
cheapening process is apparent everywhere in the play, most embarrassingly in the scene in which Anne dresses up and calls for-
mally on Peter: Corliss Archer in the shadow of Belsen. Anne
Frank's attitude toward Peter in the diary is both too adult and
too innocent for it to be turned into comic teen-agery. The play
does manage to give something of the diary's sense of a group
trapped together, their nearness forcing them into nagging resentment, open quarrels. The adapters are only able to do this, however, by finding a villain—Mr. Van Daan, who steals food—and
by giving him a contrition-and-forgiveness scene to do with Mrs.
Frank. The play is a mixture of genres—half adolescent comedy,
half spy melodrama (will the thief tell or will he not?); neither

kind of play can help but vulgarize the diary. There is an emotional reaction to *The Diary of Anne Frank,* and to *The Wall,*
that is not induced by the plays themselves. The audience, still
close to the actual horrors with which these plays are supposed to
deal, comes to the theater ready to be moved. The plays, however,
are more likely to turn the latent response than to release it. For
the most part, they call for standard sentimental reactions; they
offer, as Arthur Miller has said of *Anne Frank* (*Harper's,* August
1958), only the "subtly perverse comfort of pathos."

If *The Diary of Anne Frank* shows what happens when two
professionals decide to make a sensitive little girl's thoughts get
up and walk around stage, *The Wisteria Trees* (1950) illustrates
how another professional reacts in the face of material that is already beautifully stageworthy. It is easy to understand why
Joshua Logan should have decided to transfer Anton Chekhov's
The Cherry Orchard to the postbellum South, for there are similarities—the decay of the landed aristocracy, the growth in power
of the self-made businessman—between that place and period and
Chekhov's setting. Logan's play is almost a character-by-charac-
ter, scene-by-scene transposition of the cherry orchard to the wisteria park. The changes, however, are illuminating. Logan does
not have the subtlety that would allow him to see Peter Whitfield
(his Trofimov) as an almost slapstick character who happens, for
all his own ineffectuality, to see the inevitability of the social
change going on around him. Logan turns him into a writer of light
verse and gives him conventional American success (a job on the
Times Picayune, which is, of course, just the beginning) and Antoinette (Anya) to marry. The most revealing change is in Logan's
feeling that he has somehow to explain that last wonderful scene
of Chekhov's in which Lopahin still cannot speak to Varya, in
which they separate although everyone—even themselves—assumes that they will marry. Logan's Lopahin (Yancy), his proposal makes clear, is in love with Lucy Ransdell (Madame Ra-
nevsky). Logan's departures from Chekhov's play are in the
direction of Broadway—more congenial conclusions (the marriage
of Antoinette and Peter) and greater specificity, in motivation and
in theme (Lucy has a speech in which she explains the whole concept of the fading aristocracy); Logan's faithfulness to Chekhov
only reminds us how good the latter is and how little reason there
was for Logan to write his play.

Anita Loos's Colette, unlike Logan's Chekhov, is American by accident. Her *Gigi* (1951) tells the same story as Colette's short novel, but the tone is very different. In both works, Gigi, raised by her grandmother and her great aunt to become a courtesan, gets Gaston for a husband instead of a keeper. In Colette, the suggestion is that Gigi is what her family has always been, a woman who knows how to use her attributes—in her case, her tomboyishness, her innocence—to gain her own ends. In Loos, Gigi is a normal (American) girl in revolt against the kind of life that her elders advocate; she is even given to moralizing speeches, which suggest that she reads syndicated advice columns instead of Parisian gossip papers, as when she says of her great aunt's life: "I think you're a failure!" The play is full of bromidic stage business—the maid does the familiar fright-at-the-new-telephone routine—which seems to suggest that Miss Loos intends to be professional (on Broadway this means doing what has already been done) in her adaptation, but the real difference between the play and its source lies in the fact that the two authors are so unlike in temperament. Ketti Frings's *Look Homeward, Angel* (1957) is another play that shows, less obviously, the difference in sensibility between the adapter and the original author. The length of Thomas Wolfe's novel and its flood of rhetoric would present any adapter with a serious problem of selection. Miss Frings has sensibly limited herself to the early sections of the novel, those that deal with Eugene Gant's home and family, and his escape from them. Some things in the play—Eugene's conversation with the dead Ben in the epilogue, the corny comedy with the tombstone-buying madam in the second act, the stereotypes (right out of Wolfe) who live in the Dixieland Boarding House—are awkward enough, but for the most part the play is a reasonably effective family drama in the tradition of American regionalism. In one instance (Act I, Scene 2), Miss Frings writes extremely well when she allows Eliza's resentment, built up but unreleased in her scene with her husband, to spill over into her scene with Ben and Mrs. Pert. It is Eliza, in fact, who becomes the focus of the play and it is this change in emphasis that indicates most clearly the way an adapter's personality can overlay that of the original author. *Look Homeward, Angel* is Eugene's novel, Wolfe's self-dramatization; *Look Homeward, Angel* is Eliza's play, the same material seen through the eyes of an adapter who happens also to be a woman.

Paul Osborn's *Point of No Return* (1951) displays almost all of the hazards of adaptation. For one thing, the John P. Marquand novel on which the play is based is a long one, the bulk of which (more than three hundred pages) is a flashback, sandwiched between two sections that take place in the present. The play tries to retain the same form, but the early years at Clyde have to be jammed into the second act in so condensed a version that incidents that in the novel stretch over months follow one another immediately. Such a device violates Marquand's precise sense of behavior within social strata, but then Osborn violates that sense elsewhere in the play and with less reason. In the third act, for instance, the news of Charles's promotion is broken at a dinner that the Grays give for the Burtons. This dinner is false to Marquand since he makes clear that social behavior in the bank would preclude the Grays offering the Burtons an invitation and it is structurally inept as well since the Burtons are forced to leave the stage twice (the excuse is a phone call from a daughter at school) to let Nancy and Charles discuss their private problems. Whether Osborn is intent on ending on the Broadway upbeat or whether his sense of the implications of the situation is different from Marquand's, the play and the novel do different things. Dull though the novel is, its tone is essentially ironic; it suggests that a man follows a path in life, one ordained by his origins and by accident, and that, after the point of no return, he must continue to the end, even if he has come to suspect that there is not the reward and the joy that he once thought to find there. The play, if it means anything, says that after a man has crept and kowtowed his way to the vice presidency in a bank, he can be himself and still be accepted. Not that Osborn intends to say that; the general impression from the play is that Osborn does not know or care what Marquand is doing and that he feels that, even if he retains some of the incidents and implications of the novel, they will all be washed clean if he sees that his hero gets ahead in his business and a curtain kiss from his loyal wife.

Occasionally an adaptation fails not by comparison with the original, but with an intervening adaptation, sometimes in another medium. *Rashomon* (1959), by Fay and Michael Kanin, is an example. Although the published play proclaims that it is based on stories by Ryunosuke Akutagawa, it owes much to Akira Kurosawa's fine film (1950), which carries the same name. The

Kanins, like Kurosawa, borrow the rape and murder from Akutagawa's "In a Grove," and describe what happened through the eyes
of the murderer, the murdered man (through a medium), the raped
wife, and a passing woodcutter, who is involved only to the extent
of having stolen the murder weapon. The story and both adaptations are essays on the relativity of truth, like Pirandello's *It Is So!*
(If You Think So). Akutagawa, however, is content to let the
three principals tell their stories, each giving stature to the teller;
Kurosawa adds the woodcutter's version, a slapstick account of the
same incident, which suggests that any human event becomes
ludicrous in so far as an individual can separate himself from it.
Kurosawa also and unfortunately adds a frame story involving a
Buddhist priest and an abandoned baby, which allows him to end
on a note of affirmation that is quite irrelevant to the philosophic
point that is at the heart of the film. The Kanins borrow both the
slapstick version of the murder and the frame story; they
give much more attention to the development of the latter, seeing
the whole thing in terms of the priest's loss and regaining of faith.
The play, which makes its points too insistently, reads better than
it plays; on stage, it stands in constant comparison to the film, its
unacknowledged source, and all that it can offer (or that it
did offer) in production is a ponderous revolving stage as a substitute for the excellent photography of Kurosawa that contributed,
in each case, to the psychological authenticity of the description
of the murder.

The difficulties of the adapter that I have described above are
intensified by the reputation of the original author, by his claim
to that doubtful designation *classic*. One of the bromides of popular criticism (on paper and in the mouths of the members of any
audience) is that the play (film, television drama, ballet, opera)
is all right in its way, but that it just does not catch the spirit of the
original. Nor does it in most cases. There is a tendency to forgive adaptations of current works, as though they were somehow
fair game (still in the market place, perhaps), but let a work mature for a few years, let its author achieve the dignity of age, death,
or the attention of the academy, and enthusiasts are on hand to
catch the adapters out.
    Marjorie Barkentin came close to outwitting the purists in *Ulysses
in Nighttown* (1958), an adaptation from James Joyce's *Ulysses*,

which she made with the help of Padraic Colum. Except for the introduction of Stephen and Bloom, which she takes from earlier chapters of the novel (adaptation, like source, opens with the familiar, "Stately, plump Buck Mulligan . . ."), Miss Barkentin sticks fairly closely to Joyce's Nighttown section, which is in dialogue in the original. Her work is largely cutting and rearrangement. Except for changes in pronouns and nouns of address, demanded when narration is transferred to a particular speaker or when a character disappears (Power no longer goes to the funeral with Bloom, Daedalus, and Cunningham), and except for an occasional softening of complicated puns and arcane references, the words are Joyce's. The printed play uses, as stage directions, the descriptive bits that Joyce provides between speeches in the original; these, of course, are about as stageable as Ring Lardner's *Clemo Uti*. The New York production tried to suggest the quality of the Joyce passages with choreography by Valerie Bettis, but the effect unfortunately was only hectic. There is also a difficulty about the tone of the adaptation. It ends, as Joyce's Nighttown section does, with Bloom's vision of the dead Rudy. The published play contains Joyce's description, one that rules out the possibility of sentimentality:

He has a delicate mauve face. On his suit he has diamond and ruby buttons. In his free left hand he holds a slim ivory cane with a violet bowknot. A white lambkin peeps out of his waistcoat pocket.

A child on stage is something else again, and the New York production, partly because of Zero Mostel's Bloom, ended up standing with Bloom rather than off with Joyce watching Bloom. The play's virtues are Joyce's; its success is Joyce's. In most cases, the nagging discontent over details gave way, for even the sternest Joyce admirers, to the pleasure of hearing his language on stage.

Henry James has not always been lucky in his adapters, but William Archibald's *The Innocents* (1950), an adaptation of *The Turn of the Screw*, does no great disservice to the original. The play communicates the sense of evil and corrupted innocence that the book conveys. The important difference is that James's story is told by the governess, and the play, an objective recounting of the same events, does away with the ambiguity of the original. In Archibald, the ghosts of Quint and Miss Jessel are real, not only to the audience (which might make them stage conventions), but to Mrs. Grose, the housekeeper, who never sees them in the story. James provides for two interpretations. "No mere phantoms appear in this tale," writes Leon Edel (The New York *Times Book Review*, September 3, 1961). "They are ghosts we fashion in our minds, the fears with which we frighten ourselves." The governess then may be suffering hallucinations and passing her fear on to the children, which would explain Flora's behavior and Miles's death. Still, James understands the ghost story well enough to leave open the possibility of supernatural rather than psychological possession. After her first encounter, the governess describes Quint whom she had never seen in life or heard described, and Miles, in the last scene, speaks the names of Quint and Miss Jessel although neither he nor the governess has spoken them before. If Archibald sacrifices the subtlety of James in making the ghosts so obviously real (and loses a further dimension of titillation), he succeeds—and his title suggests that this is his real concern—in presenting the horrifying juxtaposition of innocence and corruption in the children. Some of his inventions are plainly theatrical—including the songs that Miles and Flora sing—but theatricality in this case is a virtue, for he cannot, as James can, build his horror on the unstated, the implicit. Given the change in emphasis, of course, the struggle for Miles's soul becomes a real tug-of-war between Miss Giddens and Quint, but Archibald manages to retain at least the ambiguity of the end of the story. Although he brings the curtain down on the governess leaning over the body of Miles, muttering hysterically, "—you are free—Miles —you're free. You're free—," there is no clear idea of whether she has been victorious or defeated.

The Innocents is close enough to the tone of *The Turn of the Screw* to pass for a respectable adaptation; alongside *The Heiress* (1947), a travesty of *Washington Square,* the Archibald play seems a model of fidelity. In the Ruth and Augustus Goetz play, which, to do them credit, is labeled "suggested by the Henry James novel," the adapters have converted James's story into a sentimental melodrama in which the turning worm resoundingly punishes both her father and her false lover. Catherine Sloper's two big scenes— the denunciation of her father and her slow ascent of the stairs while Morris pounds on the door and calls her name—are plainly not in the spirit of James's book, which might be characterized by

this exchange between Dr. Sloper and his sister, Mrs. Almond,
shortly after his announced disapproval of Morris as suitor:

> And, meanwhile, how is Catherine taking it?
> As she takes everything—as a matter of course.
> Doesn't she make a noise? Hasn't she made a scene?
> She is not scenic.
> I thought a lovelorn maiden was always scenic.

If the scenic Catherine is not James's Catherine, neither is she
quite right for the play that the Goetzes pretend to write from
time to time. They use to excess the popular psychology of
the contemporary theater, building James's hints about motivation into case histories. James describes Catherine as "uncom-
fortably, painfully shy," although her shyness never becomes path-
ological as it does with the Goetzes. James lets Catherine believe
that her father "is not very fond of me" because of her beautiful
mother who died in childbirth; the Goetzes use this as diagnosis,
converting Dr. Sloper into the tyrant-father of *A Very Special
Baby*. Not content with this cliché, they must make him love Catherine as well so that the audience will feel that her final attack on
him is effective. Having made their obeisance to psychological
drama, the Goetzes dump their incipient characterizations and
end the play in an earlier tradition of popular drama by punishing
the villains and allowing the audience to feel that the benevolent
gods of come-uppance are still in operation. In this confusion of
genres, the Goetzes retain not only some of James's characters but
a number of his lines; it is incongruous to hear their sentimentalized Dr. Sloper ("Is Cook's knee any better?") in a scene
in which he speaks the detached lines in which James is ironic about
the character's attempts at irony. The whole tone of *Washington
Square*, in fact, is dictated by the artificial, brittle, almost flip, narrative style that James uses, one that keeps the story of Catherine
Sloper, with all of the implications that the Goetzes dote on, in the
realm of high comedy.

What the Goetzes did to James in *The Heiress*, they did to
André Gide in their adaptation of *The Immoralist* (1954). Gide's
novel, the struggle within Michel between the sensual and the intellectual man, completely disappears. In concentrating on the
homosexuality and playing their old game of simplistic motivation
(they provide Michel with a schoolboy scandal and a feeling of

being unloved), they ignore the real texture of the novel, Gide's re-creation of Michel's slow awakening to sensation. Michel's attempt to convey color, sound, touch—the assault on all his senses —and the implications of his yearnings can hardly be transferred to the stage. In their attempt to find an exterior drama for the interior one of Gide, the Goetzes have escaped, as in *The Heiress,* into the comfort of the obvious. Two conflicting attitudes seem to be in operation within the play. One is propagandistic, the suggestion that we should all be intelligent about homosexuality. Despite their good intentions on this score, the Goetzes are tempted by the exotic. They convert the orchard in which Gide's Michel used to sit into a homosexual paradise (based on sound philosophic principles) that (through an Arab boy as siren) keeps luring Michel away from Marcelline; it is typical of the Goetzes that their Michel cannot be tempted in Normandy, as Gide's is, but only in North Africa, which on Broadway and off (Tennessee Williams and Meade Roberts) is a convenient symbol for fashionable corruption. Although their view of Moktir's orchard endangers their desire to be sensible about perversion, the real opposing attitude at work in the play is their desire that it should somehow fit the conventions of popular drama. Their solution is to bring Michel back to Marcelline and their child in Normandy where they will, side by side, face and fight his homosexuality; with all respect to their attempt to keep Michel's sexual proclivities intact, this is only a variation on the standard love-of-a-good-woman curtain. Ironically, in their Introduction to the published play, the Goetzes quote Gide's initial reaction to their suggestion that they dramatize the play, "In the theatre homosexuality is always a false accusation, never a fact of life." Although the play pays lip service to Gide's fact of life, the ending, implicitly at least, pays homage to the convention of the false accusation.

One of the best adaptations to reach Broadway since the end of the war is *Billy Budd* (1951), which Louis O. Coxe and Robert Chapman made from Herman Melville's "Billy Budd, Foretopman." The authors alter Melville's tale in two basic and strangely conflicting ways. First, they try to give a real setting to the story, peopling the ship with a variety of standard nautical types, where Melville concentrates on the character immediately in front of him. Second, having, as they admit, seen *Billy Budd* as a morality play, they emphasize the symbolic character of Billy, Claggart, and Captain Vere. The impulse of the authors, then, is to be both more concrete and more abstract than Melville, and here lies the difficulty of the play. By giving their morality figures a real ship to act in and by providing them with a hint of motivation (there is a suggestion that both Billy's innocence and Claggart's evil are sexual), the adapters make a gesture toward verisimilitude that their conception of the play as morality denies; as a result, the audience, having been asked to accept the characters as more than symbolic figures, is left disbelieving, particularly in Billy, partly in Claggart, even to some extent in Vere. The play's strength is its argument, its development of the problem of good and evil in relation to human law. Billy and Claggart, in the play, are more simply good and evil than they are in Melville (where Billy is "little more than a sort of upright barbarian," innocence before knowledge of evil, and Claggart is "depravity according to nature") and, in judging Billy for Claggart's death, Vere becomes a symbol too, the law that man must live by so long as he wears the "uniform of flesh." * Melville's Vere remains the commander of the ship, a man consciously putting on the symbol of command; his sentencing of Billy and his death cry ("Billy Budd, Billy Budd") make clear, by implication, man's longing for the good and his refusal of it for societal reasons. In the play this is quite specific in Vere's speech to Seymour, the preparation for his insistence on the death sentence: "But without this lawful tyranny, what should we have but worse tyranny of anarchy and chaos? . . . Oh, if I were a man alone, manhood would declare for Billy." By comparison to Melville, whose characters twist and turn as you hold them, changing symbolic value with each new light, Coxe and Chapman are as neat as the writers of ancient morality plays. It is this neatness that is their greatest virtue. Their characters are occasionally complicated by the demands of psychological realism that they have not completely discarded, but, since they never attempt the ambiguities that seem to come naturally to Melville, they are at their best when they let their philosophical play speak as directly as the morality play has always done.

The problems of adaptation are not simplified, as generations of novelists have discovered, when an author decides to make

* The first version of the play, produced in 1949 off Broadway, had that title.

a play of his own novel or short story. Ideally, the conflict of temperaments should disappear, leaving only the struggle to refashion material that has been conceived for another genre. Ideally, but not actually, not always. Take *The Cold Wind and the Warm* (1958) as an example. A conflict in love has provided the plot motivation in every one of S. N. Behrman's comedies of ideas and, when he came to make a play of *The Worcester Account,* he, as if by reflex action, saw the difficulties of Willy Lavin in terms of a triangle, if an unconventional one; it is as though the playwright Behrman had come as an outsider to adapt the work of Behrman the reminiscence writer. In the same way, the Wolcott Gibbs who wrote the *New Yorker* stories about Fire Island is not quite the Gibbs who turned them into the comedy *Season in the Sun* (1950). The original pieces—sometimes effective, sometimes flat—were no more than sketches, incidents that expressed the author's indulgent fondness, tinged occasionally with acid, for Fire Island and its summer visitors. In the adaptation, he retains much of the original—characters, situations, dialogue—but ties the fragments together with an unfortunate plot, complete with bald moralizing ("But they're *people.* They're funny and they're *alive*"), in which his hero must come to accept "your time and that means accepting the people who go to make it up. . . ." It is the kind of play for which Gibbs, the reviewer—still another temperament— often expressed elegant contempt.

Sometimes the change of tone results when the original author —whether through his or a producer's nervousness—takes a collaborator, a professional who is supposed to and sometimes does bring the sure touch of commercial success with him. Thus, Joseph Fields helped Peter DeVries vulgarize *The Tunnel of Love* (1957), and Joshua Logan put the mark of his excess on Thomas Heggen's *Mister Roberts* (1948), making broad and farcical what was once quiet and rueful. So crass a consideration could not have made Harvey Breit Budd Schulberg's collaborator on *The Disenchanted* (1958), for Breit was innocent of Broadway success. Whatever brought the two men together, their joint effort is fairly straight sentiment. Having pared away most of the novel's environmental detail, something that Schulberg does well, the adapters are left simply with the collapse of an unattractive and unconvincing central character. Neither the frame story (the bogey of Hollywood) nor the flashbacks (that cliché about the twenties

—the dancing that stopped too quickly—and the standard destructive love) give Manley Halliday substance; not even the reflected presence of F. Scott Fitzgerald, on whom Halliday is based, can turn the water of self-pity into the wine of compassion.

The plays in the paragraph above, with the possible exception of *The Disenchanted,* are not examples of attempts to adapt narrative works so much to the stage as to a concept of the stage involving the idea of Broadway success. The changes are as much ideational as they are structural. The author who hopes really to catch the feel of his original work is something else again. Sometimes, as in Joseph Hayes's *The Desperate Hours* (1955), when the original work is a fairly obvious kind of popular fiction—in this case a thriller—the adaptation can be both faithful and commercial. In both novel and play, Hayes sets out to write a crime melodrama with periodic small climaxes designed to excite the audience and then relieve that excitement in preparation for the next build; in both forms, he succeeds. He also intends to make a small philosophic point, that there is a basic difference between the Hank Griffins and the Dan Hilliards, between those who kill and those who, even with provocation, cannot kill, but this point— which might not stand up under careful psychological probing —is always incidental to the suspense. Hayes's chief job, in adapting, is to cut away material, to focus on the conflict between Griffin and Hilliard, which means that indications of the frightened and resentful adolescent beneath the façade of the self-possessed criminal have to come earlier in the play than they do in the novel; his chief structural chore is to see that the small climaxes come with the act curtains.

According to the Foreword to the play version of *Compulsion,* Meyer Levin must have had something like *The Desperate Hours* in mind, for he says that he intended the play to be "a melodrama of philosophic implications." His finished product is more accurately a philosophic play with melodramatic undertones, for whatever interest it has lies in its ideas rather than its action. In transferring the novel to the stage, Levin makes a major change; he moves the focus to Judd Steiner and Artie Straus, away from the newspaperman-narrator whose wartime experience with a near rape teaches him something about himself and the forces that worked on the two criminals. As a study in motivation, the play is diagnostic; the characters are explained rather than created. As a philosophic statement, it is almost paradigmatic. In Act I, following the theories of the superman, Judd is convinced that he has control of his actions, that free will is operative. In Act II, under the influence of his lawyer and the psychiatrists, he comes to believe that "we were slaves, victims of a mechanistic universe of cause and effect." In the end, in the present (the play retains the frame story, the newspaperman's visit to the jail years later), Judd walks the middle way: "Somewhere, a man must assume responsibility for his actions. . . . Neither a king nor a slave, but a man." The play that I have been describing here is the one that Levin published in 1959, not the one, billed as "Producer's Version," that Michael Myerberg presented on Broadway in 1957. From all accounts, that version, written in part by Robert Thom, was rather more interested in the sensational than the philosophical and psychological implications of the Leopold-Loeb case. In the Foreword quoted above, Levin gives a long, pained account of his quarrels with producer, director, and writing assistant in trying to get his own *Compulsion* on stage. His account, like William Gibson's *The Seesaw Log,* is only one side of the story, but it is a useful reminder that the problems of adaptation, like those of all forms of play writing, are not all aesthetic these days.

Herman Wouk's *The Caine Mutiny Court-Martial* (1954) illustrates how a novelist can jettison the bulk of a book and hold onto its theme. The play, based on only the trial section of the novel, is as interesting a courtroom drama as the novel is a sea story—that is, at the level of events, the fascination of what happens next. In both forms, however, Wouk's story is peopled with characters who, despite his concern for psychological accuracy (he admits to studying case histories to write Queeg), are essentially false, stalking-horses behind which the author moves, ready to fire his ideational blast. The play, like the book, is two-faced. Having presented a Queeg who terrorized his ship and endangered it during a typhoon, Wouk allows Barney Greenwald to clear Queeg—spiritually, at least—of all guilt on the grounds that he served in the peacetime Navy and that those boys (as though it were not their job) had to bear the brunt of the early years of the war. This point of view, annoying enough when the novel was published in 1951, was even less acceptable by the time the play was produced, after three more years had slipped between the audience and any lingering wartime reverence for the armed forces.

Seldom has an author, in adapting his own novel, been successful in creating a work that is both faithful to the original and an attractive play in its own right. Carson McCullers's *The Member of the Wedding* (1950), Alfred Hayes's *The Girl on the Via Flaminia* (1954), and Truman Capote's *The Grass Harp* (1952) are the only three examples that come to mind. The Capote play is the least interesting of the three. In the play, as in the novel, Dolly Talbo to save her dropsy cure (the gift of the gypsies) from her martinet sister Verena runs away from home and lives in a treehouse. She is accompanied by Catherine Creek, the Negro servant who pretends to be an Indian, and her nephew Collin (he is a combination of the novel's Collin, a barely formed, near adolescent, and Riley Henderson, a flashy, tough, lonely young man), and is joined by Judge Charlie Cool, a man in search of a place and another person. Outraged, Verena enlists the aid of local authority (the sheriff, the parson) to force the runaways out of the tree, back into conventional society. The opposing forces collapse when their opposition has consequences—the accidental shooting of Collin—and the outsiders return, supposedly having both learned and taught by their withdrawal to the treehouse. This double effect is made evident through the humanization of Verena and the discovery of self in Dolly. Deserted and robbed by Dr. Morris Ritz, her partner in the attempt to get the dropsy cure, Verena is able to speak her need for Dolly, and the latter, who has wanted "Verena to see this woman that I am," can return to the house, which she has owned in spirit and Verena in fact, ready to share it with her sister. Since the play is not the whole story of Dolly Talbo, as the novel is, it focuses on the resolution of the conflict and becomes too specific in the process. Dolly is forced to make an uncharacteristic speech, moralizing in tone; "I can see now that in a vain self-pitying corner of myself I've always felt that *I alone* knew what was right. Just as you did, Verena. And people who believe they alone are right can do nothing but deliver ultimatums." Verena, in her turn, asks if she may go herbing with Dolly and Catherine. The two sisters are not so much changed by events, as they are in the novel, as sentimentalized by genre.

Capote also makes changes in the social implications in the play.

In both versions of *The Grass Harp,* the Judge describes Dolly as "a spirit, a pagan" and adds, "Spirits are the accepters of life; they grant its differences, and consequently are usually on the right side." If Dolly's later speech about ultimatums somewhat confuses the issue, it is clear through play and novel that there are sides to be taken. Those in the treehouse, seekers after love and beauty, are at odds with society, particularly that represented by Verena and her allies—money, authority, self-righteous religion. These last forces are considerably softened in the play, where there is no scene as blunt as the one in the novel in which the Reverend Buster tears the money away from Sister Ida, the revivalist with the hungry children. Neither Sister Ida, unhappily, nor this kind of nastiness appears in the play, but even so the forces that give lip service to virtue are decidedly unpleasant. Capote's restraint in picturing them, one assumes, is to make Dolly's return acceptable. In the novel, he is willing that Dolly should come back to a world that will not be sweetened by her return. There is a group of characters in the novel who are neither with Dolly nor against her. These include the barber, whose gossip is basically sympathetic, and Mrs. County, the baker's wife, who sends rolls to Dolly and meals to Catherine, who is arrested in the book. Mrs. County's line, "Leading citizens have to behave themselves; otherwise the entire place goes to pieces," carries in its few words the novel's resolution, the abandoning of the treehouse, of the romantic gesture. The same line is used in the play, but here the barber and the baker's wife, having come to persuade Dolly out of the tree, join her there when the sheriff arrives. The theatrical value of this scene is apparent to anyone who, lump in throat, has waited for the reluctant citizen in the Western to take up his gun and join the posse, but the gesture does destroy the function of those characters as they existed in the novel. The play, then, becomes a relatively sweet one in which the good people prove finally, if temporarily, stronger than the evil. The novel, which is not about Dolly's victory in the tree, but about her whole life (the grass harp cannot tell your story until you are dead), has a much stronger underlay of sadness.

The Grass Harp, to its disadvantage, is full of echoes from Carson McCullers. The Judge's explanation of love, "A leaf, a handful of seed—begin with these, learn a little what it is to love. First, a leaf, a fall of rain, then someone to receive what a leaf has taught you, what a fall has ripened," might have come from the mouth, certainly has come from the metaphysics, of the bum in "A Tree. A Rock. A Cloud." Much of the byplay between Catherine and Collin suggests, at a considerable distance, that between Berenice and Frankie in *The Member of the Wedding*. Capote's borrowings from Mrs. McCullers are not nearly as important as what he has not been able to borrow—a quality, a tone, a substance (a tree, a rock, a cloud). There is an archness in the play version of *The Grass Harp* that the novel avoids, but, in comparison to *The Member of the Wedding,* both novel and play seem to be self-conscious constructions, built by a clever and talented craftsman out of materials he has used successfully before and which have had some vogue. The oddness, the obliquity, the wistful stasis that seem synthetic in *The Grass Harp* are organic to *The Member of the Wedding. Member* is a better play than *Harp* not simply because Mrs. McCullers has retained the flavor of the original, but because the original has substance as well as flavor.

Mrs. McCullers' play, like her novel, is the story of Frankie Addams, caught at that moment between childhood and adolescence when she feels most strongly her loneliness, her sense of disconnection. In her case the feeling is heightened by her theatrical-literary inclination ("Oh, I am sick unto death"), by her absence of family (her father is a widower who pays little attention to her), and, most of all, by her part in the kitchen threesome— with Berenice Sadie Brown, the cook, and John Henry, her seven-year-old cousin. Berenice, because she is a Negro and because she has spent her life trying and failing to find again the love she had with the long dead Ludie, and John Henry, who is an owlish miniature adult as well as a child, form with Frankie a community of the disconnected, an uneasy alliance that has made Berenice's kitchen both sanctuary and prison. Although Berenice has T. T. Williams to court her and her church to attend, Frankie the town to roam in, and John Henry a house next door to go home to, the kitchen, for the summer of the novel, is their reality. The single set heightens this effect in the play; everything that happens outside it—for instance, Frankie's trip through the town in which she tells everyone that she is to be a member of the wedding—has to be refashioned, retold, to fit the experience of the kitchen. The three participants have built a ritual—the dinner that goes on for hours, the three-handed bridge game—which is most obvious in the pat-

tern of their talk, chatter that takes them again and again over familiar ground, but which touches often on Frankie's desperate desire to break out, to get away, to join with something or someone.
The play has had to telescope the talk of a long summer into the
first two acts; lines that are remembered in the novel, recalled
from weeks earlier, must follow one another immediately. The
result is a kind of disjointed dialogue that is effective in several
ways. It is often touchingly funny; characterization lies in the likenesses and the differences between the lines; in total, the conversation communicates the peculiar quality of the kitchen and the summer, the sense of a time and place cut off from both past and future.
In "Plato in Dixie," an article on McCullers and Capote (*Georgia
Review,* Summer 1958), Frank Baldanza discusses their novels
in terms of the Platonic symposium. His concern is more with substance than with structure, but, following his lead, it might be
useful to think of Frankie, Berenice, and John Henry as involved
in a parody symposium that not only explores its subjects but reveals its participants. There are earlier theatrical examples of
this kind of thing—one thinks of the philosophic discussions in
Chekhov's *Three Sisters*—but such a use of dialogue is not native
to American drama, for our discussions tell more often than they
reveal. A case might well be made for *The Member of the Wedding* as the most obvious structural innovation in the recent American theater, although Shimon Wincelberg's *Kataki* makes an
estimable bid for that honor.

The remarks in the paragraph above would be particularly appropriate if all of *The Member of the Wedding* were like the first
two acts, but there is a third act. Here, a jumble of action and violence serves to get the trio and the audience out of that kitchen,
helps Mrs. McCullers bring her play to an end. By the end of Act
I, Frankie has decided that she has found in the wedding of Jarvis
and Janice the thing to which she can belong: "I know that the
bride and my brother are the 'we' of me. So I'm going with them,
and joining with the wedding." This decision changes the tone of
Act II but not its structure; here the three characters carry on the
kind of conversation that we have seen in Act I, but filtered this
time through Frankie's expectation, not her distress. With Act III,
the form changes. After the first scene, in which, as John Henry
says, "They put old Frankie out of the wedding," the catastrophe
ceases to be child-size. Almost too quickly, Mrs. McCullers kills,

with meningitis, John Henry, and with suicide, Honey Camden, Berenice's foster brother who, in his restlessness, is specifically identified with Frankie. In the final scene, Frankie has found a friend and has moved beyond Berenice and the kitchen. It is never clear, in the play or in the novel, why violence and death are necessary for Frankie's passage into adolescence; the fall and the beginning of school would have broken open the ring around the kitchen of that summer and, if a more specific event were needed, the wedding could have served. It may be that the double death in the play (in the novel Honey ends on the road gang) is a kind of emotional mannerism necessary to the genre of Southern writing to which Mrs. McCullers contributes. It is possible that the novelist and playwright has something more in mind, wants to indicate that the climactic acts of so many novels and plays are not formative, are only incidents on the edge of a process that will take place without them. In defense of this explanation—and I am not certain that I want to defend it—one might quote a speech of Frankie's from the last scene in which the ego of the child still speaks through her, not yet able to cut her world to fit what society expects, still mixing the horrible and the trivial as if their only relevance was to her:

It's peculiar—the way it all happened so fast. First Honey caught and hanging himself in jail. Then later in that same week, John Henry died and then I met Mary. As the irony of fate would have it, we first got to know each other in front of the lipstick and cosmetics counter at Woolworth's. And it was the week of the fair.

Although the play uses so much of the novel—the dialogue is often lifted directly from the original—it is worth the trouble to look at some of the changes that Mrs. McCullers has made in doing the adaptation. The two most important have to do with Honey and with sex. Honey's difficulties, in the novel as in the play, are the result of his being a Negro unable to act the part that a small Southern town expects of him. In the novel, all this is implicit, indicated only in the moments in which Honey mockingly adopts the speech of an uneducated, uncle-tomming colored boy. The play is quite explicit, particularly in the scene in Act II in which Honey refuses to work for Mr. Addams and elicits the latter's outraged speech about "biggety, worthless niggers." As a result, a contributing theme to the work is momentarily blown up beyond the size that the play demands and, in any case, the specificity of such a scene works against the suggestivity of much of the dialogue. An incidental effect of this change is the alteration of the character of T. T. Williams. To serve as contrast to Honey, he has had to take a reduction in status from small businessman to handyman. There is a second, a structural reason for this demotion, for T. T. is used in Act III to help out at the wedding and to serve as one of the commentators on the off-stage action. The change in T. T. would be of little importance if he did not, a little disconcertingly, still retain some of the mannerisms that mark him in the novel as a middle-class businessman. The sex is a matter of elimination rather than expansion. The incident between Frankie and the soldier is, probably wisely, left out of the play. Its presence would have disrupted the play structurally and emotionally. To keep the soldier, Mrs. McCullers would have had to move the action out of the kitchen and she would have run the risk of localizing and vulgarizing Frankie's discontent. The author may have gone farther than necessary in protecting Frankie's innocence —transferring the business between her and Barney in the garage to another little girl—but Mrs. McCullers' instinct here is sound, for the conjunction of sex and adolescents on the stage is almost invariably cute, a quality that the novel avoids and one that might have been fatal to the mood of the play as a whole. Since the adaptation catches so clearly the feel of the original and even makes a virtue of its limitations—the necessary contraction of time and space—there is no condemnation intended in this lingering over minor changes.

Even more than *The Member of the Wedding*, Alfred Hayes's *The Girl on the Via Flaminia* is a play that comes in almost finished form from the novel that is its source. Hayes must have made the adaptation shortly after the novel was published in 1949 (unless, of course, the play came first) because, although the play was not produced in New York until 1954 (a successful off-Broadway production that moved uptown), it played in Los Angeles during the 1951–52 season. Almost all of the dialogue and all the key scenes in the play are also in the novel. The latter has a few additional scenes, those that could not be accommodated in the play's one—if multiple—set: the unsuccessful Sunday trip to Lake Bracciano, the depiction of the barracks, remembered episodes. In the barracks scene, there is a brief bit, no more than an image, that serves as a metaphor for the whole story: a drunken soldier, a farmer, comes in with an owl that he has captured for a pet, but he has broken its legs to keep it with him. Even without an owl as analogy, the play makes quite clear that among the circumstances that destroy Lisa is Robert's desire to have near him something he can pet, can touch, for comfort. The situation is a familiar-enough wartime arrangement in which an American soldier, who wants privacy as well as sex, the feeling of being settled, and an Italian girl, who wants to survive, agree to live together. The plot hinges on the fact that neither Robert nor Lisa is elementary enough to settle for what he calls "a deal, a simple deal" and that each makes demands beyond the business arrangement—for affection, for trust, for respect. They represent two different kinds of innocence caught at a time and place when innocence is impossible. His inability to understand why she cannot forget that she is defeated, and her inability to understand that, for all the deal, he is not demanding the rights of the conqueror, form the crippling wall through which their love must come. The breakthrough does not come until too late, when the situation that made their need and their difficulty destroys any possibility of their overcoming the one to assuage the other. The circumstances that lead to Lisa's arrest, her receiving the yellow card of the prostitute, and her suicide are, in terms of plotting, not accidental—they are carefully planted in Act I—but they are gratuitous in a much more basic way. The war and the dislocation that grew out of it are too strong to allow two individuals and their love to make an impression on it; the lovers can learn in time to cope with one another, but they are finally helpless against the impersonality that cannot distinguish between their love and the "simple deal" that they once thought to make.

The quality of the play lies in the scenes between Robert and Lisa; their first meeting in Act I (in Chapter III of the novel) is one of the best American-European encounters that I know. The societal situation that lies beyond them, that is implicit in their unhappy love affair, is occasionally done directly in the novel in which Hayes supplies paragraphs—intrusive sometimes—that interrupt the flow of a scene to take us into the city, the country, the war, the moment in history, the pity of it all. The force of the play proves that such paragraphs are unnecessary. In fact, the depiction of Lisa and Robert is so well done that one tends to forget

that there is a certain flatness in the rest of the characters—
Adele, the sympathetic landlady; Ugo, "more of an old man
than he is a Socialist"; Nina, who is efficiently what Lisa cannot
bring herself to be; Antonio, the embittered ex-officer—which
forces them to become simply part of, or commentators on, the circumstances against which the lovers struggle. Antonio is presented
more fully in the novel, a third kind of innocence violated, the
boy who was wounded for the glory of an Italy that has become a
rubbish heap on which one barters flesh for coffee and cigarettes;
this basic character remains in the play, but he does not, as he does
in the novel, share center stage with Lisa and Robert. The play is
the stronger for his having stepped aside. At least one of the minor
characters—the English soldier—is so corny a stereotype that he
is almost embarrassing to have to listen to, but even so obvious a
blemish as he becomes unimportant in the face of the fact that
The Girl on the Via Flaminia is our most effective play about the
American soldier overseas and that the novel on which it is based
is one of the most moving to come out of the war.

Despite the cheerful note on which this chapter is ending, the
recognition that there is quality in *The Member of the Wedding*
and *The Girl on the Via Flaminia,* the recent addiction to adaptation has produced no more than a handful of plays that are interesting in themselves and even fewer that communicate the feeling of the works on which they are based.

Let us beware of Poetry announced by placards.
—MICHEL DE GHELDERODE

"There can never be / a play worth listening to except in verse,"
says Hubert, the playwright in *Many Loves,* who has just finished
writing three plays in prose. There, in the speaker and the
spoken, stands the position of verse in the contemporary American theater—the yearning for it and the willingness, the eagerness
even, to do without it. As though the best modern drama were not
in prose, however poetic its conception, our theater has retained
a pious attitude about verse. Even the crassest Broadway businessman, the producer who would never touch a verse play, is likely
to make public obeisance to the form, public confessional of his
part in the guilt that accrued when Ibsen killed Shakespeare where
three roads meet. Our dramatists, particularly those who have a serious idea of their function as artist, are likely to make public
sacrifice, offering up a play in verse of sorts, to the possibility of
the higher drama. Much of Maxwell Anderson's career as a playwright consisted of that ritual. Barrett H. Clark, in *Maxwell Anderson, The Man and His Plays,* quotes the playwright as having once
said, "If we are going to have a great theater in this country somebody has to write verse, even if it is written badly." With no talent
for verse, he saw himself as that someone, although in the years
since the war, the vision was less clear, materialized just once in
Anne of the Thousand Days. The mantle was taken up, briefly
and unhappily, by N. Richard Nash in *See the Jaguar* and
Arthur Miller in *A View from the Bridge.* In both cases, what is

supposed to be ennobling turns out simply pretentious; Nash's play has been forgotten except by a few collectors of phenomena and Miller's has been rewritten with Alfieri's speeches now in prose.

Arch Oboler, with *Night of the Auk* (1956), might serve as a model for the playwright who hopes his language will lift his play out of the ordinary. A philosophical melodrama that creates some excitement as science fiction, Oboler's play presents the conflict among the crew of a space ship, returning to Earth after a first trip to the Moon, only to find that the words of triumph spoken by the megalomaniacal backer of the expedition have set off an atomic war. The play's point is that the guilt for the war lies not simply in the triggering egotism but in the attitudes of the scientist Bruner and the soldier Russell, one of whom withdrew from the world in horror, the other so much in it that he refused to see the implications behind the facts and tools with which he worked. The play ends on a note of muted affirmation, as two survivors, Bruner and the stereotyped young radio operator, who has earlier spoken the stock young man's speech about how the old men ruined the world, head for Earth or death and, if the first, a possibility of rebuilding. Out of what material? "Words, words, words," to borrow a phrase from the Dane who learned too late the difference between action and expression. Out of the holocaust, Bruner suggests, may come men with "idealism," "ever-renewing hope," and "true compassion"; earlier, he says to the self-absorbed Rohnen: "Give *yourself* a name! / Reach to heaven for it—in final understanding—in love!" In these phrases lies Oboler's failure as a poet and as a dramatist, even as a man who wants seriously to warn us that we stand on the edge of extinction. The mock-poet hunts the great themes with abstractions as ammunition; the poet creates an image that gives "true compassion" meaning without the need of the label. *Night of the Auk* has serious dramatic difficulties, as in the static discussion in Act III in which characters who have no validity beyond the ideational insist on defining one another, but for the most part the play's faults are verbal. The language that, in the Introduction to the published play, Oboler calls variously "free prose," "free verse," and "free-soaring prose" displays his almost perfect ear for cliché ("The masses eat, sleep, / Make their love, break wind, and die"; "We are all alone, / Each to himself. . . ."). Beyond this, Oboler indulges in a kind of cute wordplay that is sup-

posed to be enlivening, but which is as spiritless as it is confused
in its metaphor. For example, take Mac on the chances of making
radio contact:

> The microwaves are a magician's trick,
> But if the abracadabra saws the girl in half,
> We'll hear the rabbit through the trumpet!

Since Oboler is not and scarcely pretends to be a poet (thus
the equivocation about whether his language, free though it is, is
prose or verse) and since *Night of the Auk* was so resounding a
flop on Broadway, so long a look at what it does and does not do
is perhaps out of place in this chapter. Still, it does serve as an
example of what happens when a playwright who is really a prop-
agandist gets trapped by the lingering bromide that there is
something automatically elevating in verse. Most of the prose
playwrights who have taken to verse—as Anderson and Miller
indicate—display, if not the same, at least equivalent gauche-
ness.

As dramatists are attracted to verse, so poets are attracted to
drama. Although many contemporary poets have experimented
with the form, directly or through translation, very few have been
able to break through the wall (*of course I'm for verse in the
theater, but is the audience ready for it?*) that separates them from
the commercial theater. In the years since the war, only Archibald
MacLeish and Robinson Jeffers have invaded Broadway, and the
latter managed to do so only by pretending that he was Euripides
and by using Judith Anderson, who, as Medea, displayed the force
of a Sherman tank, to spearhead the attack. MacLeish, of course,
had some reputation as a playwright, the result of his radio plays
from the thirties, particularly *The Fall of the City*, long before
J. B. (1958) came to Broadway. For a time, he put verse drama
aside for, among other things, the prose plays of *The American
Story*, but he returned to verse in the early fifties. *The Trojan
Horse* (1952), "intended for reading without scenery or for radio,"
is the public quarrel about whether or not the giant horse should be
brought within the walls, an explanation, asked for at the opening,
of why "that town is fallen." The argument between Laocoön and
the demagogic Third Councillor is over whether the horse that is
the symbol of Troy is an image on a ring to be worshiped in pri-

vate or a massive public monument, whether, by extension, being a Trojan is a matter of private conviction or public declaration. As usual, as the myth tells us, the lip patriots win. MacLeish's concern in the play would appear to be contemporary. Written in a year in which public avowals of loyalty were considered not only desirable but necessary, the play records the kind of hysteria that builds around a symbol that outstrips reality; an irate woman, abusing The Girl, one of the play's two narrators, says, "Those who talk against the horse / Talk against Troy, against religion." Blind Man, the other narrator, comments ironically, "Some, / Deceived no doubt by their own senses, / Think Troy's image may conceal / Troy's enemies." The short play ends as the demagogue, demanding reverence for the image rather than the fact of Troy, oversees the dragging of the horse into the city, and Cassandra sings her song of destruction.

This Music Crept by Me upon the Waters (1953), performed on the BBC and at the Poets' Theatre in Cambridge, Massachusetts, is another one-act play, this one about contemporary characters in a contemporary setting. The action (the inaction, rather) takes place in the Antilles, where one group of people wait dinner on another. An intimation comes to both groups, induced by the magic of the moon, in which, for an instant, each person senses the possibility of living in the immediate moment, not in the expectation of something to come. All but two of the characters quickly return to normal or pretend to, but Elizabeth and Peter almost act in the spirit of the moment, almost leave together, when the momentary disappearance of Peter's wife (she has not fallen over the cliff; she is in the kitchen cooking potatoes) calls him back to the reality that, by comparison to the moment in the moon, is unreality. There are problems both dramatic and poetic with the play. The absence of characterization is a first drawback, but even if we were to accept the characters as contemporary types and not as flesh-and-blood people, if we were to be more interested in the idea of the play than in its relevance to human beings, the incident on which the play's meaning hangs is too banal. The play insists that the experience under the moon is an extraordinary one, and yet, for his one dramatic moment, for that action that must give living substance to what is still an abstraction, MacLeish can come up with nothing more inventive than the near love affair that turn-of-the-century sentimentalists (see Henry Arthur Jones's

Mrs. Dane's Defense) used in the duty-over-love plays. The failure of Elizabeth and Peter to act decisively is intended as an illustration of the play's single idea, that man can stand only the search for happiness, that the experience of it is too exquisite except for "a child or those like children." MacLeish's verse, for the most part an iambic line of varying length, like that in *J. B.*, does little to enrich the idea. There are a few metaphorical attempts to express it—the best finds that the child "Meeting happiness in a summer's door / Can take it by the hand and run with it"—but for the most part MacLeish depends on reiteration that, as in these lines of Elizabeth's about the natives of the island, reduces metaphysical conceit to verbal kidding around:

> *They* have no time to lose. They live
> Now. Not late, not soon, but now.
> They can't lose now. They live there.

Some of the same kind of wordplay is evident in *J. B.* and, on occasion, is clever beyond the demands of a particular scene, as when J. B., trying to comfort Sarah after the bomb has killed their last child, gets entangled in a passage in which words are introduced, then echoed, with meaning doubling back on itself:

> God is there too, in the desperation.
> I do not know why God should strike
> But God is what is stricken also:
> Life is what despairs in death
> And, desperate, is life still. . . .

It is possible that the simple iteration of words like *life* and *death, desperation* and *God,* might give to an audience who half heard this passage a sense that J. B. was speaking the right words to Sarah, but these lines do not offer the comfort (however ironical) of "The Lord giveth, the Lord taketh away." They argue a theological point and do so in a tone that approaches banter. The lines disappear in the Broadway version of the drama, part of a telescoping of action that removes the suggestion in the original that there are two bomb blasts, but even the Broadway J. B., who speaks more directly than his earlier self, is likely to slip into the same portentous play. More often, MacLeish gives these brightly clever lines to Nickles, where, flippant mask to his misery, they serve a useful dramatic purpose. They can be silly—"Those stars

that stare their stares at me— / Are those the staring stars I see"
—but then so can Nickles. Such verbal games are most effective in
the songs ("a kind of tuneless tune") that Nickles sings: "If God
is God He is not good, / If God is good He is not God"; "If God is
Will / And Will is well / Then what is ill? / God still? / Dew tell!"
Between book and Broadway, there was a thinning of the verse, a
movement toward spareness, directness, but in neither version is
there the pull of necessity; neither idea nor emotion depends on
the verse; it remains decoration.

Neither idea nor emotion—*J. B.* has difficulties on both these
grounds. The two versions of the play seem to be doing two different things, although MacLeish intends that J. B.'s affirmation in the
Broadway play be understood in the original. In both cases, he
wants to test a contemporary Job, who, racked by the biblical horrors brought up to date (atomic bomb, automobile accident, sex
crime), is torn between God and Satan, between the acceptance
of life without understanding and its rejection. Although the discontent in Mr. Zuss's lines indicates that J. B.'s capitulation to God
has not been complete, the burden of the original play is placed
on Sarah, who returns to J. B. with the message: "You wanted
justice and there was none— / Only love." It is as though Mac-
Leish were insisting, with Matthew Arnold, that the world has
"neither joy, nor love, nor light, / Nor certitude. nor peace, nor
help for pain," and, although he finds his comfort where Arnold
did, he cannot let his protagonist make the plea, "Ah, love, let us
be true / To one another!" It is Sarah who says, "Blow on the
coal of the heart." The three false comforters, who bring J. B.
the Marxist, the theological, and the psychological explanations
for his sufferings, are brushed aside by J. B. and his creator, but
MacLeish has not been able to avoid the greatest cliché of the fifties,
the conviction that love cures boils. Ironically, since Broadway is
the natural breeding ground for this bromide, it was Elia Kazan,
who had helped William Inge hammer the same message home in
The Dark at the Top of the Stairs, who pointed out the error of
MacLeish's ways. "The problem J. B. has been confronting has
nothing to do with love," he wrote to MacLeish, "so we cannot sat-
isfactorily solve it through love." * Even if love were the solution,
as Kazan points out, Sarah is hardly the character to express it:

* This and other Kazan remarks on the play are from the notebooks and
letters printed in *Esquire* (May 1959).

"It's even somehow smug and arrogant of her to give an answer to a man who, after all, is *the one* who's been through the struggle." Not only does Sarah take the spotlight from J. B. in delivering her inappropriate message of love, but the message itself has no connection with her as a character; we see her wifely virtues in the Thanksgiving Day dinner scene (she is something of a nag) and her sorrow in later scenes, but we are never (in either version of the play) aware that she loves J. B., and so she comes in at the end as though she had picked up the declaration, with the forsythia twig, in the wings as she steps on stage.

Sensibly, in his revision for Broadway, MacLeish shifts the conclusion of the play to J. B. After the biblical exchange with the Distant Voice, J. B. mutters again the fine-sounding words that are meaningless in his mouth (a recognition scene that was not completely clear in the production), and then he rejects the direct appeals of both Nickles and Zuss, "Neither the / Yes in ignorance . . . / the No in spite. . . ." The love creeps back at the end, although it is J. B. this time who urges Sarah to blow on the coal of the heart, but it is now secondary to the more specific acceptance: "We *are* and that is all our answer. / We are and what we are can suffer." Kazan, who grew up professionally in the Group Theatre, sees J. B. as an image of mid-century America and the play as a question, "Will America be able to take it when it comes?" It is a fair conception of the play and an indication of what is wrong with it. MacLeish intends not only to ask the question but to answer it, to hold out a positive image of man, but the story he chooses defeats him. "He can't act and you know it," Mr. Zuss says of J. B., meaning that he is a person and not a performer, but the line, inadvertently, says more than that. J. B. is only acted upon; he is as inoperative as any of Samuel Beckett's characters. Suffering may be action to that other Becket, T. S. Eliot's, but a playwright who wants to celebrate man has to create a character who embodies positiveness. J. B.'s final words are neither the end of the action nor the end of the argument. They are empty words, like those of Nickles and Zuss. The play resembles a sermon, an uplifting message in an ugly world, which may be why it was treated with reverence by so many reviewers.

The difficulty in accepting the play's conclusion as anything other than a fine sentiment may be aggravated by the hero's failure to exist in human terms. He is conceived as the type of the

American businessman, but his suffering, which should bring out the man within the type, only changes his category—from businessman to victim. It might be possible to put flesh on either of these types and to elicit audience sympathy for them, but *J. B.* never succeeds in doing that. "I've just got to get someone who can help me make the audience feel the human core of the play," Kazan wrote to Richard Rodgers, as though he suspected that the "human core" was too well hidden in what MacLeish had written. It is. J. B. and his family remain laboratory specimens, experimented upon by forces beyond them. Kazan's theatrical trickery, which, as usual, was amusing in its own way, hardly helped. In the production, the audience first saw J. B. at a Thanksgiving dinner that, because of the pink-and-white children that the casting director had found, was pure Norman Rockwell. A satirical point was made, but J. B., who is supposed to be a sympathetic not a satirical character, was marked from that moment on. The scenes in which disaster is announced, in which J. B. might, in happy circumstances, free himself of satire and stereotype, are flat and uninteresting as MacLeish presents them. Kazan tried to pump them full of life by injections of his familiar nervous artificiality—stridency of music, movement, and light—but all that he succeeded in doing was to distract attention from what the play as a whole was trying to do and to lose a small point MacLeish is making about the ways (accidentally, venally, impersonally) bad news is broken.

In demanding that the audience suffer for and with a hero who cannot command its sympathy, MacLeish pulls attention away from the frame of the play, the re-enactment of the quarrel of God and Satan by the two broken-down actors. In doing so, he lessens the emphasis on the one character in the play—the whining, acid Nickles—who takes on flesh. In the Broadway revision, at Kazan's suggestion apparently, the two actors take part in the J. B. scenes, a device that not only avoids the first-this-then-that split of the original but also gives a picture of a Nickles who is more involved in J. B.'s state of mind than is the hero himself. Despite the vividness of Nickles as a character and the appeal of the play within a play, there are disquieting things about the frame action. The play-acting, the assumption of masks, the equation of costumes and vestments, all these suggest that God and Satan are man made and that J. B.'s struggle is with a projection of his own longing for an ordering force outside himself. Yet the Distant Voice, who speaks God's lines and disconcerts the players, is part of the action. Sarah assures us at the end: "The candles in churches are out. / The lights have gone out in the sky." Is the voice, then, a prompter, as Nickles calls him, and, as such, is he deity or stage device? Granted that *J. B.* is nonrealistic theater, still poetic license does not preclude a certain logic of device and symbol. The presence of the voice suggests either that MacLeish is making a theological point that calls the end of the play in doubt, or that, delighted with the possibilities of the theater, he is treating it as a toy. With his frame story, then, as with his development both of character and idea, MacLeish in *J. B.* gives the impression that he is at once too serious and too frivolous to write a substantial play.

Robinson Jeffers' reputation as a playwright rests on only two plays, his adaptation of *Medea,* which Judith Anderson did on Broadway in 1947, and *The Cretan Woman* (1954), which had a successful off-Broadway run. Shortly before the opening of *Medea,* Michael Myerberg offered his own dramatic version of Jeffers' *Dear Judas,* a production that, even with Lehman Engel and Johann Sebastian Bach collaborating on the music, made little impression on Broadway. The Jeffers *Medea*—judging by other translations of the play—follows closely the pattern of Euripides: the establishing of Medea's jealousy and the cause of it (Jason's having left her to marry Creon's daughter, the princess of Corinth), the development of her plan for vengeance in the course of confrontations with the other principals, and the final disaster. Jeffers' conception of Medea is somewhat different from that of Euripides. In the original, jealousy has taught Medea cunning; she tacks to the wind of each visitor, flattering and playing upon their weaknesses and vanities, until she gains time to commit her murders. Jeffers attempts to use the same kind of scene, but he conceives his Medea as so violent that her contempt and anger cannot mask themselves. From her first cry, "Death" (in Euripides there is simply an unworded, off-stage moan), she is presented with such intensity that dissimulation is impossible for her. In the scene with Creon, she snarls so between her attempts at sweetness that his decision to give her a few hours' grace is inconceivable. If I seem to be taking exception to a scene in a poetic, pseudo-Greek play on realistic grounds, there is justice in my doubts, for much that Jeffers does in *Medea* has the look of latent realism about it.

Granted that he has always been attracted to figures, particularly women, whose passions drive them wildly, still it is impossible to escape the suspicion that part of the force with which he pushes his Medea comes from a need to make the audience understand how she can destroy her own children. Similarly, he adds a scene in which Jason plays with the two boys, an affectionate moment that makes the audience suspect that Medea's ghastly crime is not done in a vacuum, that the obviously self-absorbed organization man that both Jeffers and Euripides make of Jason is, in the former version, capable of grief. Not only does Medea's passion throw doubt on the credibility of some of the scenes in which she must appear, but it cripples the development of the play. Since Jeffers introduces Medea at the height of her anger and since he cannot allow it to diminish, he has a character who has reached her emotional destination before the journey begins. Ironically, it was this dramatic defect that accounted for the play's success; the part demands a tour-de-force performance, and Miss Anderson, in providing it, made an occasion of the play.*

Despite the added intensity, Jeffers' Medea is basically the character out of Euripides, the woman possessed by an irrational force. Still, the play is more than a portrayal of a destructive love. Working from the fact that Medea is an outsider from Colchis, considered a barbarian by sophisticated Corinth, Jeffers manages an implicit social commentary, one that displays his own distaste with a contemporary society that he finds both too effete and too commercial. For the most part, this theme is implicit—for instance, in the suggestion that Jason's behavior toward Medea is the result of overcivilization, the manipulation of passion for gain. Sometimes, however, Jeffers, like his heroine, cannot hold himself in. A disgruntled voice from Carmel seems to be speaking through Medea when she says to the inquisitive Corinthian women: "I understand well enough / That nothing is ever private in a Greek city; whoever withholds anything / Is thought sullen or proud—(*With irony*) undemocratic / I think you call it." All of the Jeffers plays, like their Greek originals, have voices speaking rationally, sanely,

* Harold Clurman was one of the few reviewers who attacked Miss Anderson's performance. *Lies Like Truth* (pp. 88–89) has a wonderfully vivid description of the actress on stage, but, although there is justice in Clurman's criticism, Jeffers' demands on the actress playing Medea are partly responsible for the faults in Miss Anderson's performance.

asking the protagonists to avoid, as Aegisthus says in *The Tower Beyond Tragedy,* the "mere madness" that "Lies over the wall of too-much." In *Medea,* however, Jeffers seems to dismiss the speakers for moderation as casually as Medea does. The play ends not in horror but in triumph; the heroine's final words—"Now I go forth / Under the cold eyes of heaven—those weakness-despising stars:—not me they scorn"—seem less the extreme possession of a woman driven beyond Aegisthus' wall than the cold statement of a person who has acted nobly in a corrupt world, who has put passion before interest. This celebration of Medea is, at least by implication, a social, perhaps even a political, statement.

The verse of *Medea* is the familiar long, irregular Jeffers line, swollen by the crowding in of phrase after phrase. It is always difficult for me to understand why Jeffers chooses to break a line where he does. A speech of the tutor's, picked at random, which begins in midline,

> Old servant of my lady, why do you
> stand out here, keeping watch in solitude
> With those grim eyes?

might as easily be

> Old servant of my lady, why do you stand out here,
> Keeping watch in solitude with those grim eyes?

In either case the actor will be forced to phrase according to sense (the longest pause will follow "lady"); in neither case, nor in much of Jeffers' work, do line divisions lead the speaker either to the rhythm or the sense of the line. A further drawback to Jeffers as a writer of dramatic verse is that his line, built as it is of a great number of phrases, is often aurally clear piece by piece without being comprehensible as a whole.* The use of metaphor in *Medea* is also a problem. The choice of metaphor should, ideally, reflect

---

* The reading of the verse is as much at fault here as the writing. Verse is ordinarily read one of two ways on the contemporary American stage. Either the actor decides to go for sense and reads it simply as prose, or else he embraces the idea of verse as verse and develops a reverent intonation that robs it of meaning. The Jeffers heroines are a special case since it is possible for them to substitute grand passion for both verse and meaning. When I saw *The Cretan Woman,* for instance, I understood very little of what Phaedra (Jacqueline Brooks) was saying, but I did know (it was a small theater) that she was upset about something.

the work in some way—the theme, the tone—and it is clear that
Jeffers' concern with the violent, the natural, in Medea has led him
to the animal world for his descriptive epithets. The effect, however, edges on the ludicrous. Creon is a *dog;* Jason is a *dog;* Medea
refuses to be "a bitch with pups" although, according to the Nurse,
she is "like a fierce hound at fault." Still, she insists on being something wilder, "some yellow-eyed beast" who would lie on "the
hounds' bodies"; she is frequently a bird, a falcon by choice; in
one extended passage the First Woman reminds her that the
generic *beast* and the specific *lioness, wolf-bitch,* and *eagle* do
not kill their own young, which places her in a category beyond
animal imagery. There are also a great many metaphors, both
natural and inanimate, that serve to separate Medea from the
human world; *stone* appears frequently. At one point the Nurse
says, "She is like a stone on the shore / Or a wave of the sea,"
meaning simply that she will not listen, but conjuring up a picture
of a Medea who is at once still and in constant motion. There are
other metaphors that are so standard ("Hate is a bottomless cup")
that the force has gone out of them, and there are direct ("dusty
death") and analogous ("loathing is all") Shakespearean echoes.
Medea finally comes to seem as poetically uninteresting as it is
dramatically insufficient and ideationally annoying.

In 1950, Judith Anderson appeared again as a Jeffers heroine,
as Clytemnestra in a brief run of the poet's adaptation of his early
poem *The Tower Beyond Tragedy.* The adaptation consists of
little more than the invention of characters to speak the narrative
lines of the poem which is written, for the most part, in dialogue.
Jeffers' treatment of the *Oresteia* is unusual for the intensity of
the incest between Electra and Orestes and for the strip tease that
Clytemnestra does to distract the soldiers; I understand that this
last was somewhat muted in production. *Tower* is typically Jeffers
in Cassandra's prophetic speeches about contemporary society
and in the hero's withdrawal into some community with nature
that rejects the human. Since the play is really the 1927 poem, it
belongs in an examination of recent American drama only because its production is a testimonial to the impression *Medea* had
made on Broadway three years earlier.

The Cretan Woman is the best of the Jeffers plays. Using Euripides only for the basic story, Jeffers writes scenes of confrontation that the Greek play avoids—Phaedra's attempt to seduce

Hippolytus, her accusation scene with Theseus, his stabbing of Hippolytus. Although *The Cretan Woman* belongs to Phaedra as much as the earlier play does to Medea, Jeffers does not force the other characters to give way to a conception of the heroine that necessarily belittles her antagonists. Here, the three principals are trapped in a series of circumstances, initiated by Phaedra's love-hate for Hippolytus and fed by the psychological characteristics of all three. By making Hippolytus a homosexual, Jeffers does lose some of the restraint-passion contrast that would be provided by a chaste Hippolytus alongside a demanding Phaedra; still, within the terms of his conception, the Hippolytus of this play functions well. In only one case does Jeffers not succeed with a leading character, and that is at the end when the lament of Theseus seems to ask us to accept him as a great man fallen; we have seen him only as a blunt but confused old soldier, and there is nothing more than pathos in his realization that he has killed the only two people he loves. The tragic doings at Troezene are put in an unusual light by the Chorus of begging women who, even though they are forced to become part of the action, remain aloof from it: "If this great house ever falls—I wish it no evil—I wish my boy had the looting of it." It is possible that Jeffers intends that the beggars, whom hunger keeps from the artificialities of the court (much is made of how the Nurse has tried to tempt the love-sick Phaedra with delicacies), should contribute to the theme of the play. Certainly, the point is that Phaedra, who is from Crete, who thinks of herself as a civilized woman "in exile here / Among savages: the fierce little cut-throat tribes of Greece," is torn by a passion that strips away her veneer of civilization. The same force destroys both Hippolytus, who thinks that "we control our own wills and acts / For good or evil," and Theseus, whose career of killing (Phaedra calls him "an old gray wolf") has been masked in policy. The burden of his last speech is his regret and wonder that he failed to act in a civilized manner, with understanding rather than by instinct. Aphrodite has the last word, and she directs it toward the audience, the men of "future days," warning them that, however certain they become of themselves and their control over the world, "There is always a lion just beyond the firelight."

The theme, then, is a familiar one with Jeffers. The verse, too, has the mannerisms that we have come to expect of him. There are, as usual, the animal metaphors, although not so many as there are in Medea. Here, the metaphors that get out of hand are those, so plentiful in *The Tower Beyond Tragedy*, in which sex and death are joined; Phaedra's scene with Hippolytus is very reminiscent of the last one between Electra and Orestes in *Tower*. It is the tone rather than the controlling image (the equation of penis with sword or spear is an ancient literary usage) that gives the following speech its peculiar quality:

You have a good lance there:
That boar-spear with the great metal head, your toy that you play
   with: will you do me a kindness, fellow?
You say you are not unfriendly to me— Stick it into me!

The bluntness becomes ludicrous like the line in *Tower*, accidentally funny because of the sexual imagery that surrounds it, in which Agamemnon describes Cassandra as "A piece of our goods out of the snatch of Asia. . . ." *The Cretan Woman* also has its share of poetic clichés; for example, on at least two occasions Jeffers trots out the moth and the flame. Despite a few incongruities, the verse is more direct than that in *Medea*, and the play as a whole is much more successful in letting the action carry the theme.

The only other poet to attract any attention in the postwar American theater is William Carlos Williams, whose *Many Loves* was added to the off-Broadway repertory of The Living Theatre in 1959, and his play is a twenty-year-old experiment which has more prose than verse in it; come to think of it, the verse that it does have is pretty much prose. The play's organization is thematic although there is a thin plot that holds the three disconnected episodes together. A young playwright, whose ambition is to write a new verse for the theater, has written three short prose plays about love, which we see in rehearsal; in and around these plays, we get a fourth play, in verse, which deals with the triangle formed by Hubert (the playwright), Peter (his lover and financial backer), and Alise (his fiancée and leading actress). Peter's remark about the setting, "This is the usual avant-garde décor, / isn't it, Hubert?," might be extended to the whole play. Vaguely Pirandellian, the play fails to make any illusionary capital on the device of trying to connect the audience directly with what is going on, even though there are a few portentous remarks in Williams' stage directions about "an illusion of the theater more profound than an audience is ever allowed to see." Since this device has been a theatrical commonplace at least since *Hellzapoppin!*, probably since *The Knight of the Burning Pestle,* it demands something more than the vague self-mockery of *Many Loves* to give it meaning. The play has as little to offer in terms of subject as it does in structure. There are varieties of love, but what then? Except for the woman's monologue in the third episode, in which talk is a kind of sex, and some brief funny business about an hermaphroditic rabbit in the first episode, there is very little of interest either in Hubert's story or his plays.

It is a little difficult with *Many Loves* to decide how much of it is supposed to be a joke. The Living Theatre production tended to play the whole thing as parody, but then that organization always plays as though it were kidding itself and its material. When one reads *Many Loves,* the episodes appear to be dully straight and only the frame story (the counterplay, Williams calls it) has the look of a joke about it. The episodes are really no problem because, except for the bits mentioned above, they are too flat to be either funny or serious; but the frame story is another matter. All the business about Hubert's artistic pretensions ("suggestive of the Greek theater," he says of the second episode) might be simply satirical if it were not that, under the skirl of his insistence, we get Williams' concern with the way poetry operates in a prose world. The play's subtitle, "Trial Horse No. 1," forces a comparison between Williams and Hubert, who also calls what he is doing "a trial-horse." Although Williams may share Hubert's concern with a verse "more suited to ourselves, / our times," and although he may put Hubert's story into "modern verse," I prefer to think that Hubert is a comic character. In any case, the verse that tells his story is, except for a few mock-rhetorical passages, indistinguishable from prose, and the other plays in Williams' recent collection (*Many Loves and Other Plays*)—except for the early libretto, *The First President* (1936) and the songs in *Tituba's Children* (1950), the book for a comic opera that never materialized—are in prose.

The treatment of the love theme in *Many Loves* is interesting in relation to the other Williams plays, for he seems to be preoccupied with the idea of love as an ambiguous relationship in which the lover both embraces and tries to escape his situation. This is done either specifically ("I got to get out of this place") or implicitly (all of Clara's speeches in the third episode are

about being trapped) in the episodes and is echoed in the counterplay where Peter insists that Hubert cannot love because "He has /
only one ambition—to get out!" and that writing is his exit. The
conflict between the writing and the loving, the desire to get out
and the longing to stay, is seen again in the literary doctor in *A
Dream of Love,* which made a brief off-Broadway appearance in
1949; but the point in that play is that the two impulses are not
mutually exclusive, that they live together in a state of tension.
This idea of love is seen again in the heroine of *The Cure,* which
Williams began writing in 1952 and finished in 1960 for the pub-
lication of the collected plays, but, for Connie, it is nursing not
writing that is her identification and her exit. Primarily, *The
Cure* is the presentation of a relationship, engendered by accident,
in which the two principals manage to touch needs in one another,
so that Connie becomes mother-nurse-lover to Prospero and he
child-patient-lover to her in a delicate balance that will be broken
either by sex (which does not happen) or by violence and departure (which does). It is somewhat misleading to dwell on the
ideas that one glimpses in *A Dream of Love* and *The Cure* because the ideas that, in the abstract, might attract attention are
pretty much buried in the dullness, the deadness of the plays.

The Poets' Theatre in Cambridge has encouraged a few other
poets to write for the theater—Richard Eberhart, for instance—
and some of the off-Broadway playwrights have worked in verse.
The most interesting recent development in the ambiguous relationship between the poets and the theater is that a number of
good poets have translated classic dramatists. Edwin Honig, for
instance, has put out a volume of Calderón, and Robert Lowell
and Richard Wilbur have done versions, respectively, of Racine's
Phaedra and Molière's *Le Misanthrope.* These translations will
find their audience mostly among readers, I suspect, although the
more imaginative university theaters will probably put them to
use. It is extremely doubtful that they will receive major productions.* At the moment Archibald MacLeish, Robinson Jeffers,

* It would be sacrilege, I suppose, to suggest that the American Shakespeare Festival at Stratford, Connecticut, would do greater service both
to the theater and to audiences by a good production of one of these
plays than by another one of their Shakespeare-in-disguise offerings—
Richard II set in Greenwich Village in the twenties, or whatever the current project is.

and William Carlos Williams are the only poets to have received a congenial welcome from the commercial theater, on or off Broadway. Productions of their work, particularly that of MacLeish and Jeffers, may have helped to still the guilt feelings that a prose theatrical world has when it thinks of the verse of the past, but none of their plays has convinced the innocent (those of us who think that what Ibsen committed was not murder but a mercy killing) that verse is an enrichment—not an affectation—of the stage.

The novelists have done little better than the poets in the American theater. Their infrequent excursions into production have, as often as not, been as unsuccessful as the attempts that playwrights—Arthur Miller and Tennessee Williams are examples—have made at the novel. There are exceptions, of course, as my chapter on adaptation indicates. A few novelists, reworking material for the stage, have written interesting plays—Truman Capote, Alfred Hayes, Carson McCullers. Although Mrs. McCullers made a successful adaptation of *The Member of the Wedding,* her one direct attempt at a play, *The Square Root of Wonderful* (1957), was disastrous. The play tells how Phillip (that dramatically dullest of all human characters—the writer who cannot write), a death figure, tries to dominate Mollie (the square root of wonderful, according to John), a life figure, using first his weakness and then his suicide as weapons; he fails. So, too, does the play, because neither Phillip nor Mollie—nor any character in the play—has the breath of life. The play is momentarily interesting at the beginning because of the oblique dialogue, suggestivity instead of statement, but the attractive oddness quickly passes, leaving only an occasional good line and sad echoes here and there of an earlier McCullers.

Two novelists, John Steinbeck and William Faulkner, produced works in the early fifties that were part novel and part play. Steinbeck calls *Burning Bright* (1950) a "play-novelette," which "is a play that is easy to read or a short novel that can be played simply by lifting out the dialogue." The exact generic designation need worry no one, for *Burning Bright,* on stage and between the covers of the book, might be accurately described as pretentious nonsense. The plot is that of a realistic family melodrama—not unlike *They Knew What They Wanted*—in which Mordeen takes a lover who can give her the child that her sterile husband wants so badly and in which Joe Saul (the husband) must first learn and then accept what has happened. In an attempt to give his sentimental story universal significance, Steinbeck makes the action continuous but changes the setting act by act, making the characters circus performers first, then farmers, finally seamen; their trades—we are supposed to believe—are inborn, not learned. As though this were not bad enough, Steinbeck invents the most improbable language for his characters to speak, as though the studied awkwardness of their lines might enhance the mythic concept: "But you are right, Friend Ed. I've got a rustle in me. It's a little itching rustle under my skin." Friend Ed, who is always called that, just as Joe Saul is always Joe Saul, uses words like "wife-loss" and "friend-right" that make one wait for him to come up with the correct label for what is going on on stage: *writer-crime.*

Requiem for a Nun in its original form, William Faulkner explains in a note at the beginning of the play version (1959), "was written not to be a play, but as what seemed to me the best way to tell the story in a novel." The novel is divided into three acts, each preceded by a long, highly rhetorical prose section that tells the history and the spiritual and social importance of the setting (the courthouse, the capitol, the jail) of the act that follows; I assume that these are supposed to throw the story of Nancy and Temple into a particular perspective, but their story is so impossible that I have never been able to contemplate long the significance of the prose passages. The play within the novel and the play outside it (of which Ruth Ford is listed as co-author) tell how the endless confession of Temple before the governor (ostensibly a plea for the life of Nancy, the maid who murdered Temple's child) and the example of Nancy herself teach Temple Faulkner's familiar redemption-through-suffering lesson. "The salvation of the world is in man's suffering. Is that it?" Gavin Stevens asks, and Nancy seems to agree. Not satisfied with the novel's extremely artificial working out of this idea, the authors try, in the stage version of the play, to find a dramatic action that will somehow illustrate the spiritual occurrence. They hit, unhappily, on the marriage of Gowan and Temple, which they endanger and then save, turning what I take to be a kind of dark night of the soul into an awkward and undramatic version of *Come Back, Little Sheba.* The deadliness of the dialogue (Temple's confession, in both versions, is certainly one of the most boring passages in contemporary literature) and the endless messing about with props ("For Christ's sake, do something," says Gowan. "Don't just stand there") only emphasize that Faulkner is never interested in any of his characters as other than figures in his thematic pattern. In *William Faulkner, From Jefferson to the World,* Hyatt H. Waggoner suggests, "The dramatic sections of *Requiem* are almost a parody, by intention perhaps a distillation, of the dramatic style of modern fiction. . . ." If so, the style has significance only within the novel, in the lyrical-factual, Faulkner-Hemingway split that Waggoner finds there; if he is right, what we get on stage is part of a literary joke torn out of context. In any case, what we get is a dramatic ritual that lacks human, if not spiritual, content.

Both Robert Penn Warren and Conrad Aiken have tried adaptations of their fiction, the first of the novel *All the King's Men* (1959), the second of the short story *Mr. Arcularis* (1957). The Warren play, produced off Broadway, is a revision of an earlier adaptation presented by Erwin Piscator at the New School Dramatic Workshop in 1948; the Aiken play is his attempt to do what he could not do in 1946 when he acted as play doctor to the English production of Diana Hamilton's adaptation of the story.* Warren's play is a skeletonized version of the novel, a nonrealistic work in which the incidents in Willie Stark's life are acted in brief scenes or narrated by those people, living and dead, who have played a part in his story. The effectiveness of the play lies in the deep involvement of all of the characters with Willie, the dramatic equivalent of the narrator's search, in the novel, for his own identity in Willie. Despite the abstract form of the play, the stepping in and out of scenes, the interconnection of past and present, the play is moving because everyone is intent on making his position clear, in creating a Willie who deserves the love or hate (or combination of the two) that he feels toward the politician. The play contains so many references to material treated fully in the novel that it is doubtful that it can stand completely alone; still the necessary cutting away is momentarily refreshing because it frees the observer of the uncomfortable feeling that I, for one, experience in the presence of the novel, a sense of a magnificent character trapped in the self-pity and convoluted style of the nar-

* Aiken's Introduction to the published play gives a good-natured but graphic account of the English equivalent of the Broadway tryout, rewrite process described so bitterly by William Gibson and Meyer Levin.

rator. Of course, Warren means the novel to be as much Jack Burden's story as it is Willie Stark's; the play belongs to Willie. *Mr.
Arcularis* is several different plays at once, but is most successful
at the simplest level, that of supernatural melodrama. As a psychological study—Mr. Arcularis' need to free himself of his guilt
about his dead mother—it is ineffective, and the grand abstractions on the meaning of life and death that sit at ease in the story
are completely unconvincing in the mouths of the characters. The
play is also burdened by a great deal of naturalistic to-do—details,
for instance, about who is drinking what—which makes the play
seem at times like an adaptation by George Kelly of an H. P. Love-
craft tale.

Although Edmund Wilson has written verse and fiction, he is
neither a poet nor a novelist; still, since he is our most important
literary critic and reviewer, mention of his play, *The Little Blue
Light* (1950), belongs in this chapter. The play, which was produced first at the Brattle Theatre in Cambridge and then for a
very brief run in New York, is a fascinating and finally self-defeating confusion; it mixes science fiction with allegorical morality
play, satirical comedy with psychological drama. The conception
of the play is more interesting than its realization. The three chief
characters are an editor who puts out a magazine that sounds
rather like the *Reader's Digest,** an effete writer of horror stories,
and a wife who changes poses act by act, is variously a career girl,
a woman about town, a *femme fatale,* but, as The Gardener says,
will "neither carry children nor carry the banner of freedom."
These three, somewhat corrupted versions of truth, art, and wom-
anhood, are the only allies of The Gardener in the struggle of
individualism against dictatorial power, represented here by the
Luke Teniakis Relief Bureau, an organization that has freed itself
of the allusionary masks of other power organizations and operates without ideology, without slogans, without publicity. The
three principals are destroyed when their resentments and recriminations set off the little blue light, a science-fiction machine that
is activated by the play of human feelings. The Gardener gets the
last word: "but I shall always be with you—somewhere, at some
man's side!" In the course of the play, he has spoken the bromides

* Ironically, one of his articles, "Can the Apache Be Saved from Extinction?," suggests an accidental anticipation of Wilson's later preoccupation
with the Iroquois.

of the Christian-Judaic tradition ("Just a few old platitudes!") in Italian, Irish, Scotch, and Russian accents, and at the end he becomes that tradition as the Wandering Jew. The difficulty with the play is that the ideational structure is much more interesting than the characters who inhabit it. Even though it is their human foibles, their irrationalities, that must destroy them, the characters never become believably human. One reason is that Wilson wants to make fun of the psychological clichés even while he provides the psychological groundwork that will finally set off the blue light. In fact, the satire in the play is so widespread, nibbling at so many contemporary attitudes, that it comes close to devouring the play as well. The play vacillates between bluntly funny lines and simple iterations of Wilson's prejudices, between melodramatic suspense (the scene with the light) and dull exposition. *The Little Blue Light* is more ambitious than and quite unlike most American plays, but without quite the style and wit to carry it off.

Since this chapter is pretty much limited to those plays that have reached production, it cannot indicate the extent to which poets and novelists eye the stage. On the evidence given here, few of the dramatic attempts of literary outsiders have been aesthetically successful and still fewer have been commercially successful. In the absence of a tradition of intellectual drama that, as in France, assumes that the literary man will write plays as naturally as he does novels and essays, it is unlikely that our poets and novelists will figure largely in any summary of American drama.

10 OFF-BROADWAY

I know darn well I can do without Broadway,
Can Broadway do without me?
—JIMMY DURANTE

There was a time when the words *off-Broadway theater* called up
a picture of a dedicated group, held together by aesthetic or ideational concerns, determined to change the state of the theater or
the state of the world. Today, the words suggest a producing unit
with a much smaller investment than Broadway demands, with a
small house to play in, with special Equity contracts, with a play
that is likely to be as safe as it is experimental. There are few off-
Broadway producing groups with any continuity—Circle in the
Square is an exception—and still fewer with a sense of mission—
The Living Theatre is a vocal exception. The early postwar years
in the history of off-Broadway theater are littered with almost forgotten names—New Stages, Abbe Practical Workshop, On Stage
—groups that did impressive work, producing new plays or reviv-
ing modern classics. By the fifties, the whole pattern of off-Broadway production had changed. It is not that more plays were
produced but that more of them were professional, in a technical
if not always in an aesthetic sense; it became important to the
off-Broadway producer to see that his cast had enough Equity
players in it to claim, under union rules, that it was an Equity company, for that designation meant, among other things, a review in
the New York *Times*. There has probably never been a theatrical
group anywhere in the world that has been indifferent to success
in some form or other, but the kind of success that off-Broadway
reached for in the fifties changed its character greatly. In the first

half of that decade an off-Broadway success was the play that moved uptown, that found an audience on Broadway after having been well received at its initial presentation; the New Stages production of Jean-Paul Sartre's *The Respectful Prostitute* and the Experimental Theatre production of Jan de Hartog's *Skipper Next to God* set the pattern early when, during the theatrical season of 1947–48, both made the jump to Broadway. In the second half of the last decade, the off-Broadway producer began to look for analogous rather than actual Broadway success. No one wanted to move any longer; the ideal was to stay, profitably, in one spot as long as possible. Theatrical historians who want to put a finger on the exact point of change had best look to the theatrical season of 1953–54. In that season several off-Broadway productions— Alfred Hayes's *The Girl on the Via Flaminia* from the Circle in the Square, Calder Willingham's *End As a Man* from the Theatre de Lys, the Jerome Moross-John Latouche musical *The Golden Apple* from the Phoenix Theatre—moved to Broadway and died lingering deaths in theaters too big for them; at the same time, the Marc Blitzstein version of the Bertolt Brecht-Kurt Weill *The Threepenny Opera* opened at the Theatre de Lys for a run that lasted well into the seventh year. It was at this moment that off-Broadway as we know it, a replica in small of the Broadway hit-or-flop mentality, was born. If there has been a theatrical revolution in the last fifteen years, ironically, it has not overthrown Broadway; it has re-created off-Broadway, changed it from a state of mind to a producing apparatus so like Broadway that only the technicians who draw up contracts can find the line between them.

At the same time, the attitude of theater professionals toward off-Broadway has changed. Traditionally, even while it served as a protest against the theatrical status quo, off-Broadway was an accidental training ground for Broadway. Out of its ferment came new ideas about writing and production; out of its activity came new playwrights, new performers, new directors. By the early fifties, the protest had diminished; off-Broadway was consciously a showcase. It is still a stepping stone to Broadway and Hollywood, but today the steps go in both directions; with the publicity and prestige that accompany the off-Broadway hit, it is now possible, even profitable, for performers and directors with Broadway reputations to work off Broadway. The same producers operate off and on Broadway, choosing their theater according to the intimacy required of the play at hand or an idea of the size of its potential audience.

Now that Broadway and off-Broadway appear to operate through the same economic (and artistic) motivation, it has become difficult to recognize an off-Broadway play. Two English plays, produced during the 1960–61 season, will illustrate the confusion. Agatha Christie's *The Mousetrap,* which ran almost ten years in the West End, and Brendan Behan's *The Hostage,* a product of Joan Littlewood's Theatre Workshop, had respectable runs in New York (192 performances for Christie, 127 for Behan), but it was the very conventional *The Mousetrap* that played off Broadway. Still there are ascertainable differences between the two sides of New York theater. Revivals, anathemas on Broadway, are a staple off Broadway, particularly productions of the modern classics (Ibsen, Strindberg, Shaw, O'Casey) and of more recent plays that failed on Broadway. In the last few years, however, the off-Broadway originals have outnumbered the revivals, although many of the new plays disappear within a week or two after they open. The increase in new production, even if an original does not necessarily mean originality, is all to the good because the more plays produced the better the chance of finding a gifted new playwright. Even though off-Broadway is more willing to take a chance on the unusual without the European seal of approval that Broadway demands, the bulk of off-Broadway production resembles the Broadway offerings. There are plays in the best realistic tradition and plays that experiment with form (off-Broadway is likely to be more self-conscious about its experimentation); there are heavy dramas and light comedies; there are musicals; there are adaptations.

There are plays by playwrights whose names are at home on Broadway. Maxwell Anderson's last play, *The Golden Six* (1958), for instance, followed Tennessee Williams' *Suddenly Last Summer* into the York Theatre. Other playwrights, like Alfred Hayes, Victor Wolfson, and Robert Ardrey, men who had never been as successful on Broadway as Anderson and Williams, came to off-Broadway earlier. Within a single season (1953–54), the Circle in the Square did Wolfson's *American Gothic* and Hayes's *The Girl on the Via Flaminia,* both adaptations from the playwrights' own novels. Ardrey's *Sing Me No Lullaby* (1954) played at the

Phoenix Theatre the next season. One of the reasons why Ardrey's play had to find a home off Broadway is that it is political, and political plays were not widely welcome in the early fifties. *Sing Me No Lullaby* describes (partly in the present, partly by flashback) how Ben Collinger, who escaped into the comfort of private success after his first political failure, decides to return to political life, to stand for the legislature in his Illinois district. His decision grows out of his horror that a friend of his student days, an eminent mathematician, should be so hounded by his political past (he was a Communist in the thirties) that he believes that he must leave the country, accept asylum in China. Ardrey's message is quite explicit; Ben says of his friend, "He has always been wrong. He was born believing that it's one side or the other. And he's being punished now by a nation that has come to agree with him." Ben, presumably, will do his part to insure an America that does not demand political conformity. At times *Sing Me No Lullaby* is openly melodramatic (the business with the radio at the end of Act I); at others, it is very like an old-fashioned thesis play. It is occasionally quite effective dramatically (the FBI interrogation scene), but most of the time it is the play's surprising and genuine concern with political ideas and their consequences that gives it what strength it has.

It is easier to understand just what Ardrey is doing in *Sing Me No Lullaby* after one has taken a look at his most recent play, *Shadow of Heroes* (1958), a play about the abortive Hungarian revolution of 1956, which was first acted in London. Although individual scenes in *Shadow* are written in the realistic tradition, the play is basically nonrealistic in its setting (packing boxes that can be shifted on stage to form rooms and to furnish them) and its structure (a chronicle of events held together by a narrator, representing a Hungarian writer, who occasionally steps into a scene to play a bit part). "This play is a document," the narrator says; more accurately it is a fictionalized documentary, a splicing together of historical material with Ardrey's version of the three-cornered friendship of Julia and Laszlo Rajk and Janos Kadar. Kadar is presented as an undisciplined Communist who learns to accept Rajk's view of the party ("I have no sympathies nor hungers above the needs of the Party") although the acceptance leads to his betrayal of both Laszlo and Julia. Ardrey's purpose requires a sentimentalization of both Kadar and Rajk (the implications of his having been Minister of Interior after 1946 are scarcely hinted), and the concentration on the struggle with the party places the action in a vacuum that fails to notice that the Smallholders' party and the Social Democrats took part in the government right after the war. Although the wash of details—names and dates and complicated maneuvers—is fascinating in a way, it finally floods Ardrey's primary intention: to use a personal story to illustrate an abstract idea (that communism, in Julia's words, spoiled "for all eternity more good men than you can mention"). *Sing Me No Lullaby,* it becomes clear, is built on the same pattern. Here the playwright uses fictional instead of fictionalized real characters, but they are stereotypical, so representative of a generation that they become almost documentary; and once again the personal story is used to exemplify an idea, this time, that America is only as strong as the unwillingness of good men to leave the country in the hands of fanatics of any persuasion. Both plays reflect the author's personal indignation, his willingness to sacrifice the play to the immediacy of the situation about which he is concerned, and, as a result, both of them—despite the contemporaneity of their subject matter—seem like anachronisms in the fifties.

If Ardrey seems to be trying to bring a thirties attitude toward the theater up to date ideationally, another and occasionally successful Broadway writer, Ben Hecht, in his invasion of off-Broadway with *Winkelberg* (1958), offers a nostalgic testimonial to the literary style of his youth, the clever saccharinity that characterized his part in the "Chicago Renaissance." Hecht means that the audience should accept the poet in his play, supposedly a portrait of Maxwell Bodenheim, as not only a drunken, antisocial lecher, but as a free spirit, a true poet as well. Unfortunately, Hecht conveys too firmly that Winkelberg is nasty, stupid, and egotistical, a sharp-tongued slob with a heart of gold (he is against being mean to people), but all that he can offer by way of poetic evidence is the kind of Hechtian rhetoric ("I was once a poet whose heart sang out of an ash can") that he forced on his proletarian poet in *Specter of the Rose* (1947), a pretentious art film for which he did the script. Although almost everything about the play is stridently old-fashioned—his bums and whores, for instance, have a pre-Nelson Algren innocence—ironically its structure is quite contemporary; using the sentimental supernaturalism of the turn of the century, Hecht sends the dead poet back to earth in search of the

"sweet dream" of his life, a device that allows him to use brief
scenes, to telescope time, and to abstract character (one actor
plays "The Enemy" in five incarnations) in a way that suggests
the combination of techniques from television and the twenties
avant-garde that are currently popular off Broadway.

So far as adaptations are concerned, off-Broadway is much more
sparing in the production of them than Broadway is. There have
been the Hayes and Wolfson self-adaptations mentioned above
and Robert Penn Warren's version of his *All the King's Men*. The
two most successful off-Broadway adaptations have been Arnold
Perl's *The World of Sholom Aleichem* (1953), the first off-Broadway production to send a company on the road, and Marjorie
Barkentin's *Ulysses in Nighttown*. *The World of Sholom Aleichem*
is a group of short plays based on Yiddish stories, only one
of which, despite the title, has Sholom Aleichem as its source. This
is *The High School,* a one-act play in many scenes, in which a cau-
tious Jewish businessman, pushed by the demands of his wife and
the longing of his son, finds himself in reluctant opposition to the
quota system in Russian schools and finds, to his surprise, that he
almost likes his new attitude. What the play presents is the tentative
collapse of the *shtetl* mentality, the making the best of an unpleasant situation (the story uses, almost like a refrain, variations on the
line, "A Jew is used to such treatment"), with only a wry and self-
mocking humor as comfort and defense. A good example of *shtetl*
comedy and the best of *The World* is *Bontche Schweig,* based on
an I. L. Peretz story, in which the title character, a born victim,
passes unprotesting through a life of beggary and pain, to receive,
as reward, anything in Paradise that he wants. Speaking at last
(Perl provides Bontche with a few lines, but suggests that he can—
and he should—be played in pantomime except for his request),
Bontche says, "Well, in that case—if it's true—could I perhaps
have every day, please—a hot roll with fresh butter?" The greatest difference between Perl and Peretz is that the play ends with
the angelic reaction to Bontche's request, the shamed silence, and
the story goes beyond the silence to the "bitter laugh" of the pros-
ecuting angel. Perl shows the same sentimentalizing tendency
elsewhere in his adaptations, in *The High School,* for instance,
where he makes the two boys, the Jew and the Gentile, good
friends. Sentimentality is an ingredient of most Yiddish literature,
certainly of the kind of story Perl has used, but Sholom Aleichem

and I. L. Peretz are much tougher than their adapter. The other play, *A Tale of Chelm,* is nothing more than an anecdote, decorated with jokes and sayings out of the folk tradition; much of their point depends on the audience's knowing that Chelm is the mythical town of fools, a fact that the narrator establishes, just as he translates the Yiddish words (*forspeiss, melamed*) after he has used them. This character, whom Perl uses to tie his plays together, is called Mendele, the Book Seller, presumably after the Mendele Mocher Sforim, whom Irving Howe and Eliezer Greenberg, in their *A Treasury of Yiddish Stories,* call "the patriarch of Yiddish literature." Perl is less successful in his later adaptations from Yiddish—*Tevya and His Daughters* (1957), based on the Sholom Aleichem stories. To judge by *Tevya and the First Daughter,* published in *The Best Short Plays of 1959–1960,* the play exhibits a sense of disconnection, the result perhaps of its having come from a group of stories. More important, Tevya fails to come through as anything more vital than a stereotype, and the lines seem often to have the right kind of wit but the wrong rhythm: "Since he has been in business forty-one years—he has amassed one thing: old age." I cannot pretend to be an expert on the English-Yiddish rhythm, but I cannot help feeling that "amassed" is a bad choice of word and that the sentence should begin with "forty-one years."

The problem of getting the correct rhythm is important, too, in another off-Broadway adaptation, the short play (1953) that Ellen Violett and Lisbeth Blake made from Gertrude Stein's *Brewsie and Willie.* In her short novel (a long conversation really) Stein transmutes the speech of the American soldier into her own prose style, recognizing in the process that her use of repetition and interruption provides an imitation (the oblique accuracy of the impressionist) of the aimlessness and earnestness of GI talk. Her adapters do not try to reproduce the Stein speech, although many of the actual lines are hers; they try instead, and with some success, to hold onto the desultory flow of the Stein conversation, but to free the individual lines of repeated phrases. The adapters manage to convey the sense of confusion and concern that Stein's characters display and to suggest, with Stein, that "we can't help ourselves if we do mind, and we do mind, we'd like the answer now yes we would. . . ." The play's Willie remains Stein's blunt and reluctant listener, and Brewsie is the same ruminative talker, although the adapters miss the comic edge of much of his chatter. The play does say what the novel says ("Yes, said Brewsie, do be anxious"), but it does so finally through falsification, by falling back on a sentimental stage trick. Brewsie somehow becomes a prophet for certain when, right at the end, we discover that he is an amputee.

Adaptation plays its part in the off-Broadway musical, too, but that form is still so obviously involved in the process of self-discovery that it can fit no neat description. There are, for example, the plays with music, like Langston Hughes's *Simply Heavenly* (1957) and William Gibson's *Dinny and the Witches* (1959), in which the songs are less important than the book. Hughes's comedy is based on his Simple stories, a fact that probably accounts for the irrelevant bits, like Simple's long speech about how in the next war he will be a general with white Mississippi soldiers under his command. The play is another of those neighborhood-bar comedies, like *Happy Birthday,* which collect a handful of standard types and set them talking; the bar scenes are held together by a fairly ordinary complications-of-love plot. *Dinny and the Witches,* according to its subtitle, "a frolic on grave matters," is an often inventive, occasionally funny, play about the acceptance of death as a fact of life and the consolations of love; it suggests Saroyan to some extent, not only in its elaborate eccentricity but in its finally enervating sense of its own significance. At the other extreme is the Moross-Latouche *The Golden Apple,* a carefully conceived musical in which book, music, dance, and sets were to work together to make their effects, an extension of the idea of the integrated show that Latouche and Moross had approached (with the help of three choreographers) in *Ballet Ballads* (1948). The musical transfers bits of the *Iliad* and the *Odyssey* to the state of Washington (to be near Mount Olympus) at the turn of the twentieth century, but except for a few recherché jokes (doing Scylla and Charybdis as Gallagher and Sheean) there is little to be gained by the move. The period does allow the composer and the author to make use of popular theater (the cakewalk, period melodrama) in music and scene, and there is a suggestion—though never a consistent one—that Latouche wants to make a serious satirical point about the changing values in American society. Although *The Golden Apple* as a whole never quite succeeds, it has incidental

pleasures (and had still more of them in production) that make
it an attractive pleasure.

Only within the last year or two has the musical begun really
to prosper off Broadway and, for the most part, as the popular
shows indicate, composers and writers are not nearly as ambitious
as Moross and Latouche were. The shows tend to work for small
effects, and sometimes they are happy ones. If Mary Rodgers'
Once upon a Mattress (1959) is an extremely fragile joke based
on an old fairy tale, Rick Besoyan's *Little Mary Sunshine* (1959)
is an affectionate parody of the kind of operetta that Jeanette Mac-
Donald and Nelson Eddy used to do in the movies; it succeeds
largely because the best numbers (for instance, "Do You Ever
Dream of Vienna?") come so close to working straight that the
show becomes a joke on the audience's own sentimental indulgence
as much as on the genre that is being kidded. The Harvey Schmidt-
Tom Jones *The Fantasticks* (1960) is one of the best of the off-
Broadway musicals. Based on Edmond Rostand's *Les Roman-
esques,* the musical turns the bravo of the French play into a kind
of theatrical major-domo who leads the audience into the world of
romantic make-believe. Schmidt and Jones are occasionally more
inventive than Rostand; their number "Round and Round" dis-
enchants The Girl much more effectively than does Straforel's
account of their future together in the original play. If the adapters
know how to discard, they also know how to borrow; some of the
best lines in the lyric to "It Depends on What You Pay" come directly from the bravo's long speech on rape, in the George Flem-
ing translation which is also called *The Fantasticks.* Invention or
adaptation, the musical is successfully both sentimental and satirical about its young lovers, and it makes as much ado about allusion
in and out of the theater as the most insistent Pirandello production would and is a great deal more casual about it.

Although a good musical or adaptation is welcome wherever one
finds it and although it is comforting to know that Broadway playwrights can find off-Broadway homes for works toward which
Broadway is not congenial, the legacy of expectation left us by the
Provincetown Playhouse and Eugene O'Neill demands that we
look to off-Broadway for new playwrights. We shall not find very
many. In the last year or two, as the number of original plays has

grown off Broadway, the white-hope hunters, those who keep looking for the man who will bring something fresh into the American
theater, have grown more wary. Ten years ago they embraced
more quickly, although their arms, like as not, closed on empty
space. Take Richard Harrity. When his *Hope Is the Thing with
Feathers* opened with two other one-acters, by Horton Foote and
E. P. Conkle, in 1948, one of a series of productions that the Experimental Theatre did under the auspices of the American National Theatre and Academy, it was unusual enough to create a
small stir. *Hope,* which was printed in *Theatre Arts* in 1945, is a
sentimental depression play, ten years out of its time, a gathering
of bums in Central Park trying and failing to catch a duck; most
of the characters are stereotypes, but the dialogue is efficiently
done and, at one point, when an hysterical ex-boxer is calmed by
a trick, Harrity displays a sound sense of the way conventional
characterization can be used for dramatic effect. Not long after
the play opened, Eddie Dowling took it, with two other Harrity
one-acters (*Home Life of a Buffalo,* a saccharine show-business
comedy, and *Gone Tomorrow,* a trying American variation on
the standard Irish kitchen chat) to Broadway where the production and, apparently, Harrity's playwrighting career foun-
dered. It was almost ten years before another playwright, James
Lee, was mistakenly welcomed into the creative fraternity with
the production of his *Career* (1957). An account of an actor's
struggle for success, the play is completely conventional in plot,
characterization, and sentiment (when Sam reaches stardom after
a twenty-five-year struggle, his agent asks "Was it worth it?"
and he answers, "Yes. Yes, it was worth it"); it is unusual only in
that it makes extensive use of brief scenes, which suggests that it
may have been written originally for television. Lee, unlike Harrity,
was commercially successful (the play became a big-budget
movie), but then, by 1957, off-Broadway had settled comfortably into its position as feeder and fed in the complex of the entertainment industry. Lee was fed in, too, and has, so far, not come
out with another play.

There is more than one kind of off-Broadway success, of
course; there is the coterie theater as well as the hopefully popular.
Within the last few years, old coterie producers—The Living
Theatre, for instance—have learned that it is possible to do what
they want and still touch a nerve in the general theatergoing pub-

lic. Between Harrity and Lee, there appeared a group of playwrights, more ambitious and more pretentious than they are,
whose work was little known to the general public, but which attracted, as the director Herbert Machiz says in his Introduction to a
collection of their plays, "respectful attention from those interested in what still must be called, however hackneyed the terms,
'highbrow' or *avant garde.*' " They were produced by a somewhat amorphous group called the Artists' Theatre, which operated
between 1953 and 1956, during which time it did sixteen original
plays; a subscription theater, scarcely advertised at all, restricting
itself to a few performances of each play, it understandably collapsed from lack of financial support. Seven of the sixteen plays
have now been published, three in a collection, *Playbook,* which
New Directions put out in 1956, and four more in the recent Grove
paperback, *Artists' Theatre, Four Plays*; although the plays are
not as bad as Machiz, in his enthusiasm, makes them sound, they
are plainly not the seedbed of a vital new American drama.

My reaction against the plays as a whole may be an unfortunate
one, for the best of them, Robert Hivnor's *The Ticklish Acrobat*
(1954), is an imaginative and remarkably good-humored comedy
about a Dalmatian village that withstands the invasion of an
American archeologist, just as it has absorbed so many other in-
vasions over the years. The ritual of waking up, seen at the beginning of Act I and again, clumsily, as a result of the first stages of
the dig at the beginning of the second scene, turns out, in the last
act, when the town has been stripped to its Greek days, to be a pattern that depends on the layout of the old temple. The setting and
the impetus to action give a perfect chance for the kind of facile
American-baiting that has been fashionable in some intellectual
circles in the last few years, but Hivnor happily avoids that cliché.
Although there is the suggestion of health in the continuity of the
life of the village, the villagers come in for as much kidding as the
Americans do; although there is harshness in the conception of the
archeologist as a man who would purify through destruction, he is
not a villain. The last exchange in the play is really a comment on
all the characters, including the speakers. As the Americans leave,
the mayor asks Dr. Sufi, the mystic, "Tell me, Doctor, are good
people always ridiculous?" and gets for answer: "Yes, it's a law.
Let us hope the converse is also true." The play is full of amusing
invention, characters such as Baba, the tattooed woman whose

body displays the history of art ("There is no art without suffering"), and situations, such as the festival in which Joe, the American suitor of the ticklish acrobat, wearing his baseball uniform,
acts the scapegoat. Occasionally the play seems too diffuse, unsure of its main line of action or willing to interrupt it for some
incidental business, but this is a minor flaw in a play that is both
visually and verbally funny and one which manages to be affectionate about its characters without blunting its satirical point.
Hivnor has had no play in New York since *The Ticklish Acrobat,*
but recently *The Noble Savage* (No. 3) published the Prologue
to *The Assault on Charles Sumner*; too much of a fragment to
tell us much about the whole, the Prologue suggests that Hivnor's
new work is not going to be a conventional history play.

Lionel Abel, who has translated Jean-Paul Sartre, writes a kind
of philosophical comedy in the French manner, using, as the
French often do, received myths (Greek, biblical) as the basis of
his ruminations. *The Death of Odysseus* (1953) is a one-act play
in which the titular hero, after an attempt to escape by manipulation, goes out to face certain death at the hands of Telegonous,
his son with Circe. The point, in so far as I see one, is that
Odysseus is a man of wit who must finally face the complications
of his cleverness, must learn that the philosophy of survival is no
preparation for death. *Absalom* (1956), in three acts, is an extremely confusing, often tedious, play that seems to be making an
existential point, for Absalom, despite David's insistence that "You
cannot choose to be chosen," gets his place in the tragedy by demanding it of God. In his most recent play, *The Pretender* (1959),
Abel tries the same genre in contemporary dress by examining a
rape that never took place, using as his central figure the supposedly wronged husband, a Negro novelist who, confusing himself with a Calderón hero, wants the vengeance that his honor
demands. The difficulty with Abel is that, despite occasionally
clever lines, he has very little wit; his prose style is heavy where
the genre demands polish, even elegance; he seems unwilling to
use the devices of melodrama and farce that Sartre has always used
to animate his philosophical discussion and, in the absence of such
devices, Abel's failure to create characters becomes a fatal weakness in his plays.

Other Artists' Theatre playwrights include James Merrill, John
Ashbery, and Frank O'Hara, all of whom lapse into verse occa-

sionally. Merrill's *The Bait* (1953) is a one-acter in which, in the present and in flashback, the heroine and her brother represent the life that avoids "the serious human thing / The earnest painful thing" and in which they are the bait that catches the new fiancé and the ex-husband, who, in their turn, are the bait tempting the brother and sister who must continue moving to keep off the hook of human connection. There are occasional good lines that bring one to attention ("Look at those pigeons, how can they bear it?— eating out of people's hands"), but for the most part the play is less absorbing than the idea is complicated. In *The Immortal Husband* (1955), the same author tells again the story of Aurora and Tithonous, making the inevitable point that life has meaning only in the face of mortality. The play is neatly made, the metaphors introduced and sustained, the philosophy planted and exposed periodically; and there is a kind of surface charm that, on at least one occasion—Tithonous' senile reminiscence in the last act— becomes quite effective. Merrill, however, seems not only to want to expound the life-in-death idea, but to move us by and for Tithonous and Aurora and, on that level, the play never succeeds. John Ashbery's *The Heroes* (1953) mixes the Greek heroes in a context that is part drawing-room comedy, part English murder mystery; the author is often funny after the manner of a bright undergraduate who has been exposed to Homer for the first time. Frank O'Hara's *Try! Try!* (1953) is a pointless one-acter that brings a soldier home to his wife and her lover; its language is supposed to sustain it, but as John says in the play, speaking of Jack as a letter writer, "He has a funny style, doesn't he? It seems like a pose."

Since 1959, three young playwrights have appeared off Broadway in whom, if popularity and publicity are a criterion, the future of the American theater is presumed to lie. They are Jack Gelber, Edward Albee, and Jack Richardson. Gelber, whose *The Connection* opened in 1959, was the first to be produced in New York. His play collects a group of dope addicts—an incipient psychopath, an intellectual, a folk figure, a kind of homosexual house mother, enough musicians to form a combo—and lets them spend the first act waiting for their connection and the second act getting high on the stuff he brings. Gelber's attitude toward his addicts is neither romantic (in the beat manner) nor reforming (as in *A Hatful of Rain*). Although his presentation is realistic, he intends the whole

situation to be metaphorical; he repeatedly makes the point that
we are all involved with some kind of connection, looking for our
salvation wherever we can. He does this most specifically and most
ineffectively, in Sam's direct statement:

I used to think that the people who walk the streets, the people who
work every day, the people who worry so much about the next dollar,
the next new coat, the chlorophyll addicts, the aspirin addicts, the
vitamin addicts, those people are hooked worse than me.

If too many of the connections are only verbal, Gelber does at least
try to make them dramatically. He does this best in the scene that
Solly shares with Sister Salvation in which the salvation that they
(and all of us, if we accept Gelber's view of the world) seek, the
temporary alleviation of the pain of living, is presented in the vernacular of revivalist religion. When he tries to show the same thing
in reverse, by revealing that Sister Salvation is a dope addict, he
weakens the metaphorical use of addiction and slips into the sentimentality that so often accompanies realistic treatments of the
seamier side of life; at the moment of discovery, Sister Salvation
might almost be a friend of Winkelberg. Presumably, the hooking
of Jaybird (the playwright) and 2nd Photographer is another attempt to emphasize the community of connection, but it is a
device that suffers the same drawbacks as the revelation about
Sister Salvation.

The dramatic situation that becomes a metaphor for something
greater—the one that Uncle Vanya finds himself in, for instance
—ordinarily works two ways; it has an intrinsic fascination and, in
suggesting something outside itself, becomes the type of a human
situation. Although Gelber wants that kind of significance in *The
Connection,* he never quite achieves it because, instead of letting
his gathering of junkies reach, by implication, out into the world,
he imposes the meaning on them. Even a group as special as the
one he presents might work beyond itself, but his insistence tends
to emphasize that they are different. Nor are they very interesting.
Gelber's decision not to romanticize his characters, admirable
in the abstract, catches him in an unfortunate trap. He assures us
that a heroin party is as dull as a coffee break in an insurance building, but his depiction of that assurance ends finally in a dull play.
Although Gelber gives his characters occasional sharp and funny
lines, they too quickly reveal themselves as stock figures and, by

the second act, it is difficult to pay much attention to them; not even the introduction of Cowboy and Sister Salvation can quite enliven the gathering. It is possible that my initial interest was not in character at all but in structure. Henry Hewes describes (in *The Best Plays of 1959–1960*) the form of the play as having been borrowed from jazz, "where the individual soloists take turns improvising upon an agreed-upon theme. . . ." This borrowing is underlined by the presence of the jazz musicians on stage and the musical breaks that they put between the blocks of dialogue. Unfortunately, the spoken solos are not virtuoso, so the form becomes as enervating as a jazz set in which the soloists are simply going through the motions. Finally the form breaks down, for Leach's overdose and the action (desertion or lifesaving) that follows it put us back in an older conventional theater, and all Jaybird's muttered thoughts about the play cannot mask the melodrama.

In discussing the structure of *The Connection,* I have neglected to mention the gimmick frame that surrounds it. The audience is supposed to believe that the action involving the junkies is actually taking place, that real addicts have been hired by the play's producer to improvise from the playwright's outline; two photographers are supposedly making a film of the proceedings. When the playwright and one of the photographers take dope, the Pirandellian line between the real and the imaginary is supposedly crossed. That line, however, is not drawn between the addicts and the producing group, it lies between the audience and all the actors. It is Gelber's intention to pull the audience across that line, to convince them that they are actively involved in what goes on, that they cannot be simply spectators; he tries to do this verbally in the producer's opening speech and dramatically by sending Sam (the most colorful of the addicts) to panhandle in the lobby between acts. This theatrical gimcrackery is not only inappropriate to both the tone and the theme of the main business in Gelber's play, it is generally ineffective as well. Nothing is so unconvincing in the theater (at least to me) as an attempt on the part of the characters to convince the audience that it is part of the theatrical allusion; an audience may be as imaginary as any other group of people, but it does not exist at the same level of imagination as the created character.

These remarks are not meant to champion the realistic play over the nonrealistic play, for whether the fourth wall is up or

down the audience, in any kind of conventional theatrical situation, is not part of the action. The current off-Broadway bromide,
which Gelber has accepted and which is implicit in a play like
William Carlos Williams' *Many Loves,* is that the conventional situation can be altered by a statement from the management. This
attitude is nowhere more evident than in Paul Goodman's *Faustina*
(1952), at the end of which the heroine speaks directly to the
audience ("Out there they want to see and hear, but not take part,
to be safe from taking part, frozen in immobility") and then steps
through the fourth wall and exits through the audience. "But breaking through the proscenium at the end," says Goodman, "vividly
means to me the breaking through into life, out of art." He apparently intends to suggest by this that the presence of the actress in
the audience gives a new order of reality to what has happened
on stage, but what he is really saying is that the play is over. A
play, depending on its effectiveness and the receptivity of the individual, becomes a part of the observer's life, but Goodman
and Gelber, as though distrusting their plays, demand the reverse,
that the observer become a part of the play. What they seem to
want is a kind of intellectual *Sing Along with Mitch.* Only one
play in recent years that I can think of has provided this kind
of audience-actor identity and that, ironically, never pretends to
art. Lee Maryat's *Dope* (1952) is a propaganda play, written in
a cleaned-up version of the speech of its audience, warning of the
consequences of the first shot. Sponsored by the East Harlem Prot-
estant Parish, the play was given by amateur actors on vacant lots
in that area and, according to Miss Lee (in *The Best Short Plays of
1952–1953*), the audience became one with the action, "taking
various parts and acting them out along with the actors, chiming
in on lines, shouting questions, answering." It is possible that Gelber and Goodman have been looking in the wrong place (the
theater with a box office) and at the wrong man (the playgoer
whose attendance implies an acceptance of theatrical artifice) if
they really want to break down the distance between actor and
audience.

Between 1958 and 1960, Edward Albee wrote four short
plays—*The Zoo Story, The Death of Bessie Smith, The Sandbox,*
and *The American Dream*—all of which had New York productions in 1960 or 1961. The first of these, which found its
way to American production after it had been both published

and produced in Germany, is probably the best; certainly it illustrates Albee's wit and his talent for dialogue, and in Jerry's story
of how he tried to tame his landlady's dog it shows a macabre comic
invention that is only lamely evident in the rest of the plays. *The
Zoo Story* tells how the very conventional Peter (tweeds, horn-
rimmed glasses, pipe, publishing, wife, daughters, cats, para-
keets, East Seventies) is accosted on a Sunday afternoon in Central
Park by the very conventional unconventional Jerry (single, fur-
nished room, West Side walk-up); for about half the play, Jerry
needles Peter about his life, making the kind of comic points that
any good revue skit would, but the tone shifts midway into metaphysical inchoateness as Jerry introduces the McCullers-Capote
concept of love. He finally forces Peter to kill him, presumably because his need to make contact, about which he talks so much, can
only be filled through death, and Peter apparently can only be a
man worth the contact when the act of murder assures Jerry that
he is "not really a vegetable," but "an animal." Even if we assume
that Albee seriously believes all this (go pee under the streetlamp,
we used to say when we were seven, and prove that you're a man),
it is a heavy weight for so fragile a play to bear. *The Death of
Bessie Smith* is unlike the other Albee pieces. Set in 1937, it describes, in realistic terms, how Bessie, who never appears, dies because she cannot get admission to the white hospitals in Memphis;
the play's real concern is to show that all the hospital personnel,
white and Negro, are caught, like Bessie, in the trap of the human
condition, that all, in the words of the bigoted nurse, are "tired
of my skin . . . I WANT OUT!"

In *The Sandbox*, Albee uses the bromidic comments of Mommy
and Daddy and the tough, wry remarks of Grandma, who is in the
sandbox, to satirize the conventional attitudes toward death, the
polite cover for the desire to be rid of the old and the dependent.
The same characters and the same situation are used in *The
American Dream*, although in the latter Albee has something
more on his mind. For one thing, Mommy and Daddy are obvious representatives of the typical American couple, the dominating female and the emasculated male, a use of stereotypes that
gives double meaning to Mommy's "You can't get satisfaction;
just try." The main business of the play, however, is the introduction of the handsome young man who is only a façade; "*you* are
the American Dream," says Grandma, meaning the surface, imply-

ing the absence of substance. The defining metaphor is the mutilation of the child that Mommy and Daddy adopted, smothered by affection and by restriction, wounded in the struggle between the parents; with each of its losses (heart, eyes, sex, hands, guts, spine, life), its twin suffered a comparable loss ("I no longer have the capacity to feel anything") and has become the emotionless young man we see. "Now this is a great deal more like it," says Mommy, accepting the young man as the child (the dream) that they want. The central image does its work well enough, makes Albee's point, but it does break the tone of the piece because it necessitates the young man's long speech about his losses that is played sentimentally (at least it was in the New York production). Sentimental lapses seem to be typical of Albee although he tries to mask them in a kind of wryness, apparent in Grandma's description of the contents of her boxes:

They don't have much in them . . . some old letters, a couple of regrets . . . Pekinese . . . blind at that . . . the television . . . my Sunday teeth . . . eighty-six years of living . . . some sounds . . . a few images, a little garbled by now. . . .

This kind of speech and a cliché like the death figure in *The Sandbox* give an old-fashioned air to a playwright who is usually intent on being up-to-date, verbally, structurally, ideationally. He is happiest in those speeches in *The American Dream* in which, like Samuel Beckett, he writes a variant of an ordinary line, one that asks the audience to take the words literally: "She's just a dreadful woman, but she *is* chairman of our woman's club, so naturally I'm terribly fond of her." The difficulty with Albee's work, so far as I am concerned, is that no one of his plays, not even the very short *The Sandbox,* can hold my attention; the reason is that they communicate only a pretense at seriousness. In a bad-tempered Preface to the published *Dream,* the playwright insists, for some incredible reason, that a critic has no business considering the matter of a play. If it is any comfort, my criticism is not that his matter is only the fashionable baiting of our supposedly conformist society, but that, after a closer look, the matter turns out to be simply mannerism.

Jack Richardson's *The Prodigal* (1960) is a retelling of the *Oresteia,* in which, as in the plays of Giraudoux and Sartre on which it is modeled, the costumes do not disguise the modernity of the characters. Richardson's Orestes chooses not to be involved, prefers the cynical pose or the simple life to a commitment that, whether one accepts Agamemnon's heroic view of man or Aegisthus' antiheroic one, leads to blood and discontent. In the end, Orestes returns ("I will do so under protest") to avenge his father. He does not choose his fate, as Sartre's Orestes did, but it is forced on him by the sentimental expectations of those who take part, as actors and as audience, in his story. In the last scene, Orestes and Cassandra, looking out at the sea, imagine an audience where the actual audience is, and the prophetess says, "It might be that this new gathering will demand something better for your consent than edgeworn ideals and dramatic necessity." The idea is an interesting one; the play often is not. Richardson's characters are only animated abstractions, perambulating points of view, and the argument itself has not the style and wit to overcome the shortcomings in characterization. The flaws in *The Prodigal,* however, are not fatal, as they are in Richardson's more recent play, *Gallows Humor* (1961). Two short plays joined by a central theme, *Humor* describes, first, a condemned man being entertained in his cell by a state-provided woman, and, then, the executioner trying and failing to leave his wife, his job, his boredom. The best thing about the play is its conception, the idea of the condemned as free and the executioner as condemned, but the play never lives up to its initial invention. Its simple point—that life is too regimented and planned, that surprise and excitement have gone out of living—is smothered in repetition that would be bearable only if the lines were much funnier than they are. One odd thing about *Gallows Humor* is that its metaphor for the imaginative life is murder (the condemned man's crime, the executioner's attempt to strangle his wife), just as Albee's is in *The Zoo Story;* if the Prologue in Richardson's play is accurate, if it is difficult to tell the dead from the living today, then, ironically, the playwright, the champion of life, is involved in the confusion that he is attacking. This small and apparently accidental irony does little real harm to *Gallows Humor;* the play is crippled by Richardson's habit of belaboring the obvious. His shortcomings as a playwright are implicit in the Introduction to the published *Humor,* in which it takes him two and a half pages to say that he thinks comedy is serious.

Although Gelber, Albee, and Richardson are the off-Broadway playwrights who have received the most attention recently, two other dramatists—Arnold Weinstein and Arthur L. Kopit—seem to hold out as much, perhaps more, hope for new vitality in American drama. Weinstein's *Red Eye of Love* (1961), one of the funniest plays of the last few years, is a kind of Horatio Alger story in reverse, like Nathanael West's *A Cool Million,* in which the hero is continually defeated and the heroine is on more than friendly terms with the villain. It is plain from the manner of the play (that of the silent-film melodrama) and a great number of incidental references that Weinstein has not gone to the Alger literature for a success story to turn inside out, but to the movies, that allied carrier of the American optimism myth. Although *Red Eye* gives evidence of a genuine talent for satirical invention —the hero's desire to invent a doll that will get sick and die, the meat department store—Weinstein has not written a tightly organized satire; although many of his barbs are pointed, he shoots at random, offering the pleasure of the shot instead of the certainty of a hit on target. On the evidence of this one play, Weinstein displays a lively imagination and a sense of what is genuinely funny.

The same qualities are apparent in Arthur L. Kopit's *Oh Dad, Poor Dad, Mamma's Hung You in the Closet and I'm Feelin' So Sad* (1960), which was not produced in New York until after it had been performed in Cambridge, Massachusetts, and, unsuccessfully, in London. *Oh Dad,* as the play's subtitle indicates ("A Pseudoclassical Tragifarce in a Bastard French Tradition"), is modeled on Ionesco, but Kopit has domesticated the form by using a familiar American theme. The two personalities of the heroine, Madame Rosepettle, display the emasculating American female in two of her guises: the dominating mother in the scenes with Jonathan and the frigid sex image, the iron maiden as coquette, in the scene with the Commodore. It was a combination of the two, apparently, that turned Mr. Rosepettle into a trophy, stuffed him, and put him in the closet, from which he keeps falling in the last scene, interfering with Rosalie's attempt to seduce Jonathan. Rosalie is still another kind of American female, the completely sensuous woman who pretends to be a little girl (she wears girlish pink and anklets), but as the scene on the bed indicates ("I want you . . . all for myself") she is another projection of the devouring woman. Although *Oh Dad* keeps a tight hold on its satirical theme, Kopit, like Weinstein, indicates a fondness for kidding around, for the irrelevant joke. *Oh Dad,* for instance, is full of obvious parody of Tennessee Williams. Not only do we get a mother-son traveling team, as in *Suddenly Last Summer,* but Kopit provides them with not one, but two, Venus's-flytraps and a piranha fish as well, and the fish has lines; all the names with *rose* in them suggest *The Rose Tattoo.* Although these literary jokes are amusing, particularly on first encounter, Kopit's play has more substance and a tougher kind of wit than they suggest; his talent will have freer range when he puts this kind of cleverness behind him.

For the most part, the new dramatists who have grown up off Broadway have been as conventional as their Broadway counterparts, whether their conventionality has been in terms of Broadway (James Lee) or the avant-garde (Edward Albee). There have been a few exceptions (Robert Hivnor, Arnold Weinstein), but it is too early to tell where their work will go or if, considering that Hivnor has not had a production since 1954, it will go at all. Now that off-Broadway has become Broadway in miniature, it is likely that we will get similar production patterns (if one nostalgic musical will go, why not a second, a third, a fourth). Under such circumstances, the appearance of a new playwright with talent and imagination will become as much a fluke off Broadway as on.

11 A GATHERING OF FUGITIVES

Where order in variety we see . . .
—ALEXANDER POPE

Although plays are not cattle, critics occasionally herd them as though they were, corral them, as I have done in the earlier chapters, into groups in which their likenesses make them easy to handle. We brand them, but the brands are unclear; the same plays persist in turning up in more than one corral. A few seem to belong in no particular group. Once in a while, there is a genuine stray —Jane Bowles's *In the Summer House* (1953)—that keeps to itself; more often, even the strays form family clusters.

The Bowles play is mainly about the ways of needing love. The play's heroine is a dominating woman who has persisted in giving her daughter advice instead of love and who, at the end of the play, loses the daughter to a man who has given her love. Neither this factual description, nor an emphasis on the preponderance of psychological explanation (the play does wear that brand), begins to touch the peculiar quality of the drama. Everything in the play— the action, the speeches, particularly those of the heroine—is slightly awry; Mrs. Bowles conveys a strong sense of urgency about unurgent matters and an apparent indifference to what really moves her characters, a transfer in emphasis that, I assume, is a defense made by the characters themselves. Her lines are often obliquely funny (here there is a suggestion of Williams, McCullers, Capote), and some of the scenes, those involving the ever-eating Solares family, are so broadly comic that they approach slapstick. There is justice in the criticisms of both Walter Kerr (in *How*

224

Not to Write a Play), who insists that everything happens between scenes, that the play is "one still life, then another, then another," and Louis Kronenberger (in *The Best Plays of 1953–1954*), who finds the play "effectively theatrical" but not "genuinely dramatic." *In the Summer House,* despite its obvious faults, remains strangely attractive, affecting if occasionally affected; Kronenberger quite rightly included it among the season's best plays.

Among the strays that come in groups we may as well consider the war plays first. There have not been very many of them and, for the most part, they have been neither very good nor very popular. Ralph Nelson's *The Wind Is Ninety,* which opened in June 1945 for a run (108 performances) just long enough to carry it past the Japanese surrender, might be considered the first war play in the postwar theater. The story of a dead soldier who returns to his family to soften the blow that his death will be and to teach them to face the future, *Wind* is much closer in tone to James M. Barrie's *A Well-Remembered Voice,* a typical example of World War I sentimentality, than it is to Harry Brown's *A Sound of Hunting* and Arthur Laurents' *Home of the Brave,* which opened later in 1945. Laurents' play, despite the flashbacks that show the soldiers in action, is primarily about the curing of Coney's paralysis, his acceptance of his Jewishness. *A Sound of Hunting* is a more typical war play. It concerns a squad at Cassino, the members of which disobey a direct order of the company commander and risk their own lives to try to save one man who has got himself pinned down by enemy fire. Their need, as the squad intellectual explains it, is to save the man or to know for sure that he is dead (which turns out to be the case), because the unity of the squad might disintegrate in the face of doubt, at the suspicion that the man was left behind alive as the company pulled back to a rest area. The squad is the standard collection—the Italian, the Jew, the Irishman, the Wisconsin German, the college boy—that has become the chief cliché of the war novel, play, movie; only the innocent kid and the older man are missing and the latter, from what we hear of him, is the soldier who is trapped off-stage. Brown handles these stereotypes as carefully as possible; they are plain enough, but at least he does not demand that they wear placards proclaiming their obviousness. Although the play is built around the action I have described, it is of interest mainly for the conversa-

tion that goes on among the soldiers. The talk is accurate sound-
ing, as close to GI speech as a writer can get without reproducing
that casual and innocent obscenity that sounds so false as soon as
it is committed to paper or the stage. Brown also tries to communicate the strong but masked sentimentality that was so much a part
of army life, the attitude that made it necessary for a soldier to
have both a buddy and contempt for the use of a word like
buddy. This quality is such a delicate one that it is almost impossible in a play, where, customarily, it is reduced to ordinary stage
sentiment, as at the end of *A Sound of Hunting* where Collucci
starts to eat the dead man's slice of fruit cake and then puts it back
on the table. Brown's play was a failure on Broadway, although it
contained, muted, both the horseplay (the scenes between Collucci
and Shapiro) and the romantic gesture (Collucci's destruction of
the machine-gun nest) that were to be the staples of later successes
such as *Mister Roberts* (1948), and *Stalag 17* (1951) by Donald
Bevan and Edmund Trzcinski.

Although Collucci is the principal figure in *A Sound of Hunting,*
the hero, the protagonist even, is the group. In this, too, Brown's
play is typical. Most war plays do not deal with one man in a military environment, but with the environment itself, almost as
though a squad or a crew were an individual. *The Girl on the Via
Flaminia* is an exception, but Alfred Hayes is able to consider a
single soldier largely because the action takes place in an area far
behind the fighting. The other way to focus attention on one figure
is to move up in the military hierarchy, to find a man in a position
to make decisions and to accept responsibility for them. It is true
that a decision is made in *A Sound of Hunting* and that, in reality,
the squad sergeant would be responsible, but theatrically the decision and the responsibility are absorbed by the group. In the first
successful war play, *Command Decision* (1947), William Wister
Haines comes close to finding a workable protagonist by deserting
the dugout for division headquarters, the private for the general.
Even here the emphasis shifts at the end of the second act, and
General Dennis is no longer center stage. Dennis, at his own dis-
cretion but with the tacit approval of his superior, has begun a
three-day operation that sends bombers deep into Germany, far
past fighter cover, to destroy the factories producing the new jet
fighter that presumably would give Germany control of the air.
The opposition to the completion of the operation (from the press,

from Congress, from the joint staffs) in the face of heavy losses leads to Dennis' dismissal. It is Garnett, a desk-bound professional, who must decide whether or not to fly the last strike, and by forcing the decision on him, Haines pushes Dennis to the side of the stage and, if he does not change heroes, he substitutes a concept (strategic daylight bombing) for a man. The play is interesting for its presentation of the bureaucratic stresses and strains that preoccupy the upper levels of the military departments, even in a war, and is often exciting at the simple level of whether or not the decision will be made, but it is not completely successful in projecting the mental anguish of command. In the last act, Dennis has a long speech about the horrors of command, but to convey it in personal and dramatic terms Haines falls back on an old device from *Dawn Patrol*—the death of the commander's best friend—to which he adds a second cliché, that word of the birth of the friend's son should come at the moment of his death. The play is also marred by the presence of a number of standard stereotypes—the war correspondent, the visiting Congressman, and, most annoying of all, the loyal, comic sergeant. The only other successful play to deal with the problems of command is *The Caine Mutiny Court-Martial* (1954), and Herman Wouk's play is, in a way, *Command Decision* turned inside out; where the Haines play insists that the decision is finally more important than the command (that the winning of the war takes precedence over the military status quo), the Wouk play suggests that command, competent or not, is more important than a correct decision.

Time Limit! (1956), by Henry Denker and Ralph Berkey, is the only play of any popularity to come out of the Korean War. It is possible that what small success it had was the result of its central problem, the most disturbing phenomenon of that war—the high incidence of American collaboration in Chinese prison camps—but I suspect that it succeeded, in so far as it did, as a reasonably effective melodrama. For the first two acts at least, attention is turned to process, the bit-by-bit accumulation of information that will explain why Major Cargill should have given in to brainwashing; the big scene is a standard interrogation breakdown—the one that turns up in most courtroom plays. The weakness at this level is that the interrogation scene, in which it is a witness against Cargill who does the breaking, is the melodramatic high point and Cargill's last-act explanation of why he collaborated becomes anticlimactic. The last act, then, can be sustained, if at all, only by its ideational point. In terms of idea, the play presents the conflict between the code of General Connors (who discovers that his supposed hero son has also been a collaborator, killed by his outraged fellow prisoners) that says simply that collaboration, for whatever reasons, is cowardice and treason, and the facts of Cargill that insist that there is always a breaking point and that "there ought to be a time limit because you can't ask a man to be a hero forever." At the end of the play, the investigating officer, who, as the omnipresent funny sergeant says, "believes in justice," recommends that there be no court-martial and, knowing that his recommendation will be ignored, decides to defend Cargill, presumably to establish new concepts of treasonable behavior: "This is a new kind of enemy, sir. The code isn't equipped to deal with them." The position that the authors seem to be taking at this point is colored by another ancient morality, that of the sentimental play, for Cargill, it turns out, has collaborated to save the lives of the other men in his compound. Even though *Time Limit!* is such a patchwork of conventional stage devices and attitudes, it often seems to be a direct reaction to an earlier treatment of the same material, Rod Serling's television drama *The Rack,* which was broadcast April 17, 1955. In the Serling play (which also has a general with a collaborating son), the accused comes to accept his guilt and, largely through the speech of a Chaplain, all of America is seen to take part in that guilt. The Serling character is more interesting, a man who finally broke down because of the pressure put on him and for no romantic reason, but Denker and Berkey at least open up the important problem, to what extent is the traditional code of behavior no longer operable, which Serling considers only to reject. It is incongruous to be talking about so complicated a social and political problem in the context of two such superficial plays, but the tradition of social theater in this country has produced more melodramas than it has studies in depth.

Although they are not really war plays, Irwin Shaw's *The Assassin* (1945) and Herman Wouk's *The Traitor* (1949) are from a related genre, the spy melodrama, complicated in both cases by political concerns in relation to war, hot or cold. The Shaw play is a fictionalized account of the assassination of Admiral Darlan (here called Admiral Vespery), in which the assassin is moved by a complicated pattern of motivation: his hate for Vespery; his love for his friends in the underground who will be released from prison as a result of his act; his monarchist politics (the plotter has convinced him that the removal of Vespery may lead to the restoration of the French king). Vauquin, the play's Democratic Socialist, who believes in men (be they Communists or Royalists) rather than in party affiliations, speaks the moral when he accepts the reasons for Robert's action: "Good enough. Though it would look better in the history books if you were full of simple, correct reasons and eloquent democratic slogans, and terribly anxious to die in the cause of freedom." Ironically, Shaw, who wants to make clear that heroism is not a quality that can be reduced to formula, manipulates his puppet characters to make that point as obviously and as lifelessly as any conventionally patriotic hack would do in writing the standard hero play. He even raises that standard himself when in his last scene he asks the we-who-are-about-to-die Robert to speak the admirable sentiment, implicit or explicit in every war play, that these dead shall not have died in vain: "We must not be martyrs, we must be seeds. . . ."

The Traitor is a combination of two popular forms. First of all, it is a thriller (although not a very thrilling one) that follows a recognizable formula. Wouk plants the idea that there is something suspicious in the behavior of Dr. Allen Carr (atomic scientist) and then, with a Geiger counter ticking ominously, lets Naval Intelligence confirm the suspicion. After the confirmation, the capture. Since this action brings the play only to the end of Act II, Wouk changes genre in the last act and borrows his denouement from the Bengal-Lancer kind of movie. Carr is given a chance to save his reputation (and that of the corps: the scientific community, in this case) by helping to trap the chief spy; he succeeds, but regenerated though he may be, he dies the brave death that convention demands. Neither the atomic immediacy of the situation nor the philosophical arguments about Carr's motivating belief (that if the Russians had the bomb—the play is set in 1948—a peace settlement might be negotiable) can hide the fact that the play is an old-fashioned spy romance. There is a subplot about whether or not Professor Emanuel should sign a loyalty questionnaire, which gives Wouk a chance to work one of his characteristic switches, like the one in The Caine Mutiny that turns Tom Keefer, who has all the marks of the liberal hero, into the villain of the piece. Emanuel, an old-fashioned humanist, decides to sign, despite the fact that one of the Navy Intelligence officers urges him not to do so; the conservative-liberal turnabout in this situation is so dazzling that Wouk never lets his characters stop to consider the impracticality of the questionnaire (which, given the character of the chief spy, is obvious in the context of the play), or the morality of allowing a millionaire trustee to force his concept of loyalty on an entire faculty.

It may well be that the play about the returned veteran intent on a better world than the one he left—Arthur Miller's *All My Sons* is the obvious example—is also a kind of war play. There have been few of them, perhaps because the playwrights, following the veterans, settled early into a concern with the private problem, the private comfort. *Deep Are the Roots* (1945), by Arnaud d'Usseau and James Gow, is such a veteran play, but a special one since the returned soldier in this case is a Negro. In the Preface to the published play, the authors say that a playwright should be "socially conscious," but that he should present problems not solutions; their objectivity is somewhat compromised by their insistence that "If he is accurate in his judgment, he will find himself on the side of progress, new ideas, the rebel forces, the forces of optimism." The problem that they want to examine is that of racial bigotry, of which the roots are so deep that even the supposed liberal Southerner (Alice Langdon), faced with a reactionary bromide made flesh (would you want your sister to marry a Negro?), reacts viscerally, lets herself be used by the forces of viciousness represented by her father. Since, given their view of the social play, the optimistic solution is implicit in the objective presentation, the play ends with Alice's painful confession of the racism that she wants to overcome and the agreement between her and the wronged Negro (who will not marry the sister, after all) to work together once again. Her reward (the stage likes tangible not spiritual rewards) is that her Northern novelist fiancé finds her acceptable once again. Although the play is concerned about the very real race problem and although it occasionally touches on it in terms of schools and transportation, the playwrights, by putting the unhappy love story at the heart of their play, give it an artificiality that distorts their apparent subject. It suggests those films (*Pinky, Lost Boundaries*) that came about the same time and, with the best intentions, falsified the whole racial problem in

America by choosing that very minor figure, the Negro who passes, as protagonist.

Much more was done with race problems in the films of the late forties than on stage. *Deep Are the Roots* stands alone. Since there were very few social plays, practically no message plays in the fifties, it is not surprising that dramas about and for Negro rights should never have materialized. The few plays about Negroes that turned up in the last decade are something else again. Written by Negro playwrights, they do not ignore the special difficulties involved in being a Negro in a white-oriented, white-controlled society, but they emphasize the problems that the Negro American shares with the white. Louis Peterson's *Take a Giant Step* (1953), which had a successful off-Broadway run after a Broadway failure, is a good example. It is a standard adolescent play complicated by the fact that the hero is a Negro in a white neighborhood of a New England town at the moment when his old friends, having become interested in girls, find his color an embarrassment to them. All the familiar ingredients are in the play—the abortive attempt to run away, the death of the hero's closest friend (his grandmother in this case), the introduction to sex—and the solution is the expected one, the standard end of stage adolescence: accepting the fact that being an adult is as painful as it is necessary. Although most of the characters and situations are clichés, Peterson's play is occasionally touching, and he shows a nice ear—particularly in the scenes between the boy and the grandmother—for the idiom of querulous affection within a family. Langston Hughes's *Simply Heavenly* (1957) is a less successful example of the same kind of conventional play, peopled with Negro stereotypes instead of white ones—in this case, a romantic comedy set against the background of a bar, filled for the most part with sweet eccentrics.

The most ambitious and the most successful of this group of plays is Lorraine Hansberry's *A Raisin in the Sun* (1959). The play's central situation—the decision of a Negro family to move into a white neighborhood—could have been presented with the simple anger of the thesis play, and Miss Hansberry does occasionally attack head on, as in the figure of Mr. Lindner, the representative of the Clybourne Park Improvement Association, who, using all the clichés of Christian forebearance, tries to buy out the Youngers. *Raisin,* however, is not intended as a propaganda play. Its strength is its chief character, Walter Lee Younger, whose prob-

lem is complicated by his being a Negro but is much more basic
than that. He is a victim of the American dream of success in its
most virulent form, the Willy Loman strain that suggests not that
success is possible in America, but that it is inevitable. Although
Walter wants something as specific as a liquor store, a first step on
the stairway to the heights on which he sees himself walking, his
dream for the most part is unreal, a matter of poses and images,
as these lines indicate: "sometimes when I'm downtown and I
pass them cool, quiet-looking restaurants where them white boys
are sitting back and talking 'bout things . . . sitting there turning
deals worth millions of dollars . . . sometimes I see guys don't
look much older than me——." It is inevitable, I suppose, that a
man as naïve as Walter should be wrecked on his first brush with
practicality, that he should lose the insurance money that was to
pay for the liquor store. The contrast between Walter's dream and
the facts of his life, the financier trapped in the chauffeur's job,
makes him almost as bitter at himself and his family as he is at
the rich white men whose world he covets. His mother, his wife,
his son, his sister—all of them are in a plot to defraud him of his
mythical American heritage, or so he thinks, particularly when
Lena at first refuses to let him have the insurance money; in fact,
they share his actual American heritage (ugly as it frequently is)
and are only intent, like Linda Loman, in convincing him that
they are willing to settle for something less than his dream. They
will accept a Walter Lee Younger whom they can respect as son,
husband, father, brother—a man who does not let himself be crucified on the either/or of American success but who is willing to
work for the small, the possible, dream.

Miss Hansberry arranges that they should get that Walter. At
the end of the play, unable to bring himself to sell the house on
which Lena has made a down payment, he makes a speech about
his family's pride to the confused Mr. Lindner, who has come to
buy the property. There is a certain amount of falseness in this
conclusion, for Walter has been so vividly drawn in the earlier
scenes that his conversion seems imposed from the outside; up to
this point, dignity, for Walter, has implied a material, monetary
standard. Three things contribute to the acceptability of the final
Walter, even though he never quite escapes artificiality. First, the
explicit disgust and horror that the members of his family feel for
what he is about to do, the dramatic effectiveness of which is

heightened by the depiction of his mother, whose values are in
continual conflict with his. Second, the form of the speech itself—
halting, stumbling, rambling—which suggests Walter picking his
way through his confusion and which avoids the sudden eloquence
that so often wags like an ill-fitting tail at the end of the kind of
play that *Raisin* almost is. Third, the audience that inevitably prefers the victory of virtue to the pain of dramatic consistency. If
there are extenuating circumstances that soften my doubts about
the end of the play, there is nothing—not even the explanation of
Walter's innocence—that can quite forgive the creaking mechanism of the stolen money. Much about Miss Hansberry's play is
as clumsy as it is old-fashioned, but it has virtues that commend
it. Not only are the central character and his problem important, but
the playwright's depiction of the family, particularly in the first
scene, makes use of the kind of comic line, either needling or self-
deprecatory, that suggests, not in idiom but in emotional intention,
Odets at his best.

A third group of plays that do not seem to belong in any of the
categories that I have discussed earlier are the stage biographies,
the animation of historical figures, either for their own sake or to
make some point for the playwright. If we do not consider the
symphonic outdoor dramas, to use Paul Green's designation,
which speckle the countryside every summer, and I do not intend to consider them, then the genre has never been particularly
popular in this country, certainly not as it has been in England.
There have been two recent exceptions: Dore Schary's *Sunrise
at Campobello* (1958) and William Gibson's *The Miracle Worker*
(1959). These are unusual in that they deal with the recent past
and that some of the characters (Eleanor Roosevelt, Helen Keller)
are too much alive to have become history. It is possible that their
popularity in part derived from the fact that audiences could be
expected to bring to the theater an interest in, perhaps an affection
for, the main characters in both plays. More important, as an explanation of the success of these plays, is that both of them deal
with a character who overcomes the handicap of illness (Helen
Keller's blindness and deafness, Roosevelt's infantile paralysis) and
this kind of triumph—as the editors of most popular magazines
know—is perennially appealing to audiences. In each of the plays,
the playwright has taken an inherently moving story and, in trans-

ferring it to the stage, has inevitably cheapened it by reducing the suffering to theatrical gesture. I do not intend to impugn the motives of either Schary or Gibson, but they are trapped by the genre in which they are writing. One of the reasons that dramatic representation at its best can communicate the intensity of pain is that it builds a wall around its characters, who consist only of what we know of them. The theatrical depiction of an actual person can succeed in dramatic terms only in so far as the playwright is strong enough (Shakespeare with Henry IV, or Shaw with Saint Joan) to impose his fictional conception of the man onto an audience, replacing the historical one. It is almost impossible to do this with a recent historical figure about whom people know too much and about whom they have prejudices. It is certainly impossible in *The Miracle Worker* and *Sunrise at Campobello,* where so many effects depend on knowledge outside the plays, on what Helen Keller and Franklin Roosevelt were to become. When the playwright enlists the aid of the audience by using such outside suggestion to heighten the emotional effect of a scene, he runs the risk of falsifying that whole scene, of reminding the observer that he is seeing a skeleton of conventional theatricality and that the flesh is so much more complicated, so much more fascinating, so much more rewarding to know.

Of the two plays, *The Miracle Worker* seems to me to be the more efficient. If the effects are often stagey, they at least work in the way that the playwright seems to intend. The second-act curtain is a good example. Here each of the principals sits in his own shaft of light while Annie rocks and sings "Hush, little baby"; visually and aurally this is a suspended moment in the play, one that indicates the waiting attitude that all of them have in the face of the two weeks that Annie will have alone with Helen. It is Gibson's neatness that is finally defeating because his characters become not the complicated persons that they obviously were, but sentimental stereotypes (the spunky Irish girl, the softhearted curmudgeon, the weakly cynical older son, even the spoiled child) who perform expectedly in standard scenes. In *Sunrise at Campobello,* the problem of characterization is even more obvious. Gibson, at least, had a freer hand with his characters than Schary did because there is not so much and such well-known testimony about the Kellers as there is about the Roosevelts. Schary's characters never become credible either as historical figures or as people, and the factual pressure from the outside keeps them from being workable stage stereotypes, although the family scenes do occasionally suggest *Life with Father*. The playwright tells his story, a man's triumph over a crippling disease, in terms of three nonverbal images: the man on the stretcher at the end of Act I; the man trying to get up on crutches at the end of Act II; the man at the lectern at the end of Act III. Although the images are vivid ones, it is the passages between them that should but do not convince us of the hero's strength and power. Instead of providing the dramatic force that the play needs, Schary offers the fruits of his research, the artificial comments on the political, financial, charitable, and familial doings of Roosevelt during his years of convalescence. *Sunrise at Campobello* seems much less a moving play than a frame of reference to which each member of the audience might bring his own feeling about FDR.

One of the difficulties with history plays—at least, for me—is that the minor characters are frequently well-known figures from the past, and too often their introduction into the action seems like an indulgence of the author, the playwriting equivalent of name-dropping. Al Smith's appearance in *Sunrise at Campobello,* cute though it is, has at least the excuse of the plot, the impetus toward the last scene. It is much more disconcerting to find Henry Adams and Owen Wister running in and out of the Holmes house in Emmet Lavery's *The Magnificent Yankee* (1946) or Helen Hunt Jackson popping in for a visit with Emily Dickinson in Dorothy Gardner's *Eastward in Eden* (1947). It is not that there is anything historically wrong with this conjunction of characters; it is simply that Adams and Wister in the one play, Mrs. Jackson in the other, are only points of view that help the playwrights explain their main characters, and although the functional character, the one-dimensional friend, is an occasionally acceptable device in a play, it is annoying to see him wear a label that implies a richness the dramatist will not even attempt to show. Nor does it help when, as in Lavery's play, there is an attempt to humanize the character; in this case, Lavery's lines let Holmes harp on what a bore Adams is.

The Magnificent Yankee is an episodic play that carries Oliver Wendell Holmes from his arrival in Washington in 1902 as a Supreme Court Justice, to 1933 when, past ninety and retired, he receives the new president, who honors the old man by coming directly from his inauguration to pay his respects. Although the emphasis throughout is on the joyful marriage—one of mind and spirit—of Holmes and Fanny, a number of less central points are important enough to keep recurring: the childlessness of the couple and the way Holmes's secretaries become substitute sons; his disappointment at never having become Chief Justice; the use of military language, the unspent legacy of his Civil War service. The play has no particular plot although it does seem to be designed to say again and again that life is a continuing process, that it can never be summed up until the end. For all the references to cases that came before him, people he knew, ideas that intrigued him, the play never catches Oliver Wendell Holmes except as a crusty but lovable old gent, and its real appeal, I suspect, is that it is a vehicle that allows an actor and an actress to age becomingly, from sixty to ninety, in the three acts allotted them. *Eastward in Eden* is as episodic as *The Magnificent Yankee,* but Miss Gardner's Emily Dickinson is easier to take than Lavery's Holmes. The play, which is subtitled "The Love Story of Emily Dickinson," is just that; the playwright attempts to make the poetess' love for Charles Wadsworth vivid enough to convince the audience that she could live for twenty years in twin worlds, the real world of Amherst and the ideal world of her poetry and her passion, in the second of which she is the true wife of the absent Wadsworth. The chief drawback of the play is "the high ideality of it all," to use a phrase of George F. Whicher's from a very laudatory Foreword to the printed play, in which he suggests that the portrait is factually inaccurate but spiritually correct; but Miss Gardner does succeed, at least in the early scenes, in conveying an Emily in whom the intensity and the excitement are more than that of the standard spirited girl in the period play. In the end, however, *Eastward in Eden* does not so much create Emily Dickinson as lean on her for support.

Among the most satisfactory of the history plays is Saul Levitt's *The Andersonville Trial* (1959). The reason, I suspect, is that for all the historical setting it is a remarkably contemporary play, concerned with a problem that the Nuremberg trials made part of our time and which, although Levitt could hardly have foreseen the capture of the accused, the Eichmann trial was to reawaken less than two years after the play opened on Broadway. In form, Levitt's play is little more than an ordinary courtroom drama, using most of the standard tricks of that genre. In characterization, it is competent but hardly commanding; the self-pitying defendant, the cynically clever defense counsel, the passionately moral judge advocate—all these are familiar enough. It is the idea of the play that sustains it. Major Henry Wirz is charged with "Criminal conspiracy to destroy the lives of soldiers of the United States in violation of the laws and customs of war." His defense is that as officer in charge of the Confederate Prison at Andersonville he did only his duty, giving a soldier's obedience to the officers above him. The military court hopes to sentence Wirz on the evidence of cruelty that he initiated, but, as witness after witness proves useless, the prosecution moves toward the moral accusation that has been implicit in Wirz's position from the beginning: that there is a duty greater than the military that demands that a man, a soldier, disobey unreasonable orders of his superiors. The problem in the play—and out of it—is the conflict between moral and legal guilt. The play would have been stronger in the presentation of this conflict if it had ended with Wirz's admission that he failed to disobey orders that he could not approve not out of fear or duty but simply because "—I—could not. I did not have that feeling in myself to be able to. I did not have that feeling of strength to do that." His admission illustrates vividly the crippling force of habitual obedience (contrast its celebration in *The Caine Mutiny Court-Martial*), but Levitt has added an unnecessary last scene that embodies the moral too patly. In contrast to *The Andersonville Trial,* John Patrick's *The Story of Mary Surratt* (1947) is a prime example of an historical trial organized to no purpose. Patrick's Mary is an innocent victim of a vindictive military court and there is more sentiment than significance in the playwright's maneuvers.

Jerome Lawrence and Robert E. Lee have developed their own kind of history play. Using fictional names for obvious historical figures, they cheerfully manipulate any necessary facts so that history will conform to the requirements of melodrama and the sentimental stage. In *Inherit the Wind* (1955), after having presented the Dayton monkey trial as a matter of black and white, the good guys versus the bad, knowledge versus willful ignorance, they shift to a sentimental end in which Henry Drummond (Clarence Darrow) in anger at the cynical indifference of E. K. Hornbeck (H. L. Mencken) makes a "Now cracks a noble heart" speech over the dead Matthew Harrison Brady (William Jennings Bryan). In *The*

Gang's All Here (1959), the playwrights use Griffith P. Hastings (Warren G. Harding) and his unhappy administration to indicate that they disapprove of "Government by Crony" as much as, in the earlier play, they dislike bigoted, narrow-minded religionists. There is nothing in the later play that is as effective theatrically as the courtroom sequences in *Inherit the Wind,* particularly the scene in which Drummond breaks Brady on the stand. Although the main reason for the fictional fronts to these plays is that the device frees the playwrights from the restrictions of fact, it might be assumed that it also heightens the contemporary significance of events from the past. That, at least, is the implication of the statement by the playwrights in the New York *Times* (April 17, 1955): "what happened in Dayton in 1925 was not in the remote past and could have happened yesterday." Ironically, in idea and in form, the Lawrence and Lee plays are as dated as the settings in which they appear.

The cows, I hope, have all come home.

Index

Brando, Marlon, 141
Brattle Theatre, 201
Bravo!, 79
Brecht, Bertolt, 34, 204
Breit, Harvey, 171
Brewsie and Willie, 209–210
Brigadoon, 136–137
Briggs, John, 151
Brooks, Jacqueline, 192n.
Brown, Harry, 225–226
Brustein, Robert, 46
Burning Bright, 198–199
Burrows, Abe, 79, 140, 143
Bus Stop, 41, 43, 44, 45, 46, 48
By the Beautiful Sea, 138
Bye Bye Birdie, 142–143

Caine Mutiny, The, 173, 229
Caine Mutiny Court-Martial, The, 173, 227, 237
Calderón de la Barca, Pedro, 197, 214
Call Me Madam, 77, 139, 143
Call Me Mister, 124, 125
Camelot, 122, 123, 137, 138, 153
Camino Real, 20, 23, 25, 27, 30, 31, 33, 35, 38, 73, 108
Can Can, 139, 153
Candide, 89, 148, 151–153
Capote, Truman, 122, 139, 174–176, 177, 198, 219, 224
Capra, Frank, 102
Career, 212
Carousel, 133, 135, 137, 139
Case of the Crushed Petunias, The, 19
Cat on a Hot Tin Roof, 20, 22, 27, 28–29, 35, 36, 38
Cave Dwellers, The, 94–95, 96
Celebration, 71
Channing, Carol, 124
Chapman, Robert, 169–170
Charley's Aunt, 139
Chase, Mary, 107
Chase, The, 71
Chayefsky, Paddy, 43, 53, 57, 58, 59, 61, 62, 64, 66, 71, 73–75
Chekhov, Anton, 43, 91, 162, 163, 177
Cherry Orchard, The, 91, 162
Children's Hour, The, 90
Chodorov, Jerome, 104, 108, 109, 144, 157–158
Chotzinoff, Samuel, 129, 130
Christie, Agatha, 205
Christopher Blake, 79–80
Circle in the Square, 203, 204, 205
Clark, Barrett H., 182
Clearing in the Woods, A, 43, 51, 52, 53, 54, 55
Clemo Uti, 166
Climate of Eden, The, 41, 68, 79, 80, 155
Clurman, Harold, 19, 93, 144, 191n.
Coe, Fred, 57, 61
Cohan, George M., 136
Cold Wind and the Warm, The, 87, 171

Colette, 163
Colum, Padraic, 166
Comden, Betty, 132, 142, 144
Come Back, Little Sheba, 41, 43, 44, 45, 46, 47, 199
Come Blow Your Horn, 97, 107, 108
Comes a Day, 47
Command Decision, 226–227
Compulsion, 172–173
Conkle, E. P., 212
Connection, The, 56, 215–217
Connelly, Marc, 78, 79, 100
Consul, The, 126, 127, 128–129
Cool Million, A, 222
Cornell, Katharine, 77
Costigan, James, 58, 64, 70
Country Girl, The, 92, 93, 96
Cowles, Chandler, 126
Coxe, Louis O., 169–170
Cretan Woman, The, 190, 192n., 193–195
Crime in the Streets, 63
Crouse, Russel, 77, 107, 110, 113, 133, 134, 159
Crucible, The, 3, 10–12, 13, 16, 17
Cry, the Beloved Country, 84, 130
Cue for Passion, 78
Cukor, George, 103
Cure, The, 197

Damn Yankees, 105, 141, 143
Dark at the Top of the Stairs, The, 41–48, 49, 56, 187
Dark Possession, 62
Darkness at Noon, 69, 93–94
Dawn Patrol, 227
Day the Money Stopped, The, 85
de Hartog, Jan, 204
Dear Judas, 190
Death in the Family, A, 71, 160–161
Death of a Salesman, 3, 5, 7–9, 10, 13–14, 15, 16, 17, 43, 69, 103
Death of Bessie Smith, The, 218, 219
Death of Billy the Kid, The, 62
Death of Odysseus, The, 214
Decent Birth, a Happy Funeral, A, 95
Deep Are the Roots, 230–231
Deer Park, The, 93
Deirdre of the Sorrows, 85
Denker, Henry, 227–228
Dennis, Patrick, 116, 156
"Desire and the Black Masseur," 32, 33
Desperate Hours, The, 172
Destry Rides Again, 138
Detective Story, 93–94
DeVries, Peter, 109, 171
Diary of Anne Frank, The, 154, 161–162
Dinner at Eight, 79
Dinny and the Witches, 210
Disenchanted, The, 171–172
Do Re Mi, 103, 146
Donehue, Vincent, 61
Don't Go Away Mad, 95, 96
Dope, 218

Date Due

FEB 5 1969		
JUN 10 1970		
DEC 11 1970		
NOV 23 1972		
JAN 11 1993		
NOV 16 1994		
DEC 08 1999		